Also by Frank Graham

Disaster by Default:
Politics and Water Pollution (1966)

Since Silent Spring (1970)

Man's Dominion:
The Story of Conservation in America (1971)

Where the Place Called Morning Lies (1973)

Gulls: A Social History (1975)

Potomac: The Nation's River (1976)

The Adirondack Park

The ADIRONDACK PARK

A Political History

By

FRANK GRAHAM, JR.

Special Research by Ada Graham

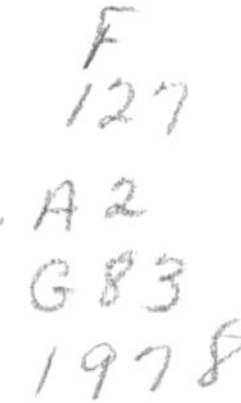

ALFRED A. KNOPF New York 1978

THIS IS A BORZOI BOOK
PUBLISHED BY ALFRED A. KNOPF, INC.

 Published in the United States by Alfred A. Knopf, Inc., New York, and simultaneously in Canada by Random House of Canada Limited, Toronto. Distributed by Random House, Inc., New York.

Library of Congress Cataloging in Publication Data

Graham, Frank [date] The Adirondack Park.

Includes bibliographical references and index.
1. Adirondack Park, N.Y.—History. 2. Conservation of natural resources—New York (State)—History. 3. Conservation of natural resources—United States—History. 4. New York (State)—Politics and government—1865–1950.
I. Graham, Ada. II. Title.
F127.A2G83 1978 974.7'53 78–54900
ISBN 0–394–42809–9

Manufactured in the United States of America

FIRST EDITION

To Harold K. Hochschild

Contents

Acknowledgments

A history of this kind is never an individual effort, and in the present case the contributions of others played an especially important role.

I want to acknowledge the help given me by three people in particular. Charles H. Callison, formerly executive vice-president of the National Audubon Society and now president of the Public Lands Institute, proposed that I write this book, just as he encouraged me to write an earlier book, *Since Silent Spring*. William K. Verner, curator of the Adirondack Museum, was generous with his time beyond the call of duty, pointing out sources I otherwise might have missed, providing hospitality at Long Lake, and critically reading the final draft of my manuscript; the defects that survive here despite his diligence should be attributed solely to my intractability. Marcia Smith, librarian of the Adirondack Museum, gave Ada and me the sort of attention researchers dream of, but do not always receive, during the course of their labors.

I also want to thank Henry L. Diamond, Harold K. Hochschild, and Peter S. Paine, Jr., for their encouragement as I began work on this history. The many courtesies extended by Craig Gilborn, director of the Adirondack Museum, made our research there a great deal easier.

Others who were most generous with their time or advice include Richard Beamish, G. Gordon Davis, William M. Doolittle, Robert F. Flacke, Courtney Jones, Richard W. Lawrence, Jr., Charles Little, Mary F. Prime, Paul Schaefer, Norman Van Valkenburgh, and Conrad L. Wirth.

In 1973 the New York State Heritage Trust made a grant to the National Audubon Society for the purpose of sponsoring a book about the political history of the Adirondack Park. The project had been conceived by Laurance S. Rockefeller and, in a real sense, grew out of his abiding interest in conservation and good land use in the Adirondack region. Funds from the grant supported my work on the book, the search for photographs, and other costs. I express my gratitude to the officers of both organizations and to Mr. Rockefeller.

My debt to Ada Graham, my partner during months of research, is noted on the title page.

Frank Graham, Jr.

Preface

There, on the very ridge-board of the vast water-shed which slopes northward to the St. Lawrence, eastward to the Hudson, and southward to the Mohawk, you can enter upon a voyage the like of which, it is safe to say, the world does not anywhere else furnish.

That was a Boston clergyman named William H. H. Murray at the outset of his 1869 best seller, *Adventures in the Wilderness*, extolling the pleasure and excitement that awaited the visitor to the Adirondack Mountains. Murray himself was later unhappy about the great surge of humanity his book impelled into the north woods, believing that what he most treasured there would inevitably disappear in the trappings of civilization. In part, his fears were justified. But ever since then, other men and women who shared Murray's enthusiasm for the Adirondacks have worked, with varying degrees of success, to save some part of the wilderness he explored and described more than a century ago. Today, the grandeur remains.

There is, in fact, no other public preserve in the United States quite like the Adirondack Park. In all the praise for our impressive National Park System, it has gone almost unnoticed that this state park is the largest of any kind in the country—at 5,927,600 acres far larger than the two national giants, Yellowstone (2,221,722 acres) and Mount McKinley (1,939,493 acres); indeed, it is larger than several states, including New Hampshire and Massachusetts. Although most Americans like to think of the wild areas of their national parks as being locked up in perpetuity, none remains so securely protected as the Adirondack Park's public land is by the "Forever Wild" clause in the New York State Constitution. It survives, the most extensive wilderness region in the populous eastern United States, its magnificent forests ornamented by two thousand lakes and six thousand miles of rivers and streams. Yet, because of the circumstances of its creation, no other large park is quite so vulnerable. There are two components to this vast tract, confusingly mingled: one is made up of private holdings, the other of public holdings collectively designated as the New York Forest Preserve; *together* the diverse holdings form the Adirondack Park. Of the park's nearly 6 million acres, 62 percent (3.7 million acres) is privately owned. Only the lesser part is state land and thus protected by the Constitution.

The New York State Legislature created the Adirondack Park in 1892 from land in large part devastated by lumbermen. The Legislature drew a "Blue Line" on the map around three million acres of private and public lands, the latter including most of the State Forest Preserve, in the Adirondack Mountains. Two years later the New York State Constitutional Convention, prompted chiefly by New York City businessmen who feared that the continuing abuse of the forest would dry up the state canal system's water sources, certified the earlier legislation (1884) that had created the Forest Preserve; the new Constitution declared: "The lands of the State, now owned or hereafter acquired, constituting the Forest Preserve as now fixed by law, shall be forever kept as wild forest lands." Article VII, Section 7, the controversial Forever Wild clause, made it plain that only the people, by amendment to the Constitution, can permit the forest to be cut, sold, or significantly altered in any way.

Intermingled with the Forest Preserve from the start lay the extensive tracts that were privately owned. In 1912 the legislators redrew the Blue Line to include some adjoining forest and defined the Adirondack Park as "all lands located within the following described boundaries," thus for the first time explicitly including the private lands as well within the park's designation.

Through the intervening years the park's defenders, self-appointed and otherwise, have beaten back many serious threats by those who wanted to exploit the mountains' resources for personal gain or even for what they saw as the public's best interests. There were attempts to amend the Constitution, calls for dams to provide water supplies or power, and squabbles over highways, campsites, bobsled runs, and other intrusions into what one observer has called "the Land of Mustn't Touch." Sometimes these disputes were decided by popular vote, sometimes by administrative decree or the opinion of the state's attorney general. Private conservation groups have lobbied and propagandized for the Forest Preserve's integrity. Men and women, all calling themselves "conservationists," have battled on opposite sides of the fence; indeed, Gifford Pinchot, who popularized the word "conservation," was among the strongest advocates of opening the preserve to lumbermen. (To avoid confusion, I have at some places in my book substituted the word "preservationists" to characterize those who put a strict interpretation on Forever Wild.)

The Adirondack Park's recent history is set against the background of a green America slowly submerging beneath an exploding population, untold acres of concrete, and enormous pollution problems. The private land within the Blue Line became increasingly a source of anxiety and dispute. Could the park, indeed, the Forest Preserve, survive uncontrolled development on those private holdings? Were "elitists" depriving local people of their chance to catch up with more prosperous areas? And now, with the Legislature's creation of the Adirondack Park Agency to regulate development on private land, is the state actually appropriating the property of its citizens?

As my book's subtitle implies, I have not written simply another celebration of the mountains' scenery, or a folksy memorial to quaint characters living in a remote region. My aim, instead, is to describe the ideas, controversies, agreements, legislation, and administration that affected the Adirondack Park from the earliest times, though in doing so I provide a background of natural and social history which either underscores or amplifies the events that took place on the political stage.

I go to some lengths to point out that the park did not evolve in isolation. I compare its formative influences with those of its contemporaries—city parks, national parks, national forests, and various public lands in other parts of the country. I show in some detail how things were done in the Adirondacks, who did them, the motives for doing them, what mistakes were made, and what was accomplished. In short, I try to distinguish between reality and illusion: are things really what they seem to be, in the park and as they affect it?

The Adirondack Park

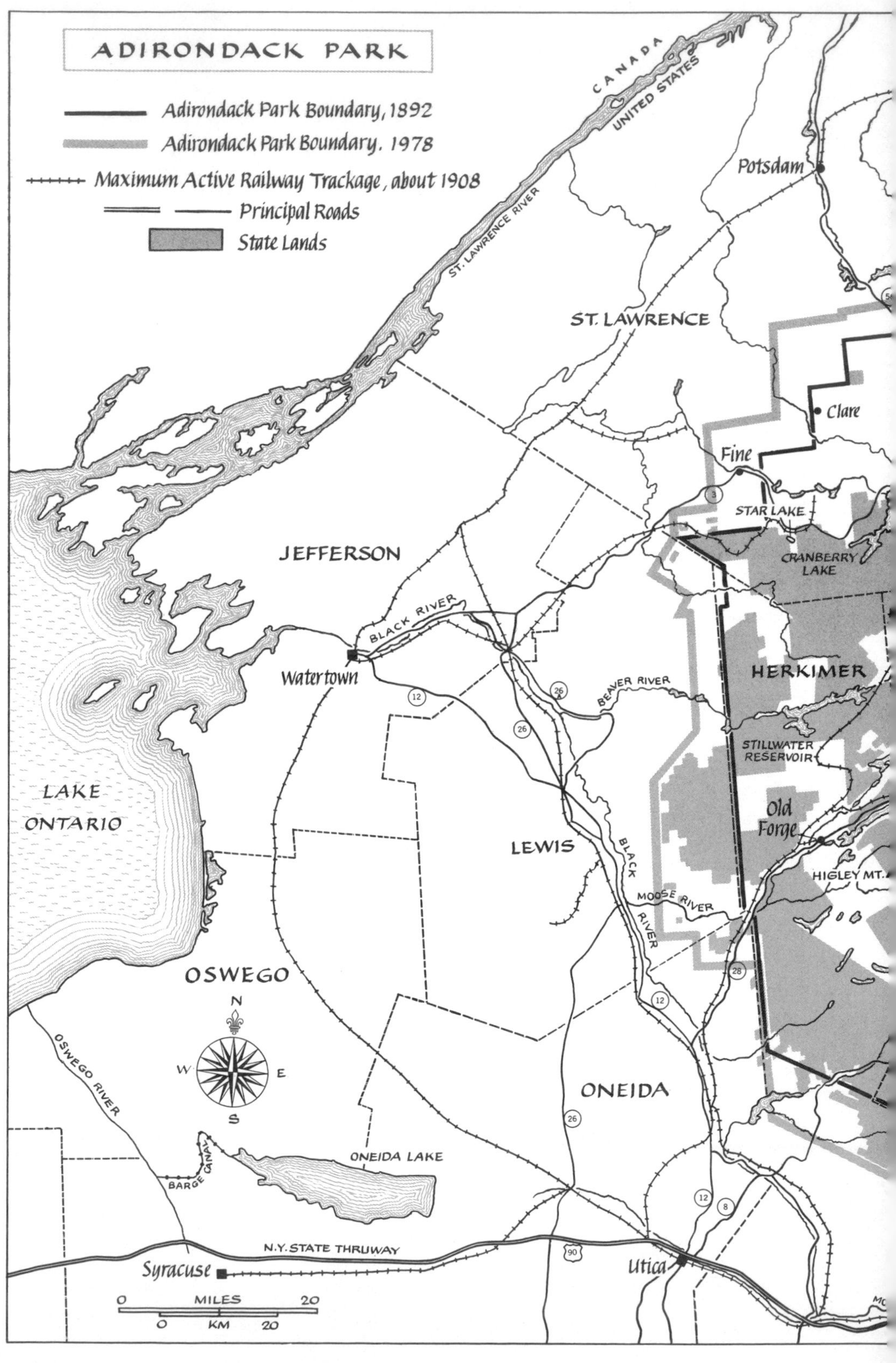
ADIRONDACK PARK
Adirondack Park Boundary, 1892
Adirondack Park Boundary, 1978
Maximum Active Railway Trackage, about 1908
Principal Roads
State Lands
CANADA
UNITED STATES
ST. LAWRENCE RIVER
Potsdam
ST. LAWRENCE
Clare
Fine
STAR LAKE
CRANBERRY LAKE
JEFFERSON
BLACK RIVER
Watertown
BEAVER RIVER
HERKIMER
STILLWATER RESERVOIR
LAKE ONTARIO
Old Forge
LEWIS
BLACK RIVER
HIGLEY MT.
MOOSE RIVER
OSWEGO
N
W
E
S
OSWEGO RIVER
ONEIDA
ONEIDA LAKE
BARGE CANAL
N.Y. STATE THRUWAY
Syracuse
Utica
0 MILES 20
0 KM 20

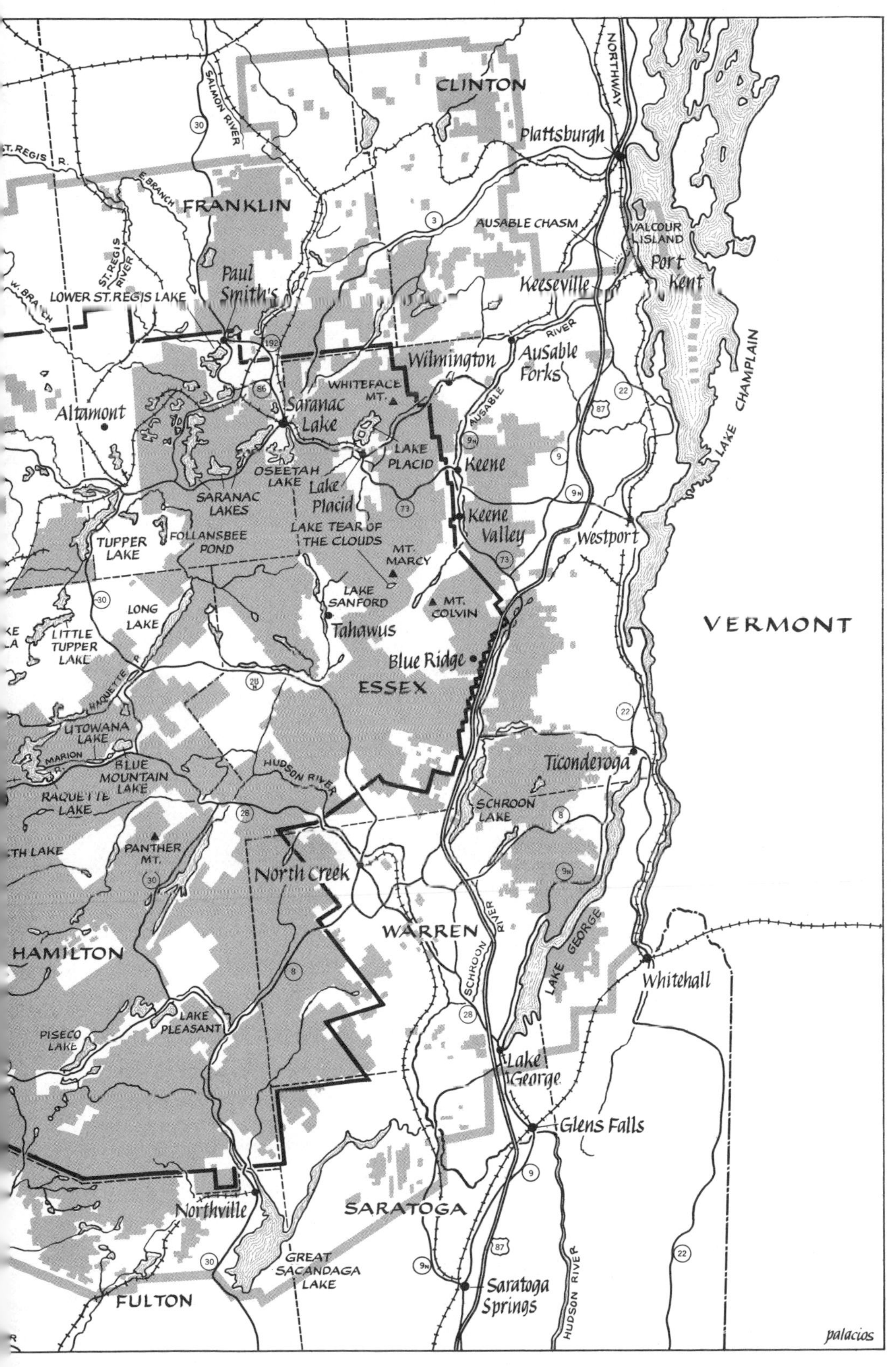

CLINTON
FRANKLIN
ESSEX
WARREN
HAMILTON
SARATOGA
FULTON
VERMONT
NORTHWAY
SALMON RIVER
ST. REGIS R.
E. BRANCH
ST. REGIS RIVER
W. BRANCH
LOWER ST. REGIS LAKE
Paul Smith's
Plattsburgh
AUSABLE CHASM
VALCOUR ISLAND
Port Kent
Keeseville
AUSABLE RIVER
AuSable Forks
Wilmington
WHITEFACE MT.
Saranac Lake
Altamont
LAKE PLACID
Lake Placid
OSEETAH LAKE
SARANAC LAKES
Keene
Keene Valley
Westport
LAKE CHAMPLAIN
TUPPER LAKE
FOLLANSBEE POND
LAKE TEAR OF THE CLOUDS
MT. MARCY
LAKE SANFORD
MT. COLVIN
Tahawus
LONG LAKE
LITTLE TUPPER LAKE
Blue Ridge
RAQUETTE R.
UTOWANA LAKE
MARION R.
BLUE MOUNTAIN LAKE
RAQUETTE LAKE
HUDSON RIVER
Ticonderoga
SCHROON LAKE
PANTHER MT.
North Creek
SCHROON RIVER
LAKE GEORGE
Whitehall
LAKE PLEASANT
PISECO LAKE
Lake George
Glens Falls
Northville
GREAT SACANDAGA LAKE
Saratoga Springs
HUDSON RIVER
30
3
192
86
9N
9
22
87
73
28N
28
8
palacios

CHAPTER I

The Great Northern Wilderness

In 1837 the village of Saratoga Springs was becoming one of the most sophisticated resorts in America. Around the effervescent alkaline springs that flowed from varied deposits of minerals in a shallow valley and were reputed to possess extraordinary restorative powers, there rose a cluster of hotels and boardinghouses, dominated by the elegant United States Hotel. The guests, who only a half dozen years before would have arrived in small numbers shaken and tired by the stagecoach ride from the cities to the south, now stepped in greater numbers and composure from trains of the Saratoga and Schenectady Railroad, which had opened in 1831, apparently with the hope of creating a busy watering place in the New York countryside to the west of the Hudson River. There were band concerts, walks at dusk in the hotel garden, flirtations on the verandas, games of forfeits in the elegant parlors—and, among the restless gentlemen, occasional small talk about the wilderness to the north. The great coniferous forest materialized just outside Saratoga. From there it stretched away northward, climbing gently at first and then in abrupt ascents under towering thunderclouds or shifting mists to blanket the mountains that as yet had no official name.

At times some of the more adventurous spirits at the resort ventured into what was usually called "the Great Northern Wilderness" to hunt or fish; the rumors described a sportsman's paradise, where big game and big fish abounded. In fact, only a few years before, a hermit named David Smith, living on the southwest fringes of the mountains, was reported to have remarked in disgust that "this place is too much frequented by hunting and fishing parties," and retreated to their dimmer recesses. The *Gazetteer of the State of New York* for 1836 noted that Lake Pleasant "has become a favorite resort for the fowler and angler," while in that same year the British author Harriet Martineau, stone deaf but indefatigable, grew weary of Saratoga's sophistication and took a boat up Lake George for a closer look at the forbidding mountains. "What a wealth of beauty is there here for future residents yet unborn," she wrote in the account of her trip.

But the mountains themselves remained largely unexplored. Indians, chiefly the Algonquins, who lived in the vicinity of Montreal, had hunted for centuries around the northern mountains. The story, often repeated, is that their rivals, the Iroquois, spoke of the forest-haunting Algonquins derisively as "Adirondacks," or "Those Who Eat Bark," though some philologists say that the word doesn't mean any such thing, and probably should be translated as "They of the Great Rocks." But no matter. The Iroquois themselves, after being driven south by their foes, also took to visiting the borders of the Adirondacks, though it is doubtful that they spent much time climbing the mountains. Thoreau, who saw Mount Katahdin in 1846, reflected in *The Maine Woods* that "the tops of mountains are among the unfinished parts of the globe, whither it is a slight insult to the gods to climb and pry into their secrets, and try their effect on our humanity. Only daring and insolent men, perchance, go there. Simple races, as savages, do not climb mountains,—their tops are sacred and mysterious places never visited by them." Presumably none of the Bark Eaters heard a different drummer.

In 1609, Samuel de Champlain approached the mountains from Canada, reaching the beautiful lake he named for himself and killing two Iroquois with a single blast of his harquebus, thereby creating an enemy for France and a tenacious ally for the English during the French and Indian Wars. The region was the scene of bloody battles through those wars and the Revolution, particularly on and around Lake Champlain and Lake George, which are connected by a narrow inlet. But the Indians, the soldiers, the beaver trappers, and the timber cruisers were transients in the mountains. A few settlers tried to remain and work the land, but, as the Adirondack historian Alfred L. Donaldson wrote, they were overwhelmed by "the odds of arctic climate, barren soil, and virtual isolation."

The mountains were and, indeed, are formidable. They are not a part of the Appalachian chain, as is so often thought, but rather are related to the great Laurentian Plateau that fans out northward through Canada; nor are they composed of the oldest rocks on earth, another occasional misapprehension, for recent isotope measurements of the anorthosite exposed by erosion in the mountains prove it to be only a little over a billion years old, far younger than similar rocks underlying Canada, South Africa, and Greenland. Nevertheless, the mountains are old even in geological terms, pushed up as a series of jagged peaks in the Paleozoic era, then worn down and rounded through the intervening ages. Closer to our own time the glaciers scoured the mountains of their vegetation and soil, leaving behind a comparatively barren but lake-studded landscape as they receded. The mountains remained as the watershed between two great rivers, the St. Lawrence on the north and the Hudson to the south. On the west flows the Black River, while the Champlain Valley borders the Adirondacks on the east before the land rises again into the Green Mountains of Vermont.

The Hudson and other river valleys around the mountains were settled early by white farmers and merchants, but even the source of the mighty Hudson remained for a long time hidden in the interior, as great a mystery as that of the Nile. (The source of the Columbia River in the Northwest, in fact, was known sixty years before the Hudson's.) It was not until 1771 that anyone showed much interest in the mountains. In that year two New York shipwrights, Joseph Totten and Stephen Crossfield, petitioned the governor of New York for a license to buy 800,000 acres in the mountains from the Mohawk and Caughnawaga Indians. The deal was made, the Indians were handed 1,135 pounds, and only when the land was surveyed later did it come to light that the Totten and Crossfield purchase amounted to 1,150,000 acres.

There were some curious sidelights to this purchase. Totten and Crossfield apparently were acting on behalf of land speculators, among them Edward and Ebenezer Jessup, who had certain other transactions in the works at the time and thought it best to conceal their part in this one. And while the local Indians did not realize a great deal from the transaction, His Majesty George III did considerably better. After getting the Indians out of the way, the buyers still had to satisfy the Crown, a procedure that Donaldson recounts "involved the payment of seemingly exorbitant fees and perquisites," all of which amounted to $40,000. The buyers, in fact, never received the patents from the Crown. The Revolutionary War broke out, the Jessup brothers favored the British side, and after the war the winners redistributed the land among new investors and some of the old ones who had come down on the right side. According to Donaldson, one of the original buyers, Theophilus Anthony of Manhattan's fashionable Murray Hill section, built a summer camp on a pond near Long Lake in 1786, thus becoming the forerunner of a million "rusticators" in the Adirondacks.*

But the state of New York appropriated a large part of what is now the Adirondacks when the Legislature passed a bill in 1779 which declared that the lands belonging to the Crown before 1776 were "forever after to be vested in the people of this state." "Forever" turned out to be a very brief time indeed, for five years later the Legislature, as desperately in need of money as legislatures usually are, passed another measure calling for "the settlement of the waste and unappropriated lands within the State" and providing for their "speedy sale." The chief lure was not the terrain, of course, but the price. While lands in other parts of the state went as quickly as the lawmakers had hoped, those in the Adirondacks were generally ignored, despite the promise that all taxes on them would be waived for seven years. Included was the so-called Military Tract of 650,000 acres in Clinton, Essex, and Franklin counties that the state made available to its veterans of the Revolutionary War, few of whom accepted the offer. Speculators finally acquired the tract at an average price of ninepence an acre. Most of the rest of the region went in one enormous bundle of nearly four million acres (at eightpence an acre) to a group headed by a speculator named Alexander McComb. Soon after the purchase, McComb ended up insolvent and in jail as a result of a banking scheme in New York City and his land was transferred to other members of his group. The state had

* Some modern Adirondackers doubt the story, believing it unlikely that anyone would have built in so remote a place, at that early date, when there was no one around the lake itself.

disposed of the mountains at prices that brought an outcry from a few farsighted individuals downstate who saw that the area might eventually become valuable as a source of timber and water and were appalled by what they felt was thievery, or at best incompetence, in letting the land go so cheaply. In later years the state would pay dearly for the giveaway.

The speculators, of course, had envisioned a trek into the "Great Northern Wilderness" as part of the young nation's expansion. This was the pattern to the south, where the immigrants, the landless, and even the owners of the exhausted tobacco-growing lands in the tidewater region of Virginia and Maryland finally moved west across the Great Valley and into the Blue Ridge and the Appalachian Mountains. But those mountains were temperate and fertile, their winters comparatively short, their slopes well clothed in forage for cattle. Throughout the eighteenth century only the trappers took much from the interior of the northern wilderness, chiefly beavers. The trade in beaver skins, which the Dutch settlers originally promoted in the state, encouraged Indians and even a few white trappers to pursue those large rodents into their mountain fastnesses, so that by the late 1830s, when the trade was petering out as European hat markets shifted to the South American coypu (or nutria) for their source of fur, it was estimated that only three hundred beavers remained in the state, all in the mountains. (New York City, the home of the Astors and other entrepreneurs enriched by the fur trade, made partial amends to the beaver by putting its picture on the municipal seal.)

Lumbering grew only slowly in the mountains, first because there were untapped supplies in Maine and elsewhere to the east, and also because of the difficulty the lumbermen had in reaching the trees and then moving them to market. But the forests in the Northeast went quickly. Under its mercantilist policy, England was determined not to be dependent on the Baltic states for the wood and other products needed by its growing navy and it looked to New England to supply them. The large pines in particular, because of their fitness for masts, were marked with the "broad arrow" by the Surveyor General of His Majesty's Woods, thus reserving them for the navy, a practice that bred resentment in the colonies. When independence came, the colonists set out to cut all the trees in the woods, authority be damned. Even as enterprising lumbermen leveled the Maine forests, others began cutting the fringes of the mountains in New York.

Until the early nineteenth century, however, removing logs from the wilderness was a complicated procedure, the logs being rafted together and floated on spring freshets down narrow streams, and occasionally hauled by teams around the falls and rapids, to the Hudson and then to the sawmills set up at Glens Falls. (The cavern under the falls there was utilized by James Fenimore Cooper as a hiding place from Montcalm's forces for Hawkeye, Uncas, and their friends in *The Last of the Mohicans.*) Then two brothers, Alanson and Norman Fox, had an idea that helped to revolutionize the lumber business. Why not send the logs *singly* down the narrow streams? They began cutting logs in the mountains, dropping them into the Schroon River, and floating them by way of the Hudson to their mill at Glens Falls. The idea caught on. Other lumbermen took up the practice, marking their own logs for identification just as cattle are branded on western ranches. There was no legal obstacle to this practice. In 1806, the Legislature had declared parts of some rivers, notably the Salmon, the Schroon, and the Raquette, "public highways," so that not only boats but also logs (always cut into thirteen-foot lengths in the Adirondacks, for some reason now lost in the mists of time) could be floated on them no matter who owned their banks. Glens Falls, which had been on the point of collapse as the nearby forests disappeared, found a new lease on life and became a center of the upstate lumbering industry. In 1824, timber in the Champlain Valley found another route to market via the Champlain Canal to Quebec.

An event occurred in 1825 that helped the lumbermen gain ascendancy in the Adirondacks for most of the rest of the century. On October 26 of that year the packet *Seneca Chief*, pulled by four gray horses, moved from Lake Erie onto the new Erie Canal. A battery of guns was fired at Buffalo to signal the opening of the canal, which three thousand men, using picks and shovels and aided by horses and oxen, had taken more than eight years to complete. As the roar of the guns drifted eastward from Buffalo, the sound was picked up in Rochester, and another battery was touched off.

In that way the boom of guns passed the word from port to port the length of the canal, 363 miles to Albany, where the people received the news only eighty-one minutes later. (Although it went unnoticed at the time, the *Seneca Chief* was not alone; both smallmouth and largemouth bass, not native to the Hudson, entered the watershed through the canal and flourished there, much to the fun and profit of later anglers.) The most important result of the canal's opening was the creation of an inexpensive and convenient route to the West. New York City's primacy as a port and a commercial center was assured, since it was situated at the critical point to take goods from the rest of the East Coast, as well as from Europe, ship them westward, and then receive the products of the newly opened West in return.

The canal also sealed the fate of the land developers in New York's wild mountains. The tide of settlement passed the mountains by, as immigrants and New Englanders alike took the new route toward fertile lands in the West.

CHAPTER II

Early Visitors

The lumbermen worked zealously in Maine's forests, stripping them of most of their big pines. Not far to the west, in New York's northern wilderness mountains, lay vast tracts, heavily forested but unwanted by farmers or, for that matter, by almost anybody else. The lumber companies were able to buy this land at bargain prices and move in to cut them. The swiftness with which they devastated the forests is astonishing at first glance, but one comes to wonder that any trees at all survived the initial onslaught in the Adirondacks.

Wood, of course, was in constant demand for buildings, furniture, ships, and most of the other primary items in the economy. Although it was not yet used in the making of paper, wood was the vital ingredient in a number of other manufacturing processes. Great quantities were burned as fuel, not only in homes but in factories as well. An Englishman, Captain Frederick Marryat, visited the salt producers at Salina (which is now part of Syracuse), New York, in the 1830s and wrote:

> Boats are constantly employed up and down the canal transporting wood for the supply of the furnaces. It is calculated that 200,000 cords of wood are required every year for the present produce; and as they estimate upon an average of about 60 cords of wood per acre in these parts, those salt works are the means of yearly clearing away upwards of 3,000 acres of land. Two million bushels of salt are boiled down every year.

Other furnaces reduced wood to charcoal and potash. Charcoal was needed as fuel in the iron and steel industries, and for a time there was an ironworks near the rich MacIntyre* Mine at the headwaters of the Hudson River, but it did not flourish. (The high cost of getting the product out of the mountains forced the mine to close eventually, but it was revived, as we shall see, under unusual circumstances in the twentieth century.)

A historian of the state's forests has described the process by which wood was turned into charcoal. The wood, he writes, was

> cut in three to five foot lengths and stacked around kindling in a circular pile, some twenty feet in diameter. Covered with earth and sod, it was fired and kept burning from ten to fourteen days before the charcoal was harvested. A good woodsman could earn four dollars or more a day cutting wood for charcoal. It was this industry, however, that rapidly destroyed forests by consuming wood in all sizes and shapes; this meant that trees too small for other uses could be harvested. As a result of the charcoal burners' operations, a forest might be stripped of all growing stock, making regeneration difficult if not impossible.

Potash, used in the manufacture of glass, soap pigments, and fertilizer, was also made from wood; the hardwood logs were burned and the lye leached from the ashes and then boiled down in large iron pots ("pot ash"). And here and there the land was cleared in the mountains by optimists who hoped to farm or graze their livestock; farmers sometimes girdled, or more often burned, the trees, their only use for the wood in that case being as ashes which mingled with the soil to fertilize it.

Soon an interest of another kind was directed toward the northern wilderness. The mountains were almost unknown; and for a long time it was believed the Catskills provided the state with its highest peaks. Though Mount Washington in New Hampshire had been climbed in 1642, apparently no one had explored the summits of northern New York. In 1830 Professor Edward Hitchcock of Amherst performed valuable geological surveys in Massachusetts, and other states funded similar programs, appointing a survey chief with a staff of assistants. William Learned Marcy, a large, gruff man with a "Websterian brow" who was then serving his third consecu-

* The mine began life as McIntyre, but later picked up an "a."

tive term as governor of New York (and who later coined the phrase "To the victors belong the spoils"), recommended to the Legislature a natural history survey of the northern wilderness. Professor Ebenezer Emmons accepted the assignment. He was a man of many talents and disciplines—geologist, mineralogist, botanist, sometime practicing physician, and professor of natural history at Williams College. (Later he made an agricultural survey of New York.)

In the summer of 1837 Emmons led a party that included several other scientists and Charles Cromwell Ingham, a prominent artist who was a founder of the National Academy of Design, into the heart of the High Peak region and up what proved to be the highest mountain in the state, an arduous climb to the summit at 5,344 feet. The party broke a trail beside the Opalescent River, the Hudson's east branch (which was devoid of fish, until stocked later, at higher altitudes because of its steep incline and many falls), and then up wooded ravines to the dense entanglement of dwarf trees that mark the approach to the alpine zone. Ingham, finding himself out of his physical class in the company of the active geologists, fainted several times on the way, but revived each time and trudged gamely along in his companions' wake. At ten o'clock on the morning of August 5, two days after leaving their base at the MacIntyre Iron Works, the explorers stood among the mosses and alpine herbage on the summit; the ice in the rocky depressions around them was half an inch thick. Emmons named the peak Mount Marcy in honor of the governor. Properly edified by the view and the features of the land he had passed on his way to the top, Ingham later made a series of sketches; they were the basis for lithographs produced by J. H. Bufford to accompany the State Natural History Survey Report that appeared the following year. Emmons, in fact, did not confine himself to naming the mountain, but provided a name for the entire mountainous region. He wrote:

> The cluster of mountains in the neighborhood of the Upper Hudson and Ausable rivers, I proposed to call the *Adirondack group*, a name by which a well known tribe of Indians who once hunted here may be commemorated. It appears from historical records that the Adirondacks or Algonquins, in early times, held all

> the country north of the Mohawk, west of Champlain, south of Lower Canada, and east of the St. Lawrence river, as their beaver hunting grounds, but were finally expelled by superior force of the Agoneseah, or Five Nations. Whether this is literally true or not, it is well known that the Adirondacks resided in and occupied a part of this northern section of the State, and undoubtedly used a portion at least of the territory thus bounded as their beaver hunting grounds.

The region now had a name, and the interior mountains were portrayed for the public for the first time in the report's lithographs. It was a public that was beginning to hunger for such scenes, either in art or in nature itself. When Ingham rendered one of his sketches into a rather lush painting of "the Great Adirondack Pass" (or Indian Pass) for exhibition at the National Academy of Design in 1839, it did not measure up to some observers' notions of what the real wilderness is like. "The rocks seem to be composed of uncut velvet," a hostile critic wrote of the painting, "the trees and bushes of the material used by milliners in ladies bonnets, and the grass of a substance from which a well-informed sheep would turn with contempt. Somebody called it 'the Great Abominable Pass.' "

At any rate, Ingham's painting is the earliest portrait in oils of the Adirondacks' High Peak region that comes down to us.* This area is the heart of the present park. At the time of Emmons' report and Ingham's portraits there was a large public ready to respond to the wildness implicit in the scene. In the first place, there was genuine surprise that so great a wilderness remained in the northeastern United States; the adventurous young were setting out for the still unexplored lands in the West, while many men who remained behind were already struck by nostalgia for the vanishing wild landscape. One of the misconceptions of our own time is that the wilderness movement is a reaction to the internal-combustion engine, but in truth that movement had its roots in the last century. When Emmons climbed Mount Marcy, Thoreau was already looking closely at the natural world around him in Concord, carping at the inroads of industry, beginning his retreat to a more natural place where he could provide a "broad margin" to his life. "It prob-

* This painting is now in the collection of the Adirondack Museum.

ably gave him more pleasure to open his door to a woodchuck than to a man," John Burroughs wrote of him. And a later critic said that nature was "a single beloved realm, a theater of operation for Thoreau's psyche." With man becoming a stranger to nature, Thoreau wrote in his *Journal* that every town must have a park, even a primitive forest, "where a stick should never be cut for fuel, a common possession forever. . . . Let us keep the New World *new*, preserve all the advantages of living in the country." If the primitive forest still existed in Africa or the American West, it was disappearing from the proximity of man. Wordsworth and Thoreau, on their respective sides of the Atlantic, were attesting to that. And yet here, only three hundred miles north of New York City and one hundred and fifty miles from Albany, lay an unspoiled "lake country," a land of forested mountains, hidden gorges, and thunderous cascades. Joel Tyler Headley, who wrote a book in 1849 about his two trips to the Adirondacks, said they bore the same relationship to New York "that the Highlands do to Scotland and the Oberland to Switzerland."

Along with an increasing sense of loss grew a taste for dramatic mountain scenery that persisted throughout the Victorian age. Byron's poems romanticized the remote crags and wind-twisted trees of Alpine lands, while in the United States, Washington Irving depicted a more accessible mountain world in his stories about the Catskills; and the painters of the Romantic era fastened on the picturesque aspects of dizzying heights and turbulent water. The Hudson River school of painters, Thomas Cole and Asher B. Durand among them, turned their backs on the traditional Biblical and classical subjects and moved gradually up the river, catching the scenery in a green-hued moment of time.

The public did not have to be trained to look at mountains with a painterly eye. In fact, travelers had become accustomed to search out the picturesque, the notion of which they had formed by looking at the landscapes of Claude Lorrain and other painters of the seventeenth century. Perhaps Robert Browning, speaking through an even earlier painter, Fra Lippo Lippi, phrased it best:

For, don't you mark, we're made so that we love
First when we see them painted, things we have passed
Perhaps a hundred times nor cared to see;

And so they are better, painted—better to us,
Which is the same thing. Art was given for that—
God uses us to help each other so,
Lending our minds out.

A scene was beautiful if it conformed to the rules of painterly composition. As late as the first half of the nineteenth century travelers and painters sometimes carried with them into the mountains a device called a "Claude glass." Claude Lorrain's paintings, as Kenneth Clark writes, displayed a vision "of a Golden Age, of grazing flocks, unruffled waters and a calm, luminous sky, images of perfect harmony between man and nature." The device that bears Claude's name and reputedly was invented by him was a sheet of convex glass, dark-tinted and framed, through which one could view the landscape as an artist's composition. It was adopted on a larger scale by one of the painters sometimes associated with the Hudson River school, Francis Guy, who learned to compose landscapes by setting up his easel in a tent, into a side of which he had cut an opening the size of his canvas. He then put a frame around the opening, stretched across it a transparent piece of black gauze and drew on it in chalk the view he observed. The chalk drawing he later transferred to canvas and thus had a painting complete with the proper perspective and proportions.

The lumbermen were now dominant in the Adirondacks, pushing on through the mountains, cutting into the great primeval forest. Buying the land cheap from the original speculators, they logged it, then let the ruins revert to the state for taxes. By 1845 there were 7,000 sawmills in New York (and 1,500 tanneries which used up enormous quantities of bark). By 1850 New York led the nation in producing lumber. But vacationers and sportsmen, who had previously stopped at Saratoga, Lake George, and elsewhere on the fringes of the mountains, were pushing in too, their heads stuffed in advance with notions of game-filled forests and majestic mountains. Charles Fenno Hoffman, an editor of the weekly journal the *New York Mirror*, was so inspired by Emmons' account of Mount Marcy that he made up his mind to climb it, though he had lost a leg in a childhood accident. Having persuaded a guide to lead him to the top, Hoffman realized partway up that the ascent was beyond his strength, and he sat down on the mountainside and broke into bitter tears. Yet he turned his experiences into the first 122 pages of his book *Wild Scenes in the Forest and Prairie*, published in England in 1839, then in the United States (1843) and Germany (1845).

The parade continued. In 1855 there appeared in the woods the Hon. Amelia M. Murray, in her sixties and maid of honor to Queen Victoria, who was on a tour of the New World. When Governor Horatio Seymour of New York invited her on an expedition to the northern wilderness, this spunky woman readily accepted and apparently had the time of her life. With Seymour, his niece, a young gentleman, and three guides, she reached Saranac Lake, and then went on to the Fulton Chain Lakes. She slept in primitive hotels and on evergreen boughs in the forest, relished the rain and even a light snowstorm, introduced the Adirondack guides to tea with lemon (since there was no milk), and made puddings from the wild fruit she collected. She even found time to make sketches, now unfortunately lost, of wild scenes and was delighted by the image of a guide carrying his boat, "with his head concealed underneath, like some nondescript shellfish." The Adirondacks figured prominently in her inevitable book.

One of the most articulate pre–Civil War visitors was S. H. Hammond, a journalist, who came to fish the Raquette River and in 1857 published a book about the Adirondacks called *Wild Northern Scenes*. Of the Raquette he wrote:

> It flows on its tortuous and winding way for a hundred miles through an unbroken forest, with all the old things standing in their primeval grandeur along its banks. The woodsman's axe has not marred the loveliness of its surroundings, and no human hand has for all that distance been laid upon its mane, or harnessed it to the great wheel, making it a slave, compelling it to be utilitarian, to grind corn or throw the shuttle and spin.

But he saw the woodsman advancing on the beautiful river, and he thought he foresaw the time when the banks of the Raquette would be cut and the river itself harnessed to man's designs. Where, then, he wondered, will men go to find the wild things and the old forests?

> Had I my way, I would mark out a circle of a hundred miles in diameter, and throw around it the protecting aegis of the constitution. I would make it a forest forever. It should be a misdemeanor to chop down a tree, and a felony to clear an acre within its boundaries. The old woods should stand here always as God made them, growing on until the earthworm ate away their roots, and the strong winds hurled them to the ground, and new woods should be permitted to supply the place of the old so long as the earth remained. There is room enough for civilization in regions better fitted for it. . . . It will be of stunted growth at best here.

For the moment the woodsman kept the upper hand, but there were others who would come along to take up Hammond's vision.

CHAPTER III

Philosophers in the Woods

"I hoped here to find new subjects for art, spiritual freedom and a closer contact with the spiritual world—something beyond the material existence," wrote William J. Stillman, artist (he was sometimes called "the American Pre-Raphaelite"), journalist, diplomat, and adventurer, of his sojourn in the Adirondacks during the 1850s.

> I was ignorant of the fact that art does not depend on a subject, nor spiritual life on isolation from the rest of humanity, and I found, what a correct philosophy would have before told me, nature with no suggestion of art, and the dullest form of intellectual and spiritual existence. . . . The humanity of the backwoods was on a lower level than that of a New England village—more material if less worldly; the men got intoxicated, and some of the women. . . . I saw one day a hunter who had come into the woods with a motive in some degree like mine—impatience of the restraints and burdens of civilization and pure love of solitude. He had become not bestialized, like most of the men I saw, but animalized, he had drifted back into the condition of his dog, with his higher intellect inert.

Nevertheless, when he went to live in Cambridge, Massachusetts, mixing with the sort of intellects he could not have found in the wilderness, Stillman was high in his praise of the Adirondacks. ("He was one of those friends of the great, whose own possibilities of greatness were dissipated by nomadic habits of mind and body," Donaldson writes of him.) Here was a true wilderness, he assured all who would listen to him, and he spoke not only of the pleasures but also of the terrors of solitude. He recounted the story of an English shoemaker who had come to live on the fringes of the Adirondacks but who wandered off into the woods one day, became lost, and perished; he was seen only once more before he died when, incoherent and his clothes in tatters, he knocked at a villager's door to ask directions, and then, before the villager could answer, panicked and rushed back into the forest. Stillman had had a similar experience of his own when he went to see a remote waterfall. Suddenly he lost his sense of direction.

> Then began to come over me, like an evil spell, the bewilderment and the panic which accompanied it. Fortunately I recognized this panic from the experiences I knew of, and was aware that if I gave way to it I was a lost man. . . . By a strong effort of the will, I repressed the growing panic, sat down on a log and covered my face with my hands, and waited . . . until I felt quite calm; and when I looked out on the landscape again I found the sun in his proper place and the landscape as I had known it. I walked back to my boat without difficulty and went home. . . .

In 1857 several of Stillman's Cambridge neighbors (including James Russell Lowell) accompanied him on a brief trip to the central Adirondacks, boating on the Raquette River, Tupper Lake, and the Saranacs. The others returned to Cambridge, but Stillman, prompted as usual by "the morbid passion of solitude" and his general inclination toward "spiritism," remained in a crude camp for the rest of the summer. The next year he organized a more elaborate expedition of ten members. The party consisted of, among others, Lowell, Ralph Waldo Emerson, Louis Agassiz, John Holmes (Oliver Wendell's brother), Judge Ebenezer Rockwood Hoar (later Attorney General in President Grant's Cabinet), and Professor Jeffries Wyman, an eminent comparative anatomist at Harvard. For a time it appeared likely that Henry Wadsworth Longfellow would join the group, but his antipathy to Emerson intruded.

"Is it true that Emerson is going to take a gun?" Longfellow asked Stillman.

Stillman replied that since everybody else was bringing a gun, Emerson had decided to arm himself too.

"Then somebody will be shot!" Longfellow thundered, and opted to remain at home.

Stillman found a perfect site, north of Long Lake, remote from any human activity and in the midst of a virgin forest, called Follansbee (now often spelled Follensby) Pond. The pond was named for a mysterious hermit who had lived on its shores and whose papers, examined after his death (according to local tradition), established him as a bona fide English nobleman. Stillman arranged for a personal guide for each member of his distinguished party, except for Agassiz, whom he kept for himself. It is difficult to realize the international esteem in which that noted autocratic Harvard zoologist and geologist was held during his heyday. When the party reached a village on the edge of the mountains, a group of local people appeared to welcome "Professor Agassiz and his friends." Emerson and the rest were virtually ignored, but the welcoming party produced from somewhere a portrait of Agassiz and, after making sure they were not confronted by an impostor, saluted him with enthusiastic speeches and handshakes. It seems that Agassiz (Swiss by birth) had touched their sense of patriotism by recently declining an offer from Emperor Napoleon III to serve as the director of the Jardin des Plantes and sit in the French Senate if he would come to live in France. "Such an incredible and disinterested love for America and science," Stillman wrote later, "had lifted Agassiz into an elevation of popularity which was beyond all scientific and political dignity."

Although Lowell named the site on Follansbee Pond "Camp Maple," the guides proved more descriptive than the poet and called it "the Philosophers' Camp." The party slept on layers of spruce and fir branches in a spruce-bark shelter erected in advance by Stillman and the guides. They drank foaming ale from "hunter's pans" and ate lake trout and venison. Agassiz and his fellow scientists collected and dissected the local flora and fauna. Lowell and others fished and hunted, Stillman painted the "philosophers" at their various pursuits, and Emerson wrote a poem called "The Adirondacks" to celebrate the expedition and its members:

Wise and polite,—and if I drew
Their several portraits, you would own

Chaucer had no such worthy crew,
Nor Boccace in Decameron.

At considerable length the poem describes the general routine of the campers. Yet the most dramatic moment had nothing to do with events at the camp, but with the arrival of news that the first cable had been laid under the Atlantic and a message sent from one hemisphere to the other:

A spasm throbbing though the pedestals
Of Alp and Andes, isle and continent,
Urging astonished chaos with a thrill
To be a brain, or serve the brain of man.
The lightning has run masterless too long;
He must to school and learn his verb and noun
And teach his nimbleness to earn his wage,
Spelling with guided tongue man's messages
Shot through the weltering pit of the salt sea.

And finally there were reflections on the different capacities of philosopher and guide, of the man of culture and the natural man, with Emerson, the great spokesman for nature, coming down on the side of civilization:

We flee away from cities, but we bring
The best of cities with us, these learned classifiers,
Men knowing what they seek, armed eyes of experts.
We praise the guide, we praise the forest life:
But will we sacrifice our dear-bought lore
Of books and arts and trained experiment,
Or count the Sioux a match for Agassiz?
O no, not we!

Before he left, Emerson, "who named the birds without a gun," got a hankering to shoot a deer, but, perhaps fortunately for all the others, Lowell downed the beast before the poet came up to it. Emerson then tried to get into the spirit of things by smoking a pipe, but it made him ill. When the August evenings at last "had a cooler breath," the party packed up and returned to Cambridge, not without promising to renew their adventure every summer. They went so far as to form an "Adirondack Club" and urged Stillman to establish a permanent campsite, which he did at Ampersand Pond near the mountain of the same name. Nothing much ever came of the club. Stillman went to live in Europe, where he became United States consul in Rome and later a correspondent for the London *Times*. The opening of the Civil War put an effective end to any further plans the philosophers had.

Twenty-five years later Stillman revisited the scene of the first Philosophers' Camp. "Except myself the whole company are dead and the very scene of our acting and thinking had disappeared down to its geological basis, pillaged, burnt, and become a horror to see." The mountains were about to experience an onslaught by the despoilers that, for its intensity and thoroughness, was in keeping with events elsewhere in the United States during the great age of extermination. But the philosophers' brief sojourn in the wilderness set the tone for other men and women of distinction who have, ever since, found refreshment for their spirits in the Adirondacks, where, like Emerson, for a short time they

let men of cloth
Bow to the stalwart churls in overalls:
They *are the doctors of the wilderness,*
And we the low-prized laymen.

CHAPTER IV

"Adirondack" Murray

Two years before the philosophers camped at Follansbee Pond, a writer of a different sort had found his way to the Adirondacks and established a more permanent campsite at Eagle Lake near the present village of Blue Mountain Lake. His name was Edward Zane Carroll Judson, but he wrote penny dreadfuls under the name of Ned Buntline. He was something of a penny dreadful character himself. He had once been lynched for killing a man in a duel in the South, but someone cut him down before the rope could finish him.

A drunk, a braggart, and a superpatriot (he was later a leader of the Know-Nothing movement), Buntline sided with the temperamental American actor Edwin Forrest in his rivalry with the English actor William Charles Macready and, during Macready's tour of the United States, led the infamous Astor Place riots, in which many people were killed, to protest the foreigner's visit. Buntline came to the Adirondacks in winter because the remote place at which he planned to work could be reached only by sled, the roads being mostly impassable at other times in the year. He lived in a camp which he called Eagle Nest, spent his time drinking, wenching (even marrying), and occasionally writing. His stories and novels (such as *The Mysteries and Miseries of New York* and *Stella Delorme; or, The Comanche's Dream*) were in great demand at the time. To ease the rush of words from his mountain lair, Buntline's publishers financed work on the roads, and buckboards henceforth carried out to civilization the eagerly awaited manuscripts at all seasons. While Ned did not contribute a great deal to the cultural history of the Adirondacks, he was a tone setter among the rusticators. Later authors of dime novels came to see the region as a setting for their own stories; Burt L. Standish, for instance, turned out novels with such titles as *Frank Merriwell's Camp; or, Yale Athletes in the Great North Woods,* and *Frank Merriwell's Magic Spectacles; or, Peril in the Adirondacks,* while Hal Standish wrote the forgettable *Fred Fearnot's Camp Hunt; or, The White Deer of the Adirondacks.* Buntline eventually went West,* where he turned an unsophisticated scout and hunter into the premier showman Buffalo Bill.

In the days when roads in the Adirondacks were mostly abominable (it took two weeks to deliver a newspaper from Malone to Saranac Lake in 1857), it must have been a heartening development when *anybody* tried to upgrade them. The buckboard (which was really a springboard with a seat in the middle, supported by two axles) was the only feasible means of "light" transportation over roads which had been chiefly cut through the wilderness by loggers. Seneca Ray Stoddard, the photographer of Adirondack scenes, recalled a trip he had made there on a stagecoach as late as 1873:

> Soon we became conscious that we had left the main road and were on one which required some little attention on our part to keep from doing injury to the interior of the coach. It was a good road—for a dyspeptic or one troubled with a poor appetite. . . . That vehicle meandered playfully over stones and stumps and into holes. It would bounce over logs when we, like rising young eagles, would soar away toward the roof. . . . our conveyance would drop down into deep holes and stop in such an emphatic sort of way that we would involuntarily feel our heads, fully expecting to find our backbones sticking up through our hats. When at long last we reached Saranac Lake, it was with a feeling of genuine goneness peculiar to those who have been without food for days and days on end.

But by the time of which Stoddard writes, the Adirondacks was not quite the unpeopled wilderness that the philosophers or Ned

* But Eagle Nest remained, expanding with each new owner until, in our time, it has been widely known as the Adirondack home of Harold K. Hochschild, the chairman of the board of American Metal Climax, founder of the Adirondack Museum, and chairman of Governor Rockefeller's Temporary Study Commission on the Future of the Adirondacks.

Buntline had penetrated fifteen or so years earlier. Not just the fringes but the interior regions were now visited (and, in the opinion of hermits and sportsmen, sometimes infested) by adventurous persons of both sexes. Some came from the cities simply to hunt and fish, others came, against all odds, to scratch a living from the hostile land. Among the latter was the abolitionist John Brown, who settled for a while with his large family on a farm near North Elba before moving on to Kansas in 1855; though he was a failure as a farmer, his rude homestead became a way station for fugitive slaves on their way to Canada. The local men, especially those around Long and Saranac lakes, served as guides for sportsmen during the summer. (Deer hunting, ever since the General Assembly passed a statute on closed seasons in 1705, had been illegal in New York between January 1 and August 1, but among the very few people taking the law seriously was Ned Buntline, who feuded with the truculent hermit Alvah Dunning because of the latter's constant violations of game laws; for the rest, even noted sportsmen took their venison wherever and whenever they found it.) But the dawn of an era can often be traced to the publication of a single book (*The Origin of Species, Studien über Hysterie,* etc.). The opening of the Adirondacks to a great flood of men, women, and children can be dated (if not ascribed) to the publication of William H. H. Murray's *Adventures in the Wilderness* in 1869.

The Reverend Murray of Boston's Park Streeet Church was probably the second most eminent preacher of his day, exceeded in fame only by the redoubtable Henry Ward Beecher. He fit the image of a church leader in many ways, a handsome, rugged, imposing man of great energy and determination (he overcame a stammer to attain eloquence in the pulpit) and an outspoken temperance lecturer; once, when the owners of a steamboat brushed aside his objections to their newly added saloon with the remark that it was "out of sight, way down below," Murray thundered in reply that this was "the exact location of hell!" At the same time he was an enthusiastic hunter and angler when such robust pursuits were considered inappropriate for a clergyman. He made a number of trips to the Adirondacks during the 1860s, and camped at Raquette Lake, perhaps using the same shanty painted into a scene depicting sportsmen at a meal at Constable Point in 1862 by Arthur Fitzwilliam Tait, which later became a well-known Currier

& Ives lithograph, "Camping in the Woods—A Good Time Coming." In 1866 one of Tait's friends mentioned in a letter to him how the lake was being spoiled by tourists and, in an apparent reference to Murray, recounted how on the previous Sunday "there were eighteen persons on Constable Point, and a minister among them performed church. Think of this and shudder." (It is ironic that thirty-five years later, when he was no longer a man of the cloth, Murray himself was concerned about the ruination of the same lake: "They even say that the little wild island I loved in the Raquette, and on whose ledge of rock, under untouched trees, I built my lodge, has been civilized by the axe and the plough, and that the divine silence of the Sabbath air is jarred into discord by the clang and rattle of a chapel bell!"

Adventures in the Wilderness was a book whose time had come, one which a fellow orator, Wendell Phillips, later said "kindled a thousand camp fires and taught a thousand pens how to write of nature." The Civil War was recently over, and people were looking for new sources of pleasure, unburdened by Puritan scruples that fettered older generations. Murray's book provided an answer. In fact, it *was* a good book. It was written in generally crisp, vivid prose, describing not only the wilderness but also how the reader could get there. There was little of the flowery writing or quaint dialect that marred so many Victorian books about rustic places. Here and there Murray exaggerated a little, and some parts of his book consisted of woodsman's tales, an aspect of his work that, according to Seneca Ray Stoddard, prompted an Adirondack guide to comment that "if his preaching is not a better guide to heaven than his book to the Adirondacks, his congregation might manage to worry through with a cheaper man."

But it was the book's facts, set in a well-delineated ambience of wilderness, that captured the reading public and sold thousands of copies at $1.50 each. Murray told his readers how much it would cost to visit the Adirondacks ($125 for one person for a month in the wilderness, which included transportation from New York or Boston and $2.50 a day for the hire of an honest guide). He advised his readers on the easiest routes to take, what clothes and sporting equipment to bring, how to deal with blackflies, and the names of reputable guides in each region. Apparently at the insistence of

Mrs. Murray, he included a section on what clothes a woman should wear in the wilderness. Murray's (or Mrs. Murray's) well-dressed woman sported a net of "fine Swiss mull," and a pair of buckskin gloves with armlets of chamois skin sewed to them to guard against blackflies and mosquitoes, a soft felt hat, "such as gentlemen wear, rather broad in the brim," to guard against sun and rain, thick balmoral boots with rubbers, a waterproof coat, and a change of flannel, and a "short walking-dress, with Turkish drawers fastened with a band tightly at the ankle."

Some of Murray's most eloquent prose went into his section on why one ought to visit the Adirondacks at all. He spoke of the attractions of the wilderness and, in case anyone had taken a notion to visit that other great "wilderness" of the Northeast, the Maine woods, he supplied a heartfelt paragraph in which he described the depredations there of the lumbermen, "the curse and scourge of the wilderness. . . . A lumbered district is the most dreary and dismal region the eye of man ever beheld." He spoke of the good hunting and fishing to be had in the Adirondacks, if one went to the proper areas. "With a guide who understands his business," Murray wrote, "I would undertake to feed a party of twenty persons the season through, and seldom should they sit down to a meal lacking either trout or venison. I passed six weeks on the Raquette last summer, and never, save at one meal, failed to see both of the two delicious articles of diet on my table."

One of the most important results of Murray's book was to publicize the Adirondacks as a place of refreshment for the body as well as the spirit. Part of his message may have been stimulated by self-interest. "If every church would make up a purse, and pack its worn and weary pastor off to the North Woods for a four weeks' jaunt, in the hot months of July and August, it would do a very sensible as well as pleasant act. For when the good dominie came back swart and tough as an Indian, elasticity in his step, fire in his eye, depth and clearness in his reinvigorated voice, wouldn't there be some preaching!" But for the rest he struck a sympathetic chord in his readers. Cities were becoming crowded, their residents subject to all the dinginess and stress the modern age associates with urban life. "'Nervous prostration' began to occur," Murray wrote in later years. "It was a new name and a new thing . . . caused by overstress and strain. . . . Clergymen, lawyers, merchants, doctors, all began to feel that the pace was too hot and too risky to keep up."

Murray especially recommended the Adirondacks to those afflicted by the century's greatest health problem. "The air which you there inhale is such as can be found only in high mountainous regions, pure, rarified, and bracing. The amount of venison steak a consumptive will consume after a week's residence in that appetizing atmosphere is a subject of daily and increasing wonder." And he went on to describe the case of a young man (he was careful to label it "extreme"), given up as a hopeless consumptive by city doctors, who had been carried into the Adirondacks, so his family thought, to die. While the guide whom his family had hired refused to accept a client who might "die on his hands," another guide took the job and "carried the young man on his back over all the portages, lifting him in and out of the boat as he might a child." Sleeping on his bed of balsam and pine, the invalid gradually inhaled "their pungent and healing odors." Day by day he grew stronger. Five months later he came out to civilization again, sixty-five pounds heavier, carrying his own boat over the portages, restored to the quick.

Adventures in the Wilderness had been in the bookstores for only a few weeks when the rush to the Adirondacks began. Hundreds of people left the cities, copies of Murray's book under their arms, the suggested clothing and equipment in their bags. (The railroads even offered free copies to the buyers of round-trip tickets.) Many followed Murray's advice about the most convenient way to reach the Adirondacks from Boston, leaving on the Boston and Albany Railroad at eight o'clock in the morning, connecting at East Albany with the Troy train and, at Troy, with the Saratoga train that deposited them at Whitehall, near Lake Champlain, at nine that night; then, after dinner on the steamboat, they returned to their staterooms and awoke the next morning to find themselves at Port Kent, New York; and from there, via coach, six miles to the Ausable House in Keeseville, where "you array yourself for the woods," and then another fifty-six miles over a plank road to their appointed meetings at five in the evening with their guides at Martin's Hotel (one of the first in the Adirondacks to attract people of wealth and leisure) on the shores of Lower Saranac Lake. In Murray's book the bearded, baldish, and peppery host, Bill Martin, received unusually high marks for his courtesy, his table, and his prices.

The result of this flood of visitors to the Adirondacks might have been anticipated. The few hotels and guides were overburdened, and visitors were often cheated by the few locals who exploited the unexpected windfall. Many tourists proceeded no farther than the Adirondacks' outer perimeter, and naturally were disappointed at the scarcity of either game or wilderness. In addition, it rained a good part of the summer, making it unnecessary for the deer to come down from the mountains to their usual watering places and lamentably increasing the intensity and duration of the blackfly season. Greenhorns, taken to the deeper woods by their guides, spent most of their time trying to learn to shoot, and in the process frightened away the game for miles around. Sportsmen who considered the Adirondacks "theirs" bemoaned the invasion; one of them, Thomas Bangs Thorpe, in an article called "The Abuses of the Backwoods" in *Appleton's Journal* that winter, attacked Murray, who "has written enough of this sort of nonsense to last a few years, at least," and, in a burst of misogyny, added of some of his readers: "We do not consider the wild woods a place for fashionable ladies of the American style; they have, unfortunately, in their education, nothing that makes such places appreciated, and no capability for physical exercise that causes the attempt to be pleasantly possible. . . . Let the ladies keep out of the woods." Other members of the press, observing the trek of disgruntled rusticators back to the cities, referred to them as "Murray's Fools."

Not all of them, in fact, returned. At least three of the optimistic consumptives died en route that year, though the woods were not full of the dead and dying, as some correspondents implied. Murray, in his own defense, pointed out that, among the many who came, three casualties "cannot be called a great rate of mortality." The book's publicity, of course, was tremendous. Correspondents debated the pros and cons of the Adirondacks in the press, Murray contributed a long "Reply to His Calumniators" to the New York *Daily Tribune*, and the noted sportswriter Charles Hallock wrote a burlesque in the style of *The Pickwick Papers* for *Harper's*, in which members of "The Raquette Club," inspired by Murray's book, make an expedition to the Adirondacks. The author himself became known ever after as "Adirondack" Murray.

But despite the jibes and the rancor, "Murray's Fools" were the vanguard of a new movement. The public's appetite had been whetted and the Adirondacks soon became a fashionable mecca of city people who wanted to get away from it all once August rolled around. Warder H. Cadbury, who is an authority on Murray and a Research Associate at the Adirondack Museum, states the problem of wilderness in the light of this seminal book: "How is the quality of wilderness to be reconciled with quantity of use, particularly when by definition quality is contingent upon low density of use? Put in another and more specific way, how can the wilderness of the Adirondacks be preserved while at the same time making wilderness and its potential values accessible to a large public?"

"Adirondack" Murray had his own doubts, as we have seen, when his old haunts became the scene of civilized activity. But on the whole he felt there was space in the Adirondacks for all. "You may put 10,000 people into the Wilderness, and localities can be found where, for the entire Summer through, no face save your guide's shall be seen, and where deer and trout shall be found in lavish abundance," he wrote to the *Tribune* during the furor. Not long afterward, Murray drifted away, giving up the ministry to raise horses in Connecticut; later he tried his hand at ranching in Texas and, as his fortunes declined, opened a restaurant in Montreal. He lived on into the twentieth century, long enough to see his beloved Adirondacks undergo enormous changes. He himself had played a large part in bringing those changes about.

CHAPTER V

The Rusticators

It became fashionable to build a summer camp in the Adirondacks. The journey in the early '70s was still an arduous one, but the reward at journey's end, the lovely lakes in their setting of mountains, was worth the hardships. Railroads were already invading the mountains (or, to paraphrase Leo Marx, the machine was in the garden). As early as 1834 the State Legislature, five years after the first railroad had been built in America and even before the Adirondacks was the name of a mountainous region, had chartered a line to run into the mountains almost to the Eckford Lakes. In 1837, the year Emmons and his party climbed Mount Marcy, the phantom railroad took the name Mohawk and St. Lawrence Rail Road and Navigation Company and outlined a route running "from Little Falls to the headquarters of the Rackett River or Southern termination of Rackett Lake through Rackett, Crotched [Forked] Lake, Long Lake and down the Rackett River." Like many other such projects proposed in the region, it was never built.

But others came in. In 1848 the Legislature passed an act incorporating the Sacketts Harbor and Saratoga Railroad Company, which was eventually sold to Dr. Thomas Clark Durant, a surgeon-turned-magnate who had been a leader in the building of the Union Pacific Railroad and of whom the *Dictionary of American Biography* says: "Reticent and quiet in manner, he was able to excite his subordinates to extraordinary exertion. In his associates he aroused deep antagonism or warm admiration." (He and Leland Stanford had tried to drive in a symbolic spike, put together with twenty-three gold dollars, at the joining of the two converging lines of the

Union Pacific Railroad in Utah on May 10, 1869, but the gold proved to be too soft and bent under their sledgehammer blows.) Naming his new line the Adirondack Railroad, Dr. Durant completed it from Saratoga to North Creek, carving a bed through the cliffs of the upper Hudson, in 1871, but it was to be another fifty-one years before the line was extended twenty miles to the iron-ore mines near Tahawus. "Murray's Fools" had already been able to take advantage of another line, that built by the Delaware and Hudson from Plattsburgh to Point of Rocks in the northeastern Adirondacks in 1868, and extended to AuSable Forks in 1874. In 1875 a line ran up the western shore of Lake Champlain.

Typical of the well-to-do city families that came to the Adirondacks in summer was that of Theodore Roosevelt. At the beginning of August 1871, the twelve-year-old Theodore left for the mountains with his mother and father, his brother, his two sisters, and a variety of aunts, uncles, and cousins. They traveled by train to Glens Falls and then by stage and steamer up Lakes George and Champlain to Plattsburgh, and by train and stage to Paul Smith's Hotel on St. Regis Lake. For ten days the Roosevelts made tours to the neighboring lakes and mountains, helping the guides portage the boats ("While crossing this portage I observed a red-backed salamander [*Plethedon erythorotus*] on a damp decayed log," the young naturalist noted in his diary one evening), and set up camps by the quiet lakes. Theodore meticulously kept his diary, and kept it scientific:

> While in Lake St. Regis we saw other kinds of wild duck (*Aythyia americana*), loons (*Colymbus torquatus*) and a great blue heron (*Ardea herodias*). I saw also a kingfisher (*Ceryle alcyon*) dive for a fish and a mink (*Putorius vison*) swam across the stream while covys of quail (*Ortyx virginianus*) and grouse (*Bonasa umbellus*) rose from the banks. On the way we had caught 8 trout which we had for supper. Father read to us from the *Last of the Mohicans*. In the middle of his reading I fell asleep. Father read by the light of the campfire.

The Roosevelts returned to Paul Smith's to prepare for the journey home. "We started by coach for Ausable Forks where some magnificent falls are," Theodore wrote. "In ascending hills, West [a cousin] and I who were behind the coach would whenever we saw a peculiarly beautiful lichen or moss jump off and get it. We collected many specimens this way. The Ausable River flows through a narrow ravine with very steep sides and as the falls are very high the effect is indescribably magnificent." Six years later, while he was a student at Harvard, his diligent peeping and botanizing bore fruit; he returned to the Adirondacks and with a classmate published at their own expense a small pamphlet entitled *The Summer Birds of the Adirondacks in Franklin County, N.Y.*, which included only those species, 97 in all, that they had seen or heard. The distinguished biologist C. Hart Merriam reviewed it enthusiastically in the *Bulletin of the Nuttall Ornithological Society* in April 1878, writing: "By far the best of these recent lists which I have seen is that . . . by Theodore Roosevelt and H. D. Minot. [It] furnishes that which was most needed, i.e. exact and thoroughly reliable information concerning the most characteristic birds of the limited region (Franklin County) of which they treat."

Many other travelers in the mountains were beginning to make use of hotels such as the one operated by Paul Smith, the most famous of the Adirondack hosts. In the early years those establishments were not anything more than the spare rooms of local woodsmen or hunters, rented to passers-by; the Hon. Amelia Murray recalled being crowded three in a room at a tiny Saranac Lake hostelry in 1855. But Paul Smith, born Apollos A. Smith, the son of a Vermont lumberman, in 1825, not only began to provide a service for tourists but finally became one of the Adirondacks' special attractions, like Mount Marcy or Ausable Chasm. "There is little doubt that the foundation of Paul's success lay in his wife's ability to cook a good dinner, and in his own to tell a good story," Donaldson writes. His own early experiences in the Adirondacks were as a hunter and trapper, but he soon set himself up in business as a guide. At the suggestion of some of his clients he built a hunters' retreat on the north branch of the Saranac in 1852. Donaldson continues:

> It consisted of one large living-room and kitchen, with eight or ten thinly partitioned sleeping quarters overhead. . . . Board and lodg-

ing was $1.25 per day; but it cost $2.00 a day to hire a guide. There was, of course, a bar on the premises, and it was run on the pay-as-you-enter principle. In one corner of the living-room stood a barrel of rye whiskey. Fastened to it by a stout string was a tin dipper. The price of a drink was four cents—probably because nickels were not in general use at the time—and the consumer thereby saved a penny. To get a drink you placed four coppers on top of the barrel, and removed the spigot from near the bottom.

Seven years later, again at the urging of his clients, Smith built a more spacious place, this time on Lower St. Regis Lake, where they could bring their wives. Almost simultaneously, Paul himself took a wife. Bit by bit over the years he added both to his land and to the hotel, so that by the time of his death in 1912 he owned over 30,000 acres (besides land which he had sold to wealthy rusticators looking for summer places of their own). As the hotel grew in size, Smith added an entire complex of buildings around it, including two dormitories for the help, stables for sixty horses, a casino (which had a special wire to the New York Stock Exchange), a four-story warehouse, an office, and a sawmill.

Part of Smith's attraction lay in the perversity which induces men of affairs to take pleasure in being mocked and insulted by a hearty publican. One of the few areas in which he went out of his way to please his guests was his approval of their craving to hunt out of season; he resolutely opposed all game laws. Four men who were or would be Presidents of the United States stayed at Smith's —Grover Cleveland, Benjamin Harrison, Theodore Roosevelt, and Calvin Coolidge—as well as entrepreneurs such as P. T. Barnum and E. H. Harriman. As time went on, this overbearing bumpkin took on some of the trappings of the autocrat. Donaldson, who knew him, writes:

In stature he was a tall, broad-framed, big-boned, powerfully built giant, well poised and balanced—a veritable Apollo Belvedere. He carried himself with youthful elasticity, erect and alert, well into his eighties. With his snow-white hair, his Van Dyke beard, his blue serge suit—usually dotted with a flower in the buttonhole—his light felt, broad-brimmed hat, he was such a trim and towering figure as the mind inevitably associates with royalty.

Mostly backwoods humor poured from the royal mouth, however, also an element in his attraction. He told tall tales with the best, and had a snappy reply for almost any question. When Paul Smith's was accorded a post office of its own, the proprietor, of course, became postmaster. One of his guests, some years later, asked him how he always managed to hold on to that political sinecure despite changing administrations. "I guess there ain't never been an administration that could change any quicker than I could," he replied.

Hotels, increasing in opulence and all of them advertising trout and venison throughout the summer (and sometimes a taxidermist's shop on the premises), soon studded the inner Adirondacks. The most ostentatious of these wilderness hotels was the Prospect House, built by Frederick C. Durant, a nephew of Dr. Thomas Clark Durant, in 1882. The young Durant set up a sawmill on Blue Mountain Lake's southeastern shore and produced an enormous, six-story frame building with three hundred rooms, rivaling the finest hotels in Saratoga. Guests paid twenty-five dollars a week on the American plan during the season. It was the first hotel in the world to equip each of its rooms with electric lights, the power being generated by a steam-driven "Edison incandescent electric light plant" on the grounds. Perhaps even more of a treat for the guests was a two-story outhouse that could be entered from the second-floor "piazzas," thus sparing the guests a chilly nighttime dash. In winter the rug that covered the expansive floor in the main parlor was cleaned by shoveling in snow from outside and then sweeping it off. The Prospect House, in part because of an outbreak of cholera in Blue Mountain Lake around the turn of the century, eventually went bankrupt; it was not even accorded the fiery end that was the fate of most old frame hotels of the era, but persisted in ever-shabbier stages on the shore of the lake (an elephantine haunted house) until its receivers finally had to pull it down.

But the Adirondacks was firmly established as one of America's most popular resorts. The Adirondack guideboat, one of the region's most distinctive and enduring creations, carried visitors to idyllic coves. Steamboats plied the lakes, not only the famous ones like Champlain and George, but also Blue Mountain Lake, Raquette Lake, and many others, carrying passengers from railheads to their hotels and avoiding the jarring, dusty rides over miserable roads. Later the wealthy visitors wanted boats of their own. Boat makers such as Fletcher Joyner of Schenectady turned out handsome craft of cedar, oiled and varnished, with brass and copper fittings. ("Joyner learned to make boats as a bird learns to build its nest," Seneca Ray Stoddard wrote.) Eventually one of the drawbacks to owning a steamboat for pleasure was that the frequency of boiler explosions caused laws to be passed that required a licensed engineer, with two years' experience in tending boilers, on each craft.

Substitutes were found. One of them was the naphtha launch, which had a great vogue on the lakes beginning about 1885 because it was clean and reasonably quiet ("The sound was the steady note of a blowtorch, deeply toned," an old-timer has said), emitting neither steam nor oily fumes; naphtha, a waste product of the early petroleum industry, had the added advantage of being cheap. Yet many subsequent builders have pointed out the anomaly of requiring a licensed operator for a boat that evaporated water in its boiler but exempting one that evaporated an explosive liquid. L. Francis Herreshoff of the boatbuilding family once wrote:

> It was the general arrangement of the naphtha launch that made it comparatively safe. The fuel tank was as far forward as possible. The engine was as far aft as was convenient with a direct drive propeller shaft, while the piping between them (condenser and fuel line) was outboard along the keel. To give the modern reader an idea of the potential danger of these infernal machines, the whistle was not blown by the pressurized vapor of the boiler but was blown by a hand driven air pump, for if the heated naphtha gasses were used there was danger of an explosion in the atmosphere as flame often came out of the stack. This was easily seen at night.

Even more popular were the electric boats that carried more than a million people across the lagoons at the Chicago World's Fair in 1893. Clean, quiet, and efficient, running on batteries hidden beneath the seats and flooring, they generated up to twelve horsepower for short spurts and produced no wake. To the great loss of all who love peaceful lakes in the wilderness, those motors were replaced after the turn of the century by the lighter, "more reliable," internal-combustion engine.

CHAPTER VI

Camps and Castles

There was a time in the gay nineties when our lakes were very fashionable and camps in much demand. So few were ever available to renters that they brought fantastic prices, probably the highest summer rentals in America. It was, if I remember aright, the Clarence Mackays who ate our frogs; but they paid $12,000 for the privilege of doing so for some six weeks. I believe the rent included ice and wood and the services of a guide, but at that time no camps had either plumbing or electricity.

This reminiscent paragraph was written by Mildred P. Stokes Hooker, who, as a girl, came to the Adirondacks with her family each summer to live for a while in a "camp" on an island in Upper St. Regis Lake. Like many another wealthy New Yorker, her father, Anson Phelps Stokes, had first brought his family to Paul Smith's, from where they often ventured into the woods to sleep on balsam boughs. Later Stokes acquired the island and in July the family moved into tents there with their voluminous baggage. All wealthy families brought great amounts of baggage, and often a horde of servants. When the Stokes family left New York for the woods in 1883, Mr. Stokes chartered a "parlor horse car" for a hundred dollars to take their belongings by rail from Forty-second Street to Au-Sable Forks. This car carried, among other things:

Anson Phelps Stokes, wife, seven children, one niece, about ten servants, Miss Rondell, one coachman, three horses, two dogs, one carriage, five large boxes of tents, three cases of wine, two packages of stove pipe, two stoves, one bale china, one iron pot, four washstands, one barrel of hardwood, four bundles of poles, seventeen cots and seventeen mattresses, four canvas packages, one buckboard, five barrels, one half barrel, two tubs of butter, one bag coffee, one chest tea, one crate china, twelve rugs, four milkcans, two drawing boards, twenty-five trunks, thirteen small boxes, one boat, one hamper.

With so much equipment it soon became obvious that tents were inadequate to hold it all, especially items that could be left there over the winter. So gradually a number of buildings went up, at first storerooms for their belongings, and later, when the tents wore out, log cabins for themselves. To store the perishables, the family built icehouses with thick, insulated walls; during the winter these buildings were filled with ice cut from the lake, which lasted all summer and sometimes for a second year. Like so many other Adirondack camps, the Phelpses' blossomed into a little village, with nearly a score of buildings, each for a special purpose, the family divided up among the cabins (the servants had their own quarters) and coming together in a separate building for their meals, and afterward going for dancing or games in a "casino" or other building. Tennis courts appeared, and inevitably the family went mountain climbing, boating, botanizing, swimming (Mrs. Stokes had been warned by the celebrated Dr. Edward Livingston Trudeau that bathing for more than twenty minutes in fresh water was dangerous, and thus she or a nurse always checked the duration of the children's dips with a watch in hand). No wonder that the Adirondacks seemed to loom so large in the lives of many wealthy men and women "from away," and that in later years they felt a proprietary interest in the mountains, putting their money, their talents, and their time into preserving them from what they saw as destructive threats. When Mrs. Hooker died in 1970 at the age of ninety, she was buried in the cemetery of St. John's in the Wilderness, close to where Paul Smith's Hotel had stood and, indeed, close to where Paul himself lies.

The private camp became the "soul" of the Adirondacks. The word "camp," when used there, is a rather bewildering term. "If ever an exact little word gradually went to seed and ran wild," says Donaldson, letting his own metaphor run wild, "not only in a wilderness of mountains but in a wilderness of meanings, it is this one.

If you have spent the night in a guide's tent, or a lean-to built of slabs and bark, you have lodged in a 'camp.' If you chance to know a millionaire, you may be housed in a cobblestone castle, tread on Persian rugs, bathe in a marble tub, and retire by electric light—and still your host may call this mountain home a 'camp.'" The early Adirondack camps were of the most primitive kind, simply tent platforms or lean-tos. Later the buildings were enclosed by walls made of unpeeled logs. Insects tended to crawl in under the bark, however, and as time went by the builders peeled and varnished the logs. The interiors were decorated with all sorts of rustic and ingenious bric-a-brac—the mounted heads of deer, unique mobiles of mounted ducks hung from rafters by bits of wire, lamps made from obsolete guns, coatracks whose "hooks" were the bent hooves of deer.

The man who elevated the Adirondack camp into an indigenous craft was William West Durant, son of the lapsed surgeon who had taken over the Adirondack Railroad. Born in Brooklyn but educated by his father in Europe, the younger Durant wandered about the Continent in his postgraduate days and made exploring expeditions to Abyssinia and the Levant. While he was still in his twenties, poking around in the sands of Egypt, his father called him back to the United States to take part in the development of the Adirondacks, where the older man had become a large landowner by virtue of his acquisition of the railroad. If the young man of the world was to live in the Adirondacks, he was going to do it on his own terms, in the style of one of the Old World potentates he had observed, and not like a backwoodsman. He became president of the Adirondack Railroad and on the shores of Raquette Lake built for himself and his family Camp Pine Knot (named for a large knot, three feet across and shaped like the hilt of a sword, found nearby).

Durant built in the style that soon became all the rage in the Adirondacks. The main building and those around it, Donaldson wrote in 1921, "were conceived, designed, and begun by Mr. William West Durant in 1879. In planning them he had the happy inspiration to combine the Adirondack features of the crude log cabin with the long low lines of the graceful Swiss chalet. From this pleasing blend there sprang a distinctive school of Adirondack architecture, and 'Pine Knot' became the prototype of the modern Camp Beautiful. Before it was built there was nothing like it; since then, despite infinite variations, there has been nothing essentially different from it." One of the buildings at Pine Knot was a four-room houseboat (with a bath and running water) that could be floated on the lake when the blackflies became too pestiferous on shore. Durant went on from height to height. At Eagle Nest (Ned Buntline's old haunt) he founded a country club complete with a nine-hole golf course. To transport the luggage of vacationers from Raquette Lake to Blue Mountain Lake on Marion River Carry (where steamboats could not maneuver), he constructed the world's shortest standard-gauge railroad, three quarters of a mile long, over which, for the first season, horses pulled streetcars Durant had bought from the Brooklyn Rapid Transit Company. Later an H. K. Porter engine (now in the Adirondack Museum) was brought in to do the job. On smaller lakes near Raquette Lake he built two large luxury camps in his famous "Pine Knot" style, Sagamore and Uncas, which, after his fortunes declined at the turn of the century, he sold to, respectively, Alfred G. Vanderbilt and J. P. Morgan. At Eagle Nest, after he had taken a fancy to a Swiss music box, four by six inches, he ordered his builders to make him a chalet of the exact design and proportions. Spending far beyond his means, his business schemes doomed to failure, his personal fortune drained by lawsuits, Durant went bankrupt at last. Though he lived throughout his declining years in New York City, taking in roomers to supplement his wife's small income, Durant left his mark permanently on the Adirondacks.

To the private Adirondack camps came not only a parade of financial and industrial giants but also a number of men and women remarkable in other fields. Putnam Camp in Keene Valley was notable in this respect. Keene Valley is one of the most beautiful regions of the eastern Adirondacks, a narrow valley about twenty-five miles west of Lake Champlain, with Marcy, Haystack, Giant-of-the-Valley, and other storied peaks creating its distant skyline. About 1877 four distinguished men—William James, the psychologist and philosopher, and the physicians Henry Bowditch and Charles and James Putnam—bought an old boardinghouse in the valley and turned it into a summer camp for their families and friends. While the camp itself never became even remotely as elaborate as those of Durant and other millionaires, it expanded in the same manner, simple, functional buildings added as they were needed. A whole way of life grew up around the original camp too. Years later, in 1941, Elizabeth Putnam McIver read a paper before the Keene Valley Historical Society, recalling the early days at the camp. She described the various buildings. One was called the Stoop, which served as the camp's parlor and library, "with two sides arranged so that they could be pushed out to form a roof over the piazza, thus opening the whole room to a glorious view of Sawtooth, Gothics, and the whole western wall of the Valley." She continued:

> The Stoop was Miss Annie Putnam's special domain. In one corner was a kerosene stove with rows of teacups and coffee cups hanging from shelves, where she made tea in the afternoon and coffee after dinner. She designed the big chimney and fireplace and burned into the wooden beam that crosses above it the quotation from Horace: "Ille terrarum mihi praeter omnes angulus ridet"—translated by one flippant young lady: "He above all others smiles at me in the corner." It was Miss Annie who arranged the curtain whereby one end of the Stoop could be turned into a stage, and who always insisted that there be some kind of organ or piano which contributed so much to the pleasure of the evenings.

While the usual recreations—mountain climbing, boating, and the like—were engaged in, the denizens of the Putnam Camp sometimes went farther afield. On hikes they carefully kept a logbook, noting the condition of the various trails or the altering of old landmarks. The hikers traced brooks to their source. They calculated the height of summits and even of certain prominent ledges by the use of an aneroid barometer. ("I am interested to find on looking at the geodetic survey maps," Mrs. McIver said in 1941, "that their calculations were not more than 10 or 20 feet out of the way.") In bad weather they retreated to the workshop, where they made furniture and toys, or undertook some necessary repair work. Dr. Bowditch even fashioned an ingenious silk-gathering contraption, "drawing the web from one of the big fat spiders found in the pasture and winding it onto a reel, operated by a little waterwheel set in a tiny waterfall in the brook."

William James, of course, was the most famous of the Putnam

regulars. Calling himself a meliorist (the world, he thought, "may be saved, on condition that its parts shall do their best"), he deeply believed in nature's capacity to refresh one's spirit and sustain one's health, and his longing for the woods he characterized as an "organic-feeling need." To a young woman he had met in the Adirondacks, he once wrote:

> We of the highly educated classes (so-called) have most of us got far, far away from Nature. We are stuffed with abstract conceptions, and glib verbalities and verbosities; and in the culture of these higher functions, the peculiar sources of joy connected with our simpler functions often dry up. . . . The remedy under such conditions is to descend to a more profound and primitive level. . . . Living in the open air and on the ground, the lop-sided beam of the balance slowly rises to the level line. The good of all the artificial schemes and fevers fades and pales; and that of seeing, smelling, tasting, sleeping, and daring and doing with one's body grows and grows. . . . I am sorry for the boy or girl, or man or woman, who has never been touched by the spell of this mysterious sensorial life with its irrationality, if so you like to call it, but its vigilance and its supreme felicity.

In 1900, in words that might have been written by a leader of the modern wilderness movement, James wrote from Europe to his son, William:

> Scenery seems to wear in one's consciousness better than any other element in life. In this year of much solemn and idle meditation, I have often been surprised to find what a prominent part in my own spiritual experience it has played, and how it stands out as almost the only thing the memory of which I should like to carry over with me beyond the veil, unamended and unaltered.

It was the presence at the Putnam Camp of men like James and the Putnams that, in fact, brought many distinguished European visitors to the Adirondacks, including Sigmund Freud and C. G. Jung.

Freud had come to the United States in September 1909 to deliver a series of lectures on psychoanalysis at Clark University in Worcester, Massachusetts. James Jackson Putnam, a Harvard professor of neurology who had become interested in the subject, attended the lectures and invited Freud and his colleagues, Sandor Ferenczi and Jung, to the family camp in the Adirondacks. The party accepted and spent three days in the woods. On September 16 Freud wrote to his family from Putnam Camp:

> Of all the things that I have experienced in America, this is by far the most amazing. Imagine a camp in a forest wilderness situated somewhat like the mountain pasture on the Loser where the inn is. Stones, moss, groups of trees, uneven ground which, on three sides, runs into thickly wooded hills. On this land, a group of roughly hewn small log cabins, each one, as we discover, with a name. One of them is called the Stoop and is the parlor, where there is a library, a piano, writing desks and cardtables. Another, the "Hall of Knights" with amusing old objects, has a fireplace in the center and benches along the walls, like a peasant dining room; the others are living quarters. Ours with only three rooms is called Chatterbox. Everything is left very rough and primitive but it comes off. Mixing bowls serve as wash bowls, china mugs for glasses, etc. But naturally nothing is lacking and is supplied in one form or another. We have discovered that there are special books on camping in which instruction is given about all this primitive equipment.
>
> Our reception at half past two consisted of an invitation to take a walk up the nearest mountain, where we had an opportunity of becoming acquainted with the utter wildness of such an American landscape. We took trails and came down on slopes to which even my horns and hoofs were not equal.
>
> Fortunately it is raining today. There are many squirrels and porcupines in these woods; the latter are invisible so far. Even black bears are said to be seen in winter.

Finally, as a contrast to the simple buildings and intellectual pleasures of Putnam Camp we may gaze in some awe on the stone castle built about 1913 in the style of a French chateau—even to its formidable towers—near Tupper Lake by a New York lawyer and financier, Edward Hubbard Litchfield. Litchfield, by his portrait a man of imposing presence with keen eyes and a neat Vandyke beard, had a taste for imposing houses and estates. During the 1850s he built an Italianate villa in Brooklyn on land that had a fine view of the harbor and Manhattan Island. Egbert Vielé, an engineer then working on Central Park, once remarked to Litchfield that his land would make an impressive park too. Pleased by the notion, Litchfield gave twenty-four acres to the city, but the plans for Brooklyn's Prospect Park were abandoned until after the Civil War. Then, when Litchfield and his wife were in Europe, the New York State Legislature, in a fit of ingratitude unusual even in politicians, appropriated more of his land, including his home, for the park.

Undaunted, Litchfield erected his Adirondack castle, using native stone and foreign ideas, on a 7,000-acre estate (which was later expanded to 14,000 acres) at a point five miles from the nearest road. A great sportsman, Litchfield naturally designed a "great hall" in his castle, partly to house his collection of 193 animal heads—elephants, giraffes, dik-diks, rhinoceroses, and the like. He also conceived the idea of raising big game animals on the estate. Toward that end he put up an eight-foot-high wire fence around the grounds and turned loose a variety of animals including moose (formerly native to the Adirondacks but extirpated as early as 1861), elk, and wild boar. His hopes, however, were dashed by nature herself. Many of the animals could not cope with the strange surroundings; others escaped when storms sent big trees crashing down on the fence and flattening it. Some boars fled to the nearby Whitney estate, where the caretaker and his sons enjoyed unexpected sport, at Litchfield's expense.

CHAPTER VII

The White Plague

Any attempt to define the image of the Adirondacks as it played its part in the political events that swirled around the wilderness during the closing years of the nineteenth century must take in the mountains' reputation for sustaining human life, particularly life threatened by diseases of the lungs. Tuberculosis, or pulmonary consumption, loomed as large in the pathology of that time as cancer does in ours; "the white plague" was especially virulent in the young, and we need only think of the *famous* young it killed in the spring of genius and beauty—Keats, Chopin, Emily Brontë—to realize its impact on the popular imagination. There were no medicines (aside from cough medicines, merely palliatives) to treat the disease. For the most part, its victims were simply shut up in their rooms or in hospitals to die. No one even knew what caused the disease; it was sometimes ascribed to a mysterious dissolution of the blood. But by the middle of the century, as "Adirondack" Murray pointed out in his paean to the northern wilderness, the notion had gotten abroad that mountain air might restore consumptives to health.

A correspondent signing himself "Wachusett" and covering the "Murray's Fools" phenomenon for the Boston *Daily Advertiser* in July 1869 wrote of the people with lung diseases flocking to the Adirondacks:

> The great majority of these people derive invaluable benefit from their visit because the great majority are those who come in time, in the first stages of a malady at first capable of cure. The singular sweetness of the air is apparent to all. . . . But there is another class

> who come here this summer equally filled with hope of thorough recovery who find nothing but the bitterest disappointment, bringing perhaps an accelerated death in its train. These are the consumptives in the later stages of disease who have tried everything else in vain. . . . It is the saddest of sights to see one of these sufferers arrested in the forest by the coming of death, the comforts with which home would surround him absolutely unattainable by any expenditure of money, no means at hand of summoning friends, no physician to be found, even departure by the route of entrance impossible now that the stimulus of hope has been withdrawn.

Murray, of course, had stressed frequent retreats to the wilderness as a means of relieving tensions and maintaining health ("Let the old, old nurse, Nature . . . take you to her bosom again; and you will return to the city happier and healthier for the embrace"), but he also saw the Adirondacks as a vast sanatorium ("I predict that the Wilderness will be more and more frequented by invalids, as accommodations are provided for their reception and comfort, and that the region will become the resort of thousands each year seeking restoration to health").

In that sense Murray was a prophet, but as talented as he was he could not on those terms have forged anything more vital than a fad for cures. To go beyond that point required a doer with more substance than earnest prose. It required a vision and a commitment. They were supplied almost immediately by one of the most remarkable men who ever lived in the Adirondacks, Dr. Edward Livingston Trudeau.

Trudeau was a curious amalgam, a dandyish man-about-town and a skilled sportsman, the Prodigal Son fired by an all-consuming passion for knowledge and service. His life was a triumph of dedication over his earlier aimlessness, a habit of life he obviously had drifted into because of his home environment. His father, James, was an odd fish, a socially prominent physician in New Orleans whose bent for the adventurous life was stimulated by his acquaintance with John James Audubon. According to Edward Trudeau's autobiography, his father was a frequent companion of Audubon's on scientific expeditions and his guide in various anatomical constructions. Although the family later boasted of the connection, the elder Trudeau was of little service to his illustrious friend. Asked by Audubon to obtain natural-history books for him when he went to live in Paris, Trudeau ignored the request, much to the great man's disgust. Trudeau, indeed, won for himself a certain spurious immortality by sending Audubon a tern he had allegedly shot at Great Egg Harbor in New Jersey. Audubon excitedly described it as a species new to North America and named it Trudeau's tern (*Storna trudeaui*). Although the tern remains saddled with Trudeau's name, and indeed continues on the American Ornithologists' Union's *Check-list of North American Birds*, it has never been seen by any reputable ornithologist on the continent and is now believed to have been shot in Chile, a place more congenial to it than the Jersey shore. In any case, the elder Trudeau gained further luster by having Audubon's son, John Woodhouse Audubon, paint a portrait of him dressed in an Osage Indian costume.

James Trudeau was highly mobile during his heyday, sampling a variety of cities and experiences. His son Edward was born in New York City and grew up in France. When young Edward returned with his father to New York, he lived the good life with no thought for future deeds of a high and noble character. For a time he served as a midshipman, pointing toward a naval career, but tragedy put an end to that ambition. A beloved brother was stricken with "consumption." Trudeau left the Navy to nurse him, and, tuberculosis not being recognized as a contagious disease, lived with him in a closed room, even sleeping with him in the same bed as he steadily grew worse. After his brother's death, Trudeau dabbled for a while in business, married, and then abruptly decided to study medicine. Shortly after he entered practice in New York in 1871, he was also struck down by tuberculosis.

Other doctors diagnosed his case as very serious. He went south for a while, but his health did not improve. Expecting death and ordered to stay away from the city, Trudeau recalled a happy hunting expedition to Paul Smith's in the Adirondacks. In 1873, accompanied by a couple of friends, he set out for the wilderness by way of Plattsburgh, but he was so weak that he could not walk without support. He made the final leg of the journey while lying uncomfortably on a mattress in a stagecoach, jolting for forty-two miles over corduroy roads. Mrs. Smith's brother carried him to his room, easing him onto the bed with the remark: "Why, Doctor, you don't weigh no more than a dried lambskin!"

Trudeau remained at Smith's for three months that summer. The following year, after a relapse, he made up his mind to return to the Adirondacks and live there year round, an almost unheard-of decision for a "city man" in those days. He brought his wife and children with him in 1874, and settled in at Paul Smith's. To everyone's amazement, his health slowly improved. In 1876 he made a permanent home in Saranac Lake, hardly a prepossessing place if one believes the early descriptions of it, such as this one, written by a clergyman from Philadelphia, the Reverend J. P. Lundy, during an enforced sojourn there for his health in 1877–78:

> The miserable hamlet of Saranac Lake—its present name twice changed from that of Baker's and Harrietstown, as if the people were ashamed of having it long known under one appellation—consists of about fifty or sixty log and frame-houses, and has a population of three or four hundred souls. It is in a little deep basin of hills on every side of it, on the main branch of the Saranac River, a few miles from its leaving the lower lake of that name, and one mile below Martin's. It is nearly forty miles distant from the terminus of the branch railroad from Plattsburg to Ausable, and is reached by daily stage. The Montreal Telegraph Company has a station here from which dispatches can be sent anywhere. It is this sheltered position of the place in winter, this daily stage and the telegraph that have given Saranac Lake its main attraction to invalids, aside from the pure invigorating mountain air.
>
> It has two country stores of the usual heterogeneous assortment of coarse dry-goods, boots and shoes, groceries, hardware, and quack medicines, but no books and magazines. An old rickety saw-mill supplies the place and neighborhood with building materials, and a steam-mill occasionally makes shingles and clapboards. There is also a small gristmill; one shoemaker but no tailor. The barber of the place is a peripatetic on crutches, going from house to house or from room to room on call, to discharge his tonsorial duties and do the main headwork of the community at the rate of twenty-five cents for each clipping and manipulation. . . .
>
> Saranac Lake has one flourishing tavern, whose landlord, it is needless to say, is the richest man in the place; and who, publican and sinner as he is, gave us the choice of a half-acre lot on which to erect our church.

Having gone on to characterize most of the natives as pastured in vice or sloth, the Reverend Lundy took care not to have his book published until after he had reached home. (It was privately printed in Philadelphia in 1880 under the title *The Saranac Exiles: A Winter's Tale of the Adirondacks,* "Not by W. Shakespeare.") The only resident for whom he had unstinting praise was Dr. Trudeau, who by that time was about to embark on his extraordinary career.

A skillful marksman as well as an enthusiastic hunter, Trudeau had keenly felt the restrictions his illness laid on him. One of his greatest pleasures was to take up a position on a hillside, now called Mount Pisgah, where there was a sheltered spot with a view looking to the distant mountains and from which Trudeau could shoot the foxes that often used the place for a runway. On his long vigils there the idea came to him that Saranac Lake would be an ideal area in which to set up a sanatorium where other, less fortunate victims of consumption might come to receive the benefits he had found. He had been deeply interested in the theories of the German physician Hermann Brehmer, who was the first to use the sanatorium treatment (rest, fresh air, and the regulation of the patient's life and habits). In 1882 Trudeau read of the discovery by another German, Robert Koch, that tuberculosis was caused by a bacillus.

Trudeau was impelled into the study that now occupied most of his time. He set up a primitive laboratory in Saranac Lake, duplicating Koch's experiments and pursuing his own research into the nature of the disease. With the help of wealthy friends, most of whom owned camps on the St. Regis and Saranac lakes, he also founded among the boulders and scanty grasses on the side of Mount Pisgah the Adirondack Cottage Sanatorium. Indeed, that was all it was at first—a one-room cottage, fourteen by eighteen feet, with a little porch and a wood stove. The cottage, built in 1884 and which came to be called "the Little Red," was in keeping with Trudeau's ideas that the patient ought not to be jammed with others in an airless dormitory, but must have privacy and plenty of fresh air. The first two patients were penniless factory girls. As other cottages went up, financed by the money Trudeau was able to squeeze from his wealthy friends, patients poured in to Saranac Lake to take the cure, and word of the great experiment spread. While wealthier patients were sent by the doctors to stay in Saranac

Lake at the various hotels and boardinghouses built to accommodate the traffic, the Cottage Sanatorium catered to those of modest means, who were treated at "less than cost." The summer people in the Adirondacks started a fair to support the sanatorium. As Mildred Hooker wrote in *Camp Chronicles*:

> This sanatorium fair became an annual event, first at Birch Island, then at Paul's [Smith's], and people vied with each other in planning salable articles. Our greatest success was with the little tent sewing baskets that mother invented. She had us cover cardboard with green and white striped material and sew the pieces together to form miniature tents. You lifted one side of the top and there inside were needles and threads, reels, scissors, etc. They went like hotcakes and we had orders for more. In later years on our biennial trips abroad mother spent much time collecting unusual things of charm and value which she knew could be sold for profit at the fair.

Alfred Donaldson, a banker whose health had collapsed and who came to the Adirondacks as one of Dr. Trudeau's paying patients (and stayed for the rest of his life to become the region's historian), described his first visit from the physician:

> Despite the intense cold outside, he wore no overcoat. His costume consisted of a fur cap which had been pulled down over his ears, a sweater that came high up around his neck, trousers folded into long lumbermen's socks, called "Pontiacs," and moccasins that gave an Indian silence to his tread.
>
> Above this picturesque apparel emerged a most unusual and impressive head. The upper part seemed abnormally large, for the broad, protruding forehead ran back into the baldness of the crown. The keen but kindly gray eyes were deep set beneath overhanging brows. The cheek-bones were prominent, the nose aquiline, and the lower face tapered into a small, sensitive mouth and clean-cut chin.
>
> His movements were rapid and lithe, and he was obviously nervous, restless, and high-strung. Yet he brought into the sick-room nothing but soothing and uplifting magic. His voice had much to do with this. It was very smooth and low. His utterance was copious and rapid, but clear and modulated. The words ran from him like silk unwinding from a spool.

Donaldson was only one of thousands atttracted to Saranac Lake and the "cure" by the magnetic Trudeau. Once the accommodations were built, the town was well suited to be a health resort. As the railroads came to the Adirondacks it was no longer terribly remote from the great population centers of the East, nor were the mountains themselves of such altitude that they caused the patients discomfort. (Saranac Lake lies 1,500 feet above sea level.) The best medical opinion of the time held that pines and other conifers provided a healthy atmosphere. As a physician wrote in the *New York Medical Journal* in 1886: "The turpentine exhaled from these pine forests possesses, to a greater degree than all other bodies, the property of converting the oxygen of the air into ozone, and, as this latter destroys organic matter, the air of such forests must be very pure, and consequently conducive to respiration." Moreover, the air in the Adirondacks is notably dry, unlike the misty, rainy climate of England's Lake Country, hostile to consumptives, to which the region is sometimes compared.

Donaldson has commented on the climate of the Adirondacks:

> The dryness of the air is due largely to the extreme sandiness and porousness of the soil, which is nowhere of a character to retain much moisture. There are very few clay beds in the Adirondacks, virtually none in the mountainous parts. Papers and books can be left in a summer camp all winter without showing a trace of dampness in the spring. This lack of humidity robs the cold of winter of its sting, and the heat of summer of its sappiness. It lends the average atmosphere an invigorating, champagne-like quality, comparable to the bouquet of fine wine.

One of the invalids soon attracted to the Adirondacks' "fine wine" was Robert Louis Stevenson. His reputation among readers on both sides of the Atlantic was immense; he had already written such classics as *Treasure Island*, *Kidnapped*, *The Strange Case of Dr. Jekyll and Mr. Hyde*, and, a mark of his versatility and virtuosity, *A Child's Garden of Verses*. With an entourage that included his wife, his mother, his stepson, and a servant, he settled into a guide's house in Saranac Lake for the winter of 1887–88 to become a patient of Dr. Trudeau. The winter proved to be ferocious, and

Stevenson and his family were unhappy in its grip. "Here we are in a kind of wilderness of hills and fir-woods and boulders and snow and wooden houses," he wrote in November to another valetudinarian author, John Addington Symonds. "So far as we have gone the climate is grey and harsh, but hungry and somnolent; and although not charming like that of Davos, essentially bracing and briskening. The country is a kind of insane mixture of Scotland and a touch of Switzerland and a dash of America and a thought of the British Channel in the skies." And, in frigid December, to another friend in England, he wrote that the mercury on the thermometer "curls into the bulb like a hibernating bear." Though Stevenson occasionally displayed his form on ice skates to admiring neighbors, he mostly kept to himself, shunning those who would thrust themselves upon his notice and retreating into his room to write a good part of *The Master of Ballantrae* (ostensibly set in the Adirondacks but of which Donaldson writes: "Let no one turn to it for Adirondack pictures. It holds none"). In the spring Stevenson fled to Samoa, where he found both the climate and the natives much more to his taste.

In our own time climate has lost its primary position in the treatment of pulmonary diseases, with doctors turning to powerful drugs such as streptomycin to control tuberculosis even in the patients' urban homes. The Trudeau Sanatorium closed for lack of patients in 1954, after having carried on its founder's research and treatment so well that it put itself out of business. The Trudeau Institute remains to carry out a variety of research projects. But there is little doubt that regulated diet and rest under a sympathetic physician like Dr. Trudeau, in the clear, brisk air of the mountains, contributed to a great many recoveries in earlier years. That the Adirondacks possessed such healing characteristics gave those who would preserve its forests and waterways an added point in the debates to which we shall now turn.

CHAPTER VIII

Parks for America

The awareness of "limits to growth" is characteristic of our own time. In the middle of the nineteenth century there was a growing suspicion that the wilderness, on which the New World seemed to hold a near monopoly, had very real limits too. "In the beginning, all the world was America," John Locke had written. The places where a man could go and live by himself for a while, confronting nature as Thoreau had done only a few years before, were dwindling. In England, Wordsworth stood aghast as the railroad invaded the picturesque Lake Country, prompting him to ask in sonnet form:

Is then no nook of English ground secure
From rash assault . . .

The American woods, as well as their wild denizens, were suffering rash assaults from a variety of directions as lumbermen, farmers, miners, market gunners, and vacationers marched on them to appropriate their slice of the rich pie. The cities, once overgrown villages, suddenly grew into stinking, disease-ridden warrens where fragile people of all ages rapidly succumbed to the impurities around them. It was only natural that remedies should be sought first where the crisis was most real, and even before 1850 there was a strenuous effort to preserve patches of greenery among the dense grids of the eastern cities. Practical Americans reasoned that, since there was a need for cemeteries, they might as well do double duty as parks. The first of the picturesque "gardens of graves," Mount Auburn Cemetery, sprouted in Cambridge across the Charles River from Boston in 1831 (and even in the twentieth century one of America's finest field ornithologists, Ludlow Griscom, did some of his most productive birding among Mount Auburn's opulent monuments and greenery). A few years later, Brooklyn created a garden of graves of its own in Green-Wood Cemetery.

But New York, its commercial and cultural growth spurred by the opening of the Erie Canal, and boasting a population of 312,000 in 1840, had left no such significant green space among its teeming streets. Probably the first man to advocate publicly a large park for the growing metropolis was William Cullen Bryant. His experience of parks and gardens in the great European cities—the Prater in Vienna, Hyde Park in London—prompted him to warn the readers of the New York *Evening Post* in 1844 that "commerce is devouring inch by inch the coast of the island, and if we would rescue any part of it for health and recreation it must be done now." And again in 1845 he wrote:

> The population of your city, increasing with such prodigious rapidity, your sultry summers, and the corrupt atmosphere generated in hot and crowded streets, make it a cause of regret that in laying out New York, no preparation was made, while it was yet practical, for a range of parks and public gardens along the central part of the island or elsewhere, to remain perpetually for the refreshment and recreation of the citizens during the torrid heats of the warm season. There are yet unoccupied lands on the island which might, I suppose, be procured for the purpose and which, on account of their rocky and uneven surfaces, might be laid out into surpassingly beautiful pleasure-grounds; but while we are discussing the subject the advancing population of the city is sweeping over them and covering them from our reach.

Andrew Jackson Downing, the prominent landscape architect, took up the cry again at the end of the decade. A large park in New York, Jackson wrote in his own magazine, *The Horticulturist*, in 1849, "would not only *pay* in money, but largely civilize and refine the national character, foster the love of rural beauty, and increase the knowledge of, and taste for, rare and beautiful trees and plants."

Downing's ideas proved extremely influential, and it is probable that the city would have given him the assignment to plan a large park had he not drowned in 1852 at the age of thirty-seven, trying to rescue his mother-in-law during one of the early steamboat disasters on the Hudson River.

The agitation for an urban park continued, fueled by commercial interests which foresaw that land values around the park would rise. (But, like businessmen in most other American cities, New York's most influential citizens did not want to include land along the rivers in the proposed park, preferring to keep the shorelines for commercial development; and thus most of our cities, unlike those in Europe, have turned their backs on the magnificent rivers that flow past them, abandoning them to pollution and blight.) Some of the city's upper crust advocated a park because it would give them an opportunity to show off their fancy horses and carriages on leisurely afternoons, while others dissented, fearing the park would become a haunt of idlers and ruffians. In the end, good intentions and the prospect of a commercial bonanza prevailed. The city fathers raised the money and a competition was announced for a plan for a large park, to be situated in a hilly, rocky "wasteland" at the northern edge of the densely settled area, until then inhabited mostly by squatters and their pigs.

Too often in our country's history politics or graft has dictated the choice of men to design our monuments. But in the nineteenth century two men, Frederick Law Olmsted and Calvert Vaux, put their enormous talents as landscape architects at their country's disposal, and their accomplishments were enormous. (Among Olmsted's later creations were New York's Riverside Park and Morningside Heights Park, Brooklyn's Prospect Park, the Back Bay parkland in Boston, Jackson Park in Chicago, Mount Royal Park in Montreal, the campuses of Stanford University and the University of California at Berkeley, the grounds of the Capitol in Washington, and the Arnold Arboretum in Brookline, Massachusetts; he also drew up a successful plan for the preservation of Niagara Falls.) In the 1850s, after a successful career in journalism, Olmsted was just branching into landscape architecture. He secured the job of clearing the land for a "Central Park" in New York (the squatters and their shacks proved the toughest part of the land to clear, the police finally having to be brought in to do the job); then he collaborated with Vaux on a design which won out over its rivals.

They created one of the most beautiful parks in the world, using rocks, grottoes, trees, and artificial lakes to superb advantage. In the process, they put a kink in the plans of wealthy young hot-rodders of the day, designing a series of winding roads through their park that were not conducive to the sort of flat-out trotting races many had hoped for with their equipage. The park, though unfinished, opened in 1858, the same year that William Stillman led his philosophers to Follansbee Pond in the northern wilderness. Even before the park was completed more than ten million city dwellers flocked to it for renewal and recreation. Its 840 acres of picturesque greenery became "the lungs of the city."

Olmsted and Vaux literally created this park. They took an unremarkable plot at the fringe of a spreading city, land indeed already somewhat blighted by squatters, pig farmers, and the operators of bone-boiling works, and through their artistry—blasting, grading, fertilizing, lake making, and the like—they formed a pleasure ground in the image of picturesque landscapes painted by Lorrain, Poussin, and their American descendants in the Hudson River school. Since God in his wisdom had not chosen to plant a paradise on Manhattan Island, Olmstead and Vaux, by order of the city fathers, proceeded to do so. (The word "paradise" is derived from the old Persian *pairi-daēza*, meaning enclosure or park.) Central Park was a prefab Garden of Eden. Olmsted himself refers to landscape architecture as "the art of . . . scenery-making." It was approved by the municipal government, not only because it would benefit the spiritual and bodily health of the people but because it would help to raise property values in the area and bring other financial blessings to the city; Central Park appealed to commercial desires as well as to the aesthetic, and that aspect greased the political wheels. Other American cities, many with Olmsted's help, staked out parks of their own.

Parks, like gardens, originally were thought of as enclosures; in England a park had been, according to the *Oxford English Dictionary*, "an enclosed tract of land held by royal grant or prescription for keeping beasts of the chase." Later the word was stretched to cover ornamental land around large mansions, and then (in the sense of a "central park") an enclosed piece of land laid out in an ornamental fashion for public recreation. It was for expansive Americans to stretch the word further, and in a letter he wrote in 1832 (but did not publish until 1841), George Catlin, the painter of western and American Indian scenes, spoke of his hope that portions of the unsettled West, with its native people, fauna, and flora, might be preserved by the government

> in a *magnificent park*, where the world could see for ages to come, the native Indian in his classic attire, galloping his wild horse, with sinewy bow, and shield and lance, amid the fleeting herds of elks and buffaloes. What a beautiful and thrilling specimen for America to preserve and hold up to the view of her refined citizens and the world, in future ages! A *nation's park*, containing man and beast, in all the wild and freshness of their nature's beauty.

Here, indeed, was a park to match America's vastness. It was not simply a pretty conceit, but the urgent expression of a man who saw even then that the glory of the West would soon be swept away by the exploitative hordes already increasing in numbers and destructiveness. A few years later Thoreau echoed the call in an article in *The Atlantic Monthly*, asking why Americans should not "have our national preserves . . . in which the bear and panther and some even of the hunter race, may still exist, and not be 'civilized off the face of the earth' . . . for inspiration and our true re-creation?"

This idea of a great preserve or park simmered among thoughtful people for several decades, until in the 1860s a place was found for the great experiment. White men had known of a spectacular valley in the Sierra Nevada at least since 1833. In that year an old Tennessee trapper named Joseph Reddeford Walker, guided by Indians, apparently viewed this area where peaks towered nearly five thousand feet above the valley floor and a magnificent waterfall plummeted twenty-four hundred feet down the face of an imposing cliff. But the valley did not receive a name until 1851, when a former mountain man, Major James D. Savage, led an expedition of militia into the mountains to hunt down a band of Yosemite Indians who had been harassing the white settlements. A member of the militia later recalled the "exalted sensation" when he first saw the valley and the cliffs of El Capitan: "The grandeur of the scene was but softened by the haze that hung over the valley—light as gossamer—and by the clouds that partially dimmed the higher cliffs and mountains." The militiamen did not inflict much damage on the Indians but they did agree that the valley should be called after them. The fame of the lovely Yosemite Valley slowly spread through California. Explorers and sightseers rode in to view its marvels. A scientist who visited the valley with a California survey team a few years later called it "not only the greatest natural curiosity in the state, but one of the most remarkable in the world." Painters such as Albert Bierstadt came to Yosemite, and illustrators and writers publicized it in various periodicals of the time.

Near the valley lay groves of some of the largest trees on earth, the sequoias, three or four thousand years old, growing three hundred feet and more and with a girth of up to thirty feet. The commercial exploitation of such an area was inevitable. In the 1850s two men stripped the bark from one of the sequoias and took it East on exhibition, then later to London, where it was shown at the Crystal Palace (unsuccessfully, because the British could not believe in the reality of such forest giants; they thought the display was a hoax). Miners, cattlemen, farmers, and lumbermen were already invading Yosemite Valley. At last some Californians realized that they had within the state a priceless treasure, a natural wonder that might become the Niagara Falls of the West. They started a movement to have the valley, which was still in the public domain, put aside as a state reservation. Among the leaders of the group was Frederick Law Olmsted.

Frustrated by penny pinching on the part of New York's park commissioners and other difficulties, Olmsted had given up his position as architect-in-chief of Central Park upon the outbreak of the Civil War and served for a time in Washington as secretary of the United States Sanitary Commission, a forerunner of the American Red Cross. In 1863 a new challenge loomed. Colonel John C. Frémont, the dashing and controversial soldier and explorer, had bought a 44,000-acre ranch near Yosemite some years before. As with so many of his business ventures, Frémont's ranch and his nearby mining properties failed, and a group of Wall Street financiers took over. Olmsted was hired to manage the ranch and he moved his family to California.

In 1864, at the urging of some influential constituents, Senator John Conness of California introduced a bill in the United States Senate to grant Yosemite Valley and the neighboring "Mariposa Big Tree Grove" to the state to be "held for public use, resort, and recreation for all time." He assured the Senate it would not cost the United States government any money and that the valley itself was "for all public purposes worthless." The bill, stipulating that the valley and the "big trees" were to be taken out of the public domain and made the full responsibility of the state (which could grant leases on portions of the land for up to ten years), easily passed both houses of Congress. President Lincoln signed the measure into law on June 30, 1864.

Governor Frederick F. Low of California accepted the land as a "public pleasure ground" for the state. He appointed a board of nine commissioners (including himself) to oversee Yosemite Park, with Olmsted acting as its unofficial chairman. Olmsted had the new park surveyed and mapped at his own expense, then prepared a report to the State Legislature in which he proposed a policy for the park's management. "It is an extraordinary document," writes Holway R. Jones, the Sierra Club's historian. "Not only does it reveal Olmsted's philosophic basis for the practice of landscape architecture, as others have pointed out, but it also anticipated by some six years the principles underlying the Yellowstone National Park legislation, which in turn may have influenced the men who drafted the 1916 act creating the National Park Service."*

In his report, Olmsted cited two reasons why Congress apparently set aside the park. One was the commercial aspect, the value to the state of a natural wonder. The second reason postulated by Olmsted was a matter that is too often overlooked by those who object to government "interference" in the use of natural resources of any kind.

"It is the main duty of government," Olmsted wrote, "if it is not

* Olmsted's key document, long lost, was uncovered only in 1952, so that it was not his text, but his ideas picked up and handed on by interested people, that became the major influence on park planners.

the sole duty of government, to provide means of protection for all its citizens in the pursuit of happiness against the obstacles, otherwise insurmountable, which the selfishness of individuals or combination of individuals is liable to interpose to that pursuit."

He went on to point out that such a natural reservation would promote the people's health. "It employs the mind without fatigue and yet exercises it; tranquilizes it and yet enlivens it; and thus, through the influence of the mind over the body, gives the effect of refreshing rest and reinvigoration of the whole system." If the government does not withhold such areas from monopoly and exploitation, Olmsted argued, the people will be closed out. He saw the commissioners as a barrier against the greed and vandalism that natural wonders invariably excite. And he wrote:

> The main duty with which the Commissioners should be charged should be to give every advantage practicable to the mass of the people to benefit by that which is peculiar to this ground and which had caused Congress to treat it differently from other parts of the public domain. This peculiarity consists wholly in its natural scenery; the restriction, that is to say, within the narrowest limits consistent with the necessary accommodations of visitors, of all artificial constructions and the prevention of all constructions markedly inharmonious with the scenery or which would unnecessarily obscure, distort, or detract from the dignity of the scenery.

Olmsted was to learn with increasing bitterness how incursions into parklands, innocent enough at first, could easily get out of hand; it was over his strenuous objections that the notorious Tweed Ring established a zoo in the midst of his splendid landscape in Central Park, and though he did not object at first to the inclusion of an art gallery in the park, he was appalled by the way the Metropolitan Museum of Art eventually swelled and overflowed the greenery.* More immediate frustrations faced him in California. The State Legislature rejected his request for an appropriation of $37,000 to protect Yosemite and the Big Trees, and the other commissioners suppressed his report. When the former Frémont estate that employed him finally lapsed into bankruptcy, Olmsted re-

* The museum's invasion of the park continues to this day.

turned to New York and his old job at Central Park. Without Olmsted, as we shall see, the state of California bungled Yosemite's management and betrayed its responsibility.

Meanwhile, the West yielded up another treasure. Probably the first white man to penetrate the Yellowstone country in what is now northwestern Wyoming and adjacent areas of Idaho and Montana was John Colter, a trapper, who viewed the geysers there during the winter of 1807–08. From that time onward other trappers occasionally passed through and rumors of the wonders of this "infernal region" filtered through to the outside world. The geysers and extraordinary rock formations surrounding them became the basis of many tall tales, tales that probably retarded outside acceptance of the facts; Jim Bridger, one of the old mountain men, recounted stories of his own creation, including one about petrified birds perched on petrified trees singing petrified songs. But as the age of beaver trapping waned around 1840, few travelers in the West had reason to pass that way. An attempt to explore the region by a detachment of army engineers in 1859 was turned back by snow. Yellowstone and its marvels sank into neglected history.

After the Civil War there was a resurgence of interest in the Yellowstone region among some explorers and scientists. A party of nineteen men under General Henry D. Washburn, a Union officer in the Civil War and later surveyor general of the Montana Territory, reached the Yellowstone River in the summer of 1870. As they crossed a plateau, the officer in charge of the party's military escort, Lieutenant Gustavus C. Doane, was enthralled by the land he saw around him. He described it later:

> The river breaks through this plateau in a winding and impassable canyon and trachyte lava over 2000 feet in depth; the middle canyon of the Yellowstone, rolling over still pools of seemingly fathomless depth. At one point it dashes here and there, lashed to a white foam, upon its rocky bed; at another it subsides into a crystal mirror wherever a deep basin occurs in the channel. Numerous small cascades are seen tumbling from the lofty summits, a mere ribbon of foam in the immeasurable distance below. This huge abyss, through walls of flinty lava, has not been worn upon the rocks; it is a cleft in the strata brought about by volcanic action

> plainly shown by that irregular structure which gives such a ragged appearance to all such igneous formations. Standing on the brink of the chasm the heavy roaring of the imprisoned river comes to the ear only in a sort of hollow, hungry growl, scarcely audible from the depths, and strongly suggestive of demons in torment below. Lofty pines on the bank of the stream "dwindle to shrubs in dizziness of distance." Everything beneath has a weird and deceptive appearance. The water does not look like water, but like oil. Numerous fishhawks are seen busily plying their vocation, sailing high above the waters, and yet a thousand feet below the spectator. In the clefts of the rocks, hundreds of feet down, bald eagles have their eyries, from which we can see them swooping still further into the depths to rob the ospreys of their hard earned trout. It is grand, gloomy, and terrible; a solitude peopled with fantastic ideas, an empire of shadows and turmoil.

Here, laid out before the intruders, was the exotic West that Easterners and even Europeans wanted to know more about—a land of majestic creatures and majestic scenery unrivaled by that of any other continent; something indisputably American, that is no myth at all, but which has provided the backdrop for some of our most cherished myths and romances. In the evenings the men sat around their campfire and talked of what they were experiencing together, and apparently the notion of setting this region apart as a national park gained substance. Such ideas, as we have seen, were already in the air. When members of the party returned to the East they told others about Yellowstone. One of them, Nathaniel P. Langford, who had been appointed governor of the Montana Territory by President Andrew Johnson (a position he never held because the appointment was defeated by Johnson's enemies), undertook a lecture tour, describing the wonders of Yellowstone and advocating that they be set aside for the enjoyment of all the people. A man who was especially taken with the idea was Jay Cooke, the financier of the Northern Pacific Railroad. If a popular tourist attraction were established in that remote area, Cooke reasoned, the railroad would become a chief beneficiary. He subsidized Langford's lectures and put up additional money to lobby in Congress for an act creating a national park in Yellowstone.

Support for the idea grew. An expedition to Yellowstone in

1871, led by F. V. Hayden, chief of the United States Geological Survey of the Territories, produced a great deal of scientific information on the wonders there, including sketches and photographs.* Langford and his friends, with valuable support from the railroad interests, were able to get bills introduced into both houses of Congress at the end of 1871. There was some opposition in Congress as the voices for development spoke up. Senator Cornelius Cole of California could not understand why such a large tract of land should be set aside. "The geysers will remain, no matter where the ownership of the land may be," he said, "and I do not know why settlers should be excluded from a tract of land forty miles square. . . . I cannot see how the natural curiosities can be interfered with if settlers are allowed to appropriate them."

But public opinion was against him. "Why will not Congress at once pass a law setting the Yellowstone apart as a great public park for all time to come, as has been done with that not more remarkable wonder, Yosemite Valley?" asked the geologist Hayden. The great herds of bison, elk, and other western big game animals had been decimated. There were those who believed that only in a refuge such as that provided by a national park could a few of the remnant animals survive. The editor of the Helena *Daily Herald* farsightedly called for a park to preserve portions of the forests which were already threatened by the westward sweep of civilization and the timbermen. ("The loss to us is trifling, but the value of these timber lands to future generations is incalculable.") But what most appealed to Congress and the public was the image of Yellowstone as an oddity, a place of "beautiful decorations," a living museum, a geological sideshow. The park was to be a kind of theatrical tableau. This notion was in keeping with the contemporary cast of mind that prompted cultural leaders to suggest Phineas T. Barnum as director of the Smithsonian Institution.

And so Congress, its members gravely assuring each other that the land was worthless for agriculture, passed the legislation creating Yellowstone National Park "as a public park or pleasuring ground for the enjoyment and benefit of the people." It was signed

* Hayden's chief photographer was William Henry Jackson, a native of Keeseville in the Adirondacks.

by President Grant on March 1, 1872. The act ordered "the preservation, from injury or spoliation, of all timber, mineral deposits, natural curiosities or wonders within said park and their retention in their natural condition," and assigned the park's administration to the Secretary of the Interior. But Congress set no penalties for a violation of its orders and gave no appropriation for administration, policing, or the building of roads. Nevertheless, one of the park's most enthusiastic supporters, *Scribner's* magazine, optimistically applauded the legislation, predicting that "Yankee enterprise will dot the new park with hostelries and furrow it with lines of travel."

CHAPTER IX

Verplanck Colvin and the Idea of a Park

In the 1870s, while Central Park, Yosemite, and Yellowstone were all coming under at least nominal protection, the forests of northern New York (the "great northern wilderness" only a few years before) were nearly defenseless. They were subsiding beneath the demands of the Gilded Age, not so much its emissaries who poured into the hotels and luxury camps to seek recreation, but its seamier side, the exploiters of the natural world who traded in forests or buffalo, whales or plume birds, until the supply was exhausted. This is not to say that rusticators themselves were not diluting, and even destroying, the wilderness they came to find. Like most people, they sought to experience the wilderness in comfort if not in luxury, and they wanted the scenery served up as presentably as possible. Orson "Old Mountain" Phelps, the celebrated Adirondack guide who thought a man should have to work for his scenery, chided the sightseers who took in the High Peaks from their guideboats. "Waal, now, them Gothics ain't the kinder scenery you want to *hog down,*" he told them. And no less an authority than "Adirondack" Murray, writing in *The New York Times* early in 1872, attested to the changes these people had wrought:

> [The] region is now ruined for the lover of solitude and nature. Stage lines connect it with the more permanently settled regions, and visitors to the number of thirty thousand are said to have hurried through it last summer. A man cannot now sit down on the border of Tupper's Lake to fish a quiet hour, without becoming the

center of a score of interested and fashionably dressed spectators. He cannot shoot at an imaginary deer without running the risk of wounding a New York belle, while his life is placed in perpetual jeopardy as he wanders along the crowded woodpaths, by the unskilled rifle practice of the young gentlemen who lie in ambush behind every tree to shoot at casual robins. In fact, if those who have latterly made the trip through the Adirondack region are to be believed, that once imposing forest solitude is now rather more crowded and decidedly gayer, than the Central Park on a summer's Saturday afternoon. This is the work of literary tourists and stage lines.

Murray, the foremost literary tourist of them all, was a chief cause of his own discomfiture, but he had had little effect, one way or the other, on the most imminent threat to the Adirondacks; this threat was not simply to solitude but to the forest itself. The charcoal industry had clear-cut vast areas. (Much of the charcoal went to fire the kilns of the local iron foundries.) The tanning industry was in a state of collapse, closing its workshops because it had greatly reduced the hemlock on which it depended for raw material. Other parts of the forest were cleared by optimistic farmers hoping to grub a living from the thin rocky soil, and thus contributed to the erosion that followed everywhere in the wake of the lumberman. ". . . if the Adirondack forests could be saved by legislation," J. B. Harrison of the American Forestry Congress once wrote, "one of the best possible measures would be 'An Act for the Discouragement of Agriculture in the North Woods.'" And meanwhile the lumbermen, spurred by the rapid industrial growth in the North during and after the Civil War, were harvesting everything they could reach. Harrison once described a trip he had made into the Adirondacks in the 1870s:

I rode through the "Schroon Country" with a man who has probably done as much as anyone to desolate this whole region. From Minerva, past Pottersville, Schroon Lake, Schroon River (Roots Hotel) and on along the Elizabethtown road past Deadwater to the new road that leads through the forest to Smith and Beede's, we traveled all day long through a blighted and hopeless land. As league after league of utter desolation unrolled before and around us, we became more and more silent. At last my companion exclaimed: "This whole country's gone to the devil, hasn't it?" I asked what was, more than anything else, the reason or cause of it. After long thought he replied: "It all comes to this—it was because there was nobody to think about it, or to do anything about it. We were all busy, and all somewhat to blame perhaps. But it was a large matter, and needed the co-operation of many men, and there was no opening, no place to begin a new order of things here. I could do nothing alone, and there was nobody to set us to work together on a plan to have things better; nobody to represent the common object."

Ecological concepts or the scientific management of natural resources had not yet filtered down to the general public, but they were already in the air, mainly formulated by a remarkable Vermonter named George Perkins Marsh. Marsh was a man of many callings. He was lawyer, businessman, farmer, geographer, naturalist, congressman, and diplomat. Perhaps the last of these professions (he served as minister to Turkey and later to Italy) helped to bring all the rest of his experience together and forced on him certain universal conclusions. He had seen the devastation man had brought down on his environment in the Middle East, deserts and eroded gullies dominating landscapes that once were forests or fertile fields.

In 1864, Marsh wrote the first great book on ecology, *Man and Nature*. More than half of it was devoted to forests and their importance in maintaining productive watersheds. Indiscriminate cutting and burning, Marsh thought, were "the most destructive among the many causes of the physical deterioration of the earth." The forest, with its dense root system, held the soil in place, preventing erosion, and was a natural cistern for water. He had seen French and German silviculture in action and believed that Americans, rather than indulging in the waste of clear-cutting wild forests, ought to grow their timber on farms specially planted to secure the most efficient harvest. He called on contemporary man to be a steward of the earth for later generations.

On August 9 of the same year that Marsh's classic was published, *The New York Times* suggested just this sort of stewardship for a specific portion of the globe, the Adirondack Mountains. According to Donaldson, the editorial was probably written by Charles Loring Brace, "author, philanthropist, and founder of the Children's Aid Society," who often spent his vacations near Lake Placid, and a regular contributor to the *Times*. He was also a close friend of Olmsted. The editorial is a seminal document in the history of the region, and an example of how this wilderness was seen from the growing metropolis at the other end of the Hudson:

> . . . Within an easy day's ride of our great city, as steam teaches us to measure distance, is a tract of country fitted to make a Central Park for the world. The jaded merchant or financier or litterateur or politician, feeling excited within him again the old passion for nature (which is never permitted entirely to die out) and longing for the inspiration of physical exercise and pure air and giant scenery, has only to take an early morning train in order, if he chooses, to sleep the same night in the shadow of kingly hills and waken with his memory filled with pleasant dreams, woven from the cease-less music of mountain streams.
>
> To people in general, Adirondack is still a realm of mystery. Although the waters of the Hudson, which today mingle with those of the ocean in our harbor, yesterday rippled over its rocks, and though on all sides of it have grown up villages and have been created busy thoroughfares, yet so little has this wonderful wilderness been penetrated by enterprise or art that our community is practically ignorant of its enormous capacities, both for the imparting of pleasure and the increase of wealth.
>
> It is true that the desultory notes of a few summer tourists have given us a vague idea of its character. We know it as a region of hills and valleys and lakes; we believe it to abound in rocks and rivulets and have an ill-defined notion that it contains mines of iron. But as yet we have never been able to understand that it embraces a variety of mountain scenery unsurpassed, if even equalled, by any region of similar size in the world; that its lakes count by hundreds, fed by cool springs and connected mainly by watery threads which make them a network such as Switzerland might strive in vain to match; and that it affords facilities for hunting and fishing which our democratic sovereign-citizen could not afford to exchange for the preserves of the mightiest crowned monarch of Christendom. And still less do we understand that it abounds in mines which the famous iron mountains of Missouri cannot themselves equal for qual-

ity and ease of working; and that its resources of timber and lumber are so great that, once made easily accessible, their supply would regulate the prices of those articles in our market.

And this access is what we are now going to secure. The gay denizens of Saratoga this season are excited by an occasional glimpse of a railroad grade running north from that town toward the Upper Hudson and aiming directly at the heart of the wilderness [Thomas C. Durant's Adirondack Railroad]. . . . With its completion, the Adirondack region will become a suburb of New York. The furnaces of our capitalists will line its valleys and create new fortunes to swell the aggregate of our wealth, while the hunting-lodges of our citizens will adorn its more remote mountainsides and the wooded islands of its delightful lakes. It will become to our whole community, on an ample scale, what Central Park is on a limited one. We shall sleep tonight on one of the magnificent steamers of the People's Line, ride a few cool hours in the morning by rail, and, if we choose, spend the afternoon in a solitude almost as complete as when the Deerslayer stalked his game in its fastnesses and unconsciously founded a school of romance equally true to sentiment with that of feudal ages.

And here we venture a suggestion to those of our citizens who desire to advance civilization by combining taste with luxury in their expenditures . . . let them form combinations, and seizing upon the choicest of the Adirondack Mountains, before they are despoiled of their forests, make of them grand parks, owned in common and thinly dotted with hunting seats where, at little cost, they can enjoy equal amplitude and privacy of sporting, riding, and driving whenever they are able, for a few days or weeks, to seek the country in pursuit of health or pleasure. In spite of all the din and dust of furnaces and foundries, the Adirondacks, thus husbanded, will furnish abundant seclusion for all time to come; and will admirably realize the true union which should always exist between utility and enjoyment.

While the *Times*'s editorial writer conjured up sufficient utilitarian horrors to set wilderness enthusiasts of later times to gnashing their teeth, he had sent abroad a notion that would take hold. Meanwhile, the Adirondacks cried out for a man like Marsh or Olmsted who could spend his great energy on the problems and fire the public with his vision. Such a man came north into the forest from Albany in the 1860s, and later provided the facts and the vision to stem the destruction. His name was Verplanck Colvin and he was the bachelor son of a lawyer and legislator; the New York *Tribune* once described the younger Colvin as "an athletic looking man of dark complexion whose features tell of resolution, pluck and ability." He fell in love with the mountains at first sight, cherishing their mysteries, but he called for their protection because of their potential commercial value to future generations.

His father had wanted him to follow a career as a lawyer in Albany, but Colvin cared only for the outdoors and his meticulous maps. He had made a trip to the Rocky Mountains in the early 1870s and returned with a portfolio of sketches. In 1870 he climbed Mount Seward to take barometric measurements of its elevation (he calculated it to be 4,462 feet, which a 1953 survey corrected to 4,367 feet), all the while marveling at the magnificent views over the forest to Whiteface Mountain in the north, the High Peaks in the east, and the Santanoni Range in the south. Two years before, speaking to a group of fishermen and hunters at the post office in the resort community of Lake Pleasant, he had called for a forest preserve and public park in the mountains. Now he saw an opportunity to reach a more influential audience. He submitted a description of his ascent and findings to the New York State Museum of Natural History for inclusion in its Annual Report to the Legislature. And he added:

> Before closing this report, I desire to call your attention to a subject of much importance. The Adirondack wilderness contains the springs which are the sources of our principal rivers, and the feeders of our canals. Each summer the water supply for these rivers and canals is lessened, and commerce has suffered. The United States government has been called upon, and has expended vast sums in the improvement of the navigation of the Hudson: yet the secret origin of the difficulty seems not to have been reached.
>
> The immediate cause has been the chopping and burning off of vast tracts of forest in the wilderness, which have hitherto sheltered from the sun's heat and evaporation the deep and lingering snows, the brooks and rivulets, and the thick, soaking, sphagnous moss which, at times knee-deep, half water and half plant, forms hanging lakes upon the mountain sides; throwing out constantly a chilly

atmosphere, which condenses to clouds the warm vapor of the winds, and still reacting, resolves them into rain.

It is impossible for those who have not visited this region to realize the abundance, luxuriance and depth which these peaty mosses—the true sources of our rivers—attain under the shade of those dark, northern, evergreen forests. The term "hanging-lake" will not be deemed inappropriate, in consideration of the fact that in the wet season a large mass of this moss, when compressed by the hands, becomes but a small handful, the rest of its bulk being altogether water; often many inches deep, it covers the rocks and boulders on the mountain sides, every foot-print made has soon a shallow pool of icy water in it.

With the destruction of the forests, these mosses dry, wither and disappear; with them vanishes the cold, condensing atmosphere which forms the clouds. Now the winter snows that accumulate on the mountains, unprotected from the sun, melt suddenly and rush down laden with disaster. For lumber, once so plentiful, we must at no distant day become tributary to other States or the Canadas. The land, deprived of all that gave it value, reverts to the State for unpaid taxes.

The remedy for this is the creation of an ADIRONDACK PARK or timber preserve, under charge of a forest warden and deputies. The "burning off" of mountains should be visited with suitable penalties; the cutting of pines under ten inches or one foot in diameter should be prohibited. The officers of the law might be supported by a per capita tax, upon sportsmen, artists and tourists visiting the region; a tax which they would willingly pay if the game should be protected from unlawful slaughter, and the grand primeval forest be saved from ruthless desolation.

The interests of commerce and navigation demand that these forests should be preserved, and for posterity should be set aside, this Adirondack region, as a park for New York, as is the Yosemite for California and the Pacific states.

In 1872 Colvin made his most famous ascent, tracing the Hudson River to its true source on Mount Marcy. Having talked about the mountains to anyone who would listen in Albany, this flamboyant young man of twenty-five was appointed by the Legislature in that year to be superintendent of a state topographical survey of the Adirondacks. He began in the Champlain Valley, where existing base lines provided key points of reference, he and his party carrying the fine instruments he had bought with his own money, moving from peak to peak, climbing in all sorts of weather, Colvin taking his measurements from dawn to dusk, pushing his men unmercifully. Some of them quit, unable to stand the pace and the rigors to which he submitted them. Colvin often mentioned their defections in his reports:

"Here the guides, dissatisfied with the severity of the labor, demanded their discharge and asked increased pay, nor could they be persuaded to proceed further, exhibiting their torn clothing and soleless gaping boots as evidence of their inability." That he prohibited the men to take alcoholic drinks with them on their trips also added to their rebelliousness. But he went on insatiably from peak to peak, climbing to regions white men (and perhaps red men too) had never penetrated and baring the Adirondack landscape as no one had before him. In September he reached Mount Marcy, thirty-five years after Ebenezer Emmons had made the first ascent. Here he located the Hudson's source and, in the official report he filed with the Legislature in 1873, he described his find:

"Far above the chilly water of Lake Avalanche, at an elevation of 4,293 feet, is *Summit Water*, a minute unpretending tear of the clouds as it were,—a lonely pool, shivering in the breezes of the mountains, and sending its limpid surplus through Feldspar Brook to the Opalescent River, the well-spring of the Hudson."

Avalanche, Feldspar, Opalescent—among all those inspiriting names and sparkling bodies of water was the pond Colvin discovered to which he gave one of the loveliest and most apt names possessed by a natural feature in the world—Lake Tear of the Clouds.

Colvin went on for some years, completing his general survey of the Adirondacks and their peaks, inveigling men into accompanying him, squabbling with the Legislature to pry from it the money he thought was due him for his services. On one of his trips he shot the largest panther ever taken in the Adirondacks, which was mounted and displayed afterward in the State Capitol; its whereabouts are now unknown. Perhaps Colvin's greatest achievement lay in publicizing the mountains through his detailed official reports and the impassioned speeches he made before various clubs and other groups. His reports during the 1870s not only are crammed with facts but read like adventure stories. (Many years later a couple of boys, Robert and George Marshall, read Colvin's early reports and were inspired by them to climb all of the highest Adirondack peaks and then go on to play vital roles in America's wilderness movement.) He described the mountains and the hardships he encountered while surmounting them, and imparted a sense of their mystery and grandeur:

> Few fully understand what the Adirondack wilderness really is. It is a mystery even to those who have crossed and recrossed it by boats along its avenues, the lakes; and on foot through its vast and silent recesses, by following the long ghostly lines of blazed and axe-marked trees, which the daring searcher for the fur of the sable or the mink has chopped in order that he may find his way again in that deep and often desolate forest. In those remote sections, filled with the most rugged mountains, where unnamed waterfalls pour in snowy tresses from the dark overhanging cliffs, the horse can find no footing; and the adventurous trapper or explorer must carry upon his back his blankets and his heavy stock of fare. His rifle which affords protection against wild beasts at times replenishes his well husbanded provisions and his axe aids him in constructing from bark and bough some temporary shelter from storm, or hews into logs the huge trees which form the fierce roaring, comfortable fire in the camp. Yet, though the woodsman may pass his life-time in some section of the wilderness it is still a mystery to him. Following the line of the axe-marks upon the trees; venturing along the cliff walls of the streams which rush leap on leap downward to form haughty rivers; climbing on the steep wooded slopes of lakes which never knew form or name on maps, he clings to his trapping line, and shrouded and shut in by the deep wonderful forest, emerges at length from its darkness to the daylight of the clearings like a man who has passed under a great river or arm of the sea through a tunnel, knowing little of the wonders that had surrounded him.

Yet behind the mist of overblown prose Colvin, as we know, did understand some of the mysteries he had passed through in the mountains. He kept on talking about their preservation and pointing to Yosemite as a model for a possible solution in New York. In 1872, speaking to the members of the Albany Institute, he said: "It has been proposed that the state reserve this region as a Wilderness

Park for sportsmen, but that is a slight matter in comparison with the reservation of it as a timber preserve, and as the grand reservoir region of the cities of the valley of the Hudson." It was in this last notion, to which he returned again and again, that Colvin touched a chord that would eventually bring the wilderness park into existence. Before the end of the century the water issue was to prove decisive in New York, even at the expense of the scientific foresters. But for the moment most of the appeals to save the mountains were based on the readily apparent destruction of trees.

New York had done little or nothing to protect its forests. Much land, cut over or burned, had been abandoned by the owners as worthless and returned to the state. Because of a lack of proper mapping and surveying, many of these parcels of state-owned land were lost in the welter of private holdings, their boundaries unknown. The only pieces bought back by the state were seven hundred acres in Clinton County so that the state prisons would have a supply of wood. (New York paid a whopping twelve dollars an acre for these woodlands, compared to the ninepence per acre for which it had sold them in the previous century.) The first constructive forestry measure came in 1867, when the Legislature passed a law providing for the partial abatement of taxes on land where the owner had planted shade trees along public highways. Two years later, perhaps having encountered skulduggery among the landowners, the Legislature specified the distance that trees of each species were to be planted from each other and warned that no tax abatement would be permitted "unless such trees shall have been set out the year previous to the demand for said abatement of tax, and are living and well protected from animals at the time of such demand."

In his appeals for state preservation of the forests, Colvin acquired a supporter in Franklin B. Hough, a country doctor who can lay claim to being America's first native-born scientific forester. Hough was a demon for work. The time away from his practice in Lowville, New York, just west of the Adirondacks, he spent studying natural history, botany, and mineralogy. He wrote histories of several upstate counties. He supervised the state census in 1865 and the federal census in 1870. It was said that Hough had two or three desks in his office and that he relaxed by shifting from one to the other, at each of which he had a different project in progress. As he traveled throughout the state and checked the statistics he had compiled on lumber products, he felt certain that New York's forests faced disaster. The state led the nation in lumbering in 1850, but overcutting, fire, and waste had sadly depleted the woods. (New York would drop to fourth place in 1880 and to seventeenth by the end of the century.) How long will New York's remaining forests last? Hough asked himself. Like George Perkins Marsh before him, he advocated the careful management of these forests and scientific replanting where they had been cut.

While Hough was primarily concerned with timber preservation and Colvin with watershed protection, other notes began to sound in the chorus urging the state to take some action. In 1871 *The New York Times*, delivering one of the first salvos in its support of the Adirondacks which has continued to this day, spoke out in an editorial:

> No railroad, or canal, or turnpike traverses it; no steam-whistle is heard in all its borders; no boat for commerce or pleasure larger than a rowboat cuts the silent waters of its hundreds of lakes or streams. Here, alone in the Eastern States, the whirl of the factory or the hum of commerce is not heard. Around this enchanted island, the waves of business and the currents of traffic, and all the storms of the busy American world seem to beat in vain, leaving its sylvan solitudes and still lakes and ancient forests as peaceful and lonely as they were when the Pilgrims first landed. . . . What princes and millionaires enjoy in the Old World—their own solitudes and undisturbed forests and preserves—would here be offered to the people without price or condition, except an observance of laws. Will not the country press, and the Sportsmen's Conventions and their organs, recommend this measure of civilization until it becomes law?"

By 1872 the climate was right, both nationally and in New York, for action, however limited. Congress was in the process of creating a great national park at Yellowstone. But in the Great Lakes states, where the lumbermen had migrated as the forests of Maine, New Hampshire, and New York dwindled, devastating fires erupted in the carelessly cut woodlands. The deadliest of them, centered on Peshtigo in northwestern Wisconsin in 1871, had swept two counties and a million and a quarter acres of their trees, soil, and lumber camps, killing twelve hundred people. Meanwhile, New York suffered from a severe drought, raising fears of uncontrollable fires there as well.

On March 15, 1872, Assemblyman Thomas G. Alvord of Onondaga County introduced a bill to appoint "Commissioners of Parks." Although the Commission of State Parks created by the Legislature that year was essentially parkless, its function was spelled out by law "to inquire into the expediency of providing for vesting in the State the title to the timbered regions lying within the counties of Lewis, Essex, Clinton, Franklin, St. Lawrence, Herkimer and Hamilton, and converting the same into a public park." The Legislature appointed several prestigious men to the commission, including Horatio Seymour, a former governor and a noted sportsman, and William A. Wheeler, a prominent north country politician who later sank into the obscurity of the vice-presidency under President Rutherford B. Hayes. Apparently added to the commission as an afterthought were Verplanck Colvin and Franklin B. Hough, but it was they who took its work most seriously.

The commission's report, when it was published in 1873, proved to be a well-reasoned document, often phrased in Colvin's colorful prose, reflecting the latter's concern for an Adirondack watershed as well as Hough's ideas about scientific forest management. Underlying the report's substance was a fear of the ultimate effect exerted on the forest by the "cut-out and get-out" tactics of the lumbermen. At the outset the commissioners affirmed their belief that "the protection of a great portion of that forest from wanton destruction is absolutely and immediately required." They described the enormous watershed provided by upstate New York and emphasized its importance to both the Erie Canal and the state's mills and factories. If the canal dried up in western New York, the commissioners predicted, "grain would decrease in value, and the farmers would be in the power of the great railroad monopolies." The forest, in this view, accumulated rainwater in its spongy soil, releasing it slowly to the lowlands so that a sufficient supply was always available. If a twelve-inch blanket of snow melted suddenly in the mountains, the commissioners calculated, and was not retained in the forest soils, the giant flood would rush into the Hudson Valley, where "it would sweep before it fields of ice, to crush and sink the strongest vessels, and ruin the warehouses on our wharves."

The commissioners recommended that the forests be managed by professional foresters, as they were in Germany, France, and Switzerland, trees being cut only when they had reached a certain size and the area replanted to provide a harvest for future generations. Although the Adirondacks, if protected from abuse, would provide recreation for the people in the form of boating, hunting, fishing, and camping, "to strengthen and revive the human frame . . . to afford that physical training which northern America stands sadly in need of," the commissioners did not envision it as another Yellowstone Park, another "pleasuring-grounds for the people." In fact, they said, "the idea of such an unproductive and useless park we utterly and entirely repudiate." The mountains, in other words, should be open to careful forestry and mining.

Colvin sent a copy of the Park Commission's report to Governor John A. Dix and asked his assistance in the creation of a state park. At first the governor was reluctant to mention the idea in his annual message to the Legislature, agreeing with the opponents of the Adirondack Park Agency a century later that potential settlers in the region should not be discouraged by the restrictions of a park. But Colvin, arguing from economic considerations as well as his own love for the mountains, underlined the threats to the priceless watershed; and in any case, he argued, only the "untillable, rocky and mountainous lands" at the heart of the mountains (what was to be the core of Laurance Rockefeller's National Park proposal in 1967) would be included in the proposed park or preserve. The proposal really involved no new lands. It would simply require the state to retain those lands that had already reverted to it for taxes rather than sell them to lumber barons of the future.

The governor's agreement to acknowledge the Park Commission's report in his message of 1874 was hardly a victory for the park enthusiasts. Dix simply mentioned the report, without comment, and the Legislature predictably ignored it. But Colvin had another outlet from which to bombard the public with his views. Because of his colorful descriptions of the mountains and his own adventures in them, the early reports he issued as state surveyor (with unpromising titles such as *Report on a Topographical Survey of the Adirondack Wilderness in New York for the Year 1873*) were widely read around Albany. He called upon the state to buy about 384,000 acres in the High Peak region (even by eminent domain) to establish a park or forest preserve. He saw this park (which he thought might be enlarged later) as bounded by the road from Keene to North Elba on the north, the Saranac Lakes on the northwest, the Raquette River and Long Lake on the west, the road from Long Lake to Blue Ridge on the south, and the Schroon Valley on the east. As the state owned only 84,000 acres in that region, 300,000 shy of Colvin's goal, the Legislature went on ignoring him.

CHAPTER X

A Constituency for the Adirondacks

But Verplanck Colvin's words were on the wind. As early as 1876 the Manufacturers' Aid Association of Watertown, New York, thinking of their water-powered industries on the Black River just west of the mountains, applauded the proposals for a park in the Adirondacks "as securing for all time to come an ample supply of water, not only for the Black River but for the sources of the Hudson River on the south and the numerous tributaries of the St. Lawrence on the north." Those ideas would soon spread beyond the north country. For the moment, the most outspoken and influential voices raised in support of preserving the mountains were those of sportsmen. The reputed abundance of fish and game was the lure that had pulled many men from the cities north into the wilderness in the first place, and these sportsmen were now chagrined to find that the general slaughter was depriving them of their favorite recreation. Certainly the fishing was ruined in rivers badly polluted by neighboring industries near all the large cities. Frederick Mather, a pioneer fish culturist who had publicly bemoaned the destruction of streams near his home, received a reply from an industrialist in 1875:

> I think there are two sides to this question. One is the manufacturing interests, Lowell, Lawrence, and a hundred other cities and towns thriving by manufacturers, and employing hundreds of thousands of operatives; and the other is, the fishing interests. Which is the greatest: If Fred Mather wants to catch fish, why don't he go where the fish are: I do.

The fish, presumably, were in the Adirondacks, but even there many of the best fishing pools were depleted. In fact, the first conservation agency established in the state was the Fisheries Commission, created by the Legislature in 1868. A part of its mission was to study the sources of noted fishing streams in the Adirondacks and the ill effects of forest destruction on both the fish and the water supply. In the 1870s the commission got deeply involved in pisciculture, at first dealing with commercial shad.* By the 1880s the commission had established various hatcheries and was stocking streams with sport fish such as rainbow trout.

New York had dabbled in game protection at an even earlier date. One popular game bird, the heath hen (an eastern race of the prairie chicken that eventually became extinct), had already been shot to scarcity by the end of the eighteenth century. In 1791 the Legislature established a closed season on this bird. Alexander Wilson, the early American ornithologist, once recalled an odd circumstance connected with the bill's passage:

> The bill was entitled "An Act for the preservation of the Heath-Hen and other game." The honest Chairman of the Assembly—no sportsman, I suppose—read the title "An Act for the preservation of the *Heathen* and other game!" which seemed to astonish the northern members, who could not see the propriety of preserving *Indians*, or any other heathen.

The fate of "big game" in the Adirondacks is the subject of some misconceptions. Moose had disappeared from the state in the 1860s, though several unsuccessful attempts were made to restock them in the region around 1877 and again during the early years of the twentieth century. They were, in fact, declining before the hunters went after them en masse. The Adirondack forests form the southern limit of the moose population; they prefer the boreal

* The development of pisciculture in the United States is a good story in itself; there was a great deal of opposition to it, in part from those who did not believe that man should interfere in the ways of nature and, from a more practical standpoint, thought that fish ladders built to ease the path of fish upriver would inevitably cause the dams to leak. Finally, there was opposition from fishmongers. It is said that when a Fisheries Commission employee visited the New York markets there were cries of "Stop this hatching. The fish are too plenty—it don't pay!"

forests of Canada, Newfoundland, and northern Maine. Although gunners undoubtedly played a part in their extirpation from the Adirondacks, a more important factor is that moose and deer are incompatible. Deer harbor a nematode parasite called brainworm, which is comparatively harmless to them. But moose living in the same region pick up the parasite from deer, with disastrous consequences, the nematode settling in the larger mammals' brains, inducing the "blind staggers" and eventually killing them. Moose were able to get along in the Adirondacks when they were heavily forested. Once the mountains were opened up by lumbering and agriculture, deer, preferring to browse on young trees and shrubs which grow up in areas recently cleared, invaded the region in much greater numbers and the moose were in trouble. The gunners simply finished off the remnants.

Wolves were never very numerous in the Adirondacks, in this case because deer, one of their chief prey species, were not present in large numbers. "There is much to suggest that the Adirondack wolf may have been as much a victim of environmental history as [of] man," wrote C. H. D. Clarke, a Canadian biologist who has studied wildlife in the Adirondacks. "The region originally did not have an important deer population, and the wolves were small, and inefficient hunters of other large game, and could never have been numerous." Wolves, we know now, are harmless to humans and do not even deplete deer populations to any extent. But old myths and fears die hard; in the nineteenth century there was a bounty on them in the state, and they had almost disappeared by the end of the Civil War.

That other American symbol of wilderness, the panther or cougar, all but disappeared about the same time. In 1870, incredibly, the Hamilton County Board of Supervisors raised the bounty on panthers from five to fifteen dollars. Four hunters collected the bounty that year, but not many of them did so again. The panther's scream became just a memory to the old Adirondack guides.* Black bears, on the other hand, have found the Adirondacks always to

* These secretive, wide-ranging animals which, like leopards in Africa, are able to survive at remarkably low densities, are occasionally reported from the region even today, but usually without any substantial proof.

their liking, and the coming of man with his garbage and other allurements offset whatever pressure the hunters put on them.

But when speaking of hunters and hunting, the only species that really mattered in the Adirondacks was (and still is) the white-tailed deer. Originally their best habitat was on the fringes of the mountains; in pre-Columbian America deer were especially abundant in areas where the Indians planted their corn, and they learned to find all the browse they needed in clearings made by the European settlers. Inevitably they followed man into the Adirondacks, where, in turn, the city dwellers of the late nineteenth century came after them in droves. Game laws were few and seldom enforced. One midcentury hunter told of killing as many as 150 deer in certain years in upstate New York. The deer population could have sustained itself in the face of the sportsmen's onslaught, just as it does today, but deer slaying became big business in the Adirondacks. Market gunners were sent into the mountains to kill all the "mountain mutton" they could find, not only to feed the lumberjacks in the many woodland camps and the guests in the thriving hotels, but also for shipment to game dealers who sold them to hotels and restaurants in the large cities. The market gunners established camps of their own in the forests.

"They were followed by teamsters," a man active in game protection wrote long afterward, "who loaded their sleighs with the deer carcasses and carried the venison out to distributing points for shipment to Albany and the centers of central New York and New York City as well. From the north part of the Adirondacks some of this venison was shipped to Montreal."

Two hunting techniques, "jacking" and "hounding," were especially destructive. In jacking, or jacklighting, the deer were pursued at night with bright lanterns and other lights, often in boats along the shores of lakes and ponds; blinded by the strange glare, the deer were easy marks for the hunters. Other hunters used hounds extensively. The hounds often drove the deer into lakes, where hunters followed the struggling, half-drowned animals and shot them at point-blank range, the boat handler sometimes holding the deer by the tail as the hunter fired. These hounds became so efficient that, even when not in use by their masters, they took to the woods in packs, chasing down deer (especially in winter, when the deer tend to flounder in deep snow) and tearing them to pieces. Hounding was outlawed in the state in 1877, but the cry from the "hounding lobby" forced the Legislature to repeal the ban in 1879. Market gunners, backed by associations of hotelkeepers, restaurant owners, and game dealers, exerted a powerful influence at Albany, while even wealthy sportsmen liked to hunt with hounds because they coveted the prestige of a large "bag." William J. Stillman, returning to the Adirondacks years after his experience at the Philosophers' Camp, described the game situation for the readers of *The Nation* in 1884:

> The deer, too, are being thinned out by the sportsmen, in contempt of the laws, and are killed from May until March with no notice except that growing out of hotel jealousies and personal animosities. In one month—from May to June—four years since, a party of four persons, headed by a railway "magnate" of New Hampshire, killed twenty-two deer, and this at a season when the venison is not fit to eat and every doe leaves a fawn or two to starve. This magnate is known to all this section as a persistent and perennial deer-slayer in the forbidden months, and without molestation so far. The guides will not ruin their business by informing, and the people will take no trouble where they have no personal interests.

As Stillman pointed out, there were game protection laws on the books, but even when they were enforced, which was seldom, they were riddled with flaws. The season on deer opened in August, an extremely wasteful time to kill them because the fawns were still in need of their mother's care and usually starved when the doe was shot. It was said that the opening was set to accommodate the wealthy summer vacationers in the Adirondacks. Although deer could not be shot after the first of the year, there was no limit on the number that an individual or a party was permitted to kill during the open season. By 1880 the deer had been wiped out through most of the state (a few wandered across the state line from Pennsylvania occasionally), except for the Adirondacks and parts of Long Island where a moratorium on deer hunting for several years had allowed the herds to recover. Even the Catskills were bereft of deer.

With the Adirondacks serving as the last significant haven for the state's deer herd, there was much agitation to give them added protection. A powerful conservationists' forum appeared in 1873 with the publication of a magazine called *Forest and Stream*, which its editors hoped to make "the recognized medium of communication between amateurs and professional sportsmen." In their first issue the editors spoke of their determination to fight for the forests. "Our great interests are in jeopardy—even our supply of drinking water is threatened, from the depletion of our timber-lands by fire and axe," they wrote.

Such a periodical, published in New York City and numbering wealthy and influential men among its subscribers, was bound to have a beneficial effect on the Adirondacks. In articles and editorials, *Forest and Stream* publicized the campaign to protect the Adirondack forests as well as the wild things that lived in it. It also made plain the various interests that were at war with each other over how to protect the resources that more and more people were beginning to say they valued. But, despite the exhortations of its editors, many of *Forest and Stream*'s readers seemed to be less concerned with how to save the game than who was going to kill it. City dwellers, under the banner of the "sportsman," grumbled in letters to the editor about the depredations of market gunners, poachers, and jacklighters. A farmer, writing to the editor in 1879, struck back:

> It is all very well for us to catch quail and keep them through the winter, and turn them out in the spring to breed. Who gets the first shot at them in the fall? We cannot get our sowing done and corn gathered before the 15th of November. On the 1st of November we see the New York bloods appear . . . with guns strapped on their backs and dogs on their chains. Next day they come across our farms. We are busy. The first thing we hear is some one among our quail, which we wintered over. We leave our work and go see. We find some . . . running around in our sprouts, looking for something he never killed at all. We ask him to leave the birds alone. We want them for our own shooting. He will give you some of his slang, shoot till he scares all the birds out of his reach, then leave when he gets ready. Along will come another with his setter tearing through our berry vines, destroying them more like a lion than a bird dog of high blood. Tell the man to let the birds alone, and he will tell you to "go

> there yourself." Along he goes until he meets some one's flock of turkeys, lets go on them and bags one, and his retriever bites three or four more so that they die.

Whether they wanted to protect game or to kill it, sportsmen were generally in favor of the proposal to create a forest preserve in the Adirondacks, or as *The New York Times* called it, a "people's hunting ground." Throughout the 1870s and early 1880s there had been several attempts in the Legislature to keep the state from reselling the forest land it picked up for taxes and to hold it as part of a park or forest preserve. Nothing came of the proposals until 1883, when the Legislature prohibited the further sale of lands belonging to the state in ten Adirondack counties—Clinton, Essex, Franklin, Fulton, Hamilton, Herkimer, Lewis, Saratoga, St. Lawrence, and Warren. Moreover, it supported its newfound interest in the region with cash, granting the state comptroller the authority to acquire underlying or joint titles to disputed lands and giving him $10,000 to work with, the first funds it had ever allotted directly for the purchase of Adirondack lands. The Legislature also voted $15,000 to finance Verplanck Colvin in locating and surveying the detached state lands in those counties. There was some opposition from upstate senators who argued that there wasn't any sense in holding on to lands already cut over and therefore valueless as watersheds, but more and more people were coming to believe that these lands had a value above and beyond the timber that stood on them. In 1883 the nascent resort of Lake Placid entertained some seven hundred guests at a time. One of them, writing to *The New York Times*, identified himself as among the early "habitués" who had been coming to the Adirondacks for twenty-five years but who now observed a "most melancholy change."

> . . . in climbing, for instance, the slopes of the Adirondacks beyond Keene Valley, where was once a grand and most exquisite forest, one passes only through blackened ruins and miles of bare and desolate rock, and one has the certainty that it will take another thousand years to restore that ruin—all made by a certain iron manufacturer and member of the Legislature of Keene for a return of 50 cents an acre for charcoal.

And of the desolation along streams and lake shores, this same "Old Adirondacker" wrote:

> The sole cause of this wasting of a lovely landscape is apparently to enable some lumbering company (who do not own the river banks) to float their logs. A similar desolation was begun on the Upper Raquet River between Long Lake and the Falls, simply to give more water for the odious little steam launches.

Joining the sportsmen and other visitors in the new call for the preservation of the great northern wilderness were the aesthetes—the painters and the gazers who, like Walter Pater, looked for special tints and hues on their clouds and mountains. As an artist, John W. Mansfield, wrote about the Adirondacks to *The New York Times* in 1881: "This tract of land and water contains so many beauties of nature as yet untouched by that 'gentle' but unaesthetic and decidedly uncultured woodsman that I cannot bear the idea of these ever being disturbed by his too practical and unappreciative hand."

Winslow Homer's painting of "Two Guides," one of them the bearded, unwashed "Old Mountain" Phelps, set against the Adirondack high country, stirred longings in many viewers for a return to a more primitive time and also symbolized, as one art historian writes, "the retreat of wilderness in the Adirondacks to high places." Even many industrialists and financiers, having acquired a second-generation conscience, turned aside from their fathers' excesses and sought to preserve some of the country's remaining grandeur. When some enterprising promoters proposed to buy the shoreline at Niagara Falls, fence off the view, and then charge admission, Governor Alonzo Cornell raised no objection. "Why shouldn't people pay for the privilege?" he asked. "Isn't it a luxury?" But the people of New York, swayed by Frederick Law Olmsted and other prominent citizens, generally supported Niagara's preservation as a public treasure. Under Governor Grover Cleveland the Legislature created a Niagara Reservation in 1883. (Legislators and their constituents in the Adirondacks opposed granting funds for such frippery.) Two years later the Legislature voted to acquire land for the reservation, thus setting a precedent for "buying scenery."

The Niagara Reservation was a portent of things to come in the Adirondacks. Support was building downstate for a forest preserve, but when it developed it was not fueled primarily by a sentiment for aesthetics, or even for wildlife. The issue of water supply, coupled with the specters of fire and the railroads, prevailed.

CHAPTER XI

The Fragile Mountains

The inhabitants of Persia, Egypt and Mesopotamia, and the Mediterranean nations, who once enjoyed heaven on this side of the grave, have thus perished together with their forests, leaving us a warning in the ruins of their former glory, which nothing but a plea of religious insanity can excuse us for having left unheeded for the last eighteen hundred years. The physical laws of God can not be outraged with impunity, and it is time to recognize the fact that there are some sins against which one of the scriptural codes of the East contains a word of warning. The destruction of forests is such a sin, and its significance is preached by every desolate country on the surface of this planet. Three million square miles of the best lands which ever united the condition of human happiness have perished in the sand drifts of artificial deserts, and are now more irretrievably lost to mankind than the island ingulfed by the waves of the Zuyder Zee.

This was a writer named F. L. Oswald exhorting his readers in the pages of the *North American Review* in 1879 to look around them and see what disasters they faced as their own forests disappeared. It is hard for most of us today, living partly isolated from the natural world and relying on steel or plastic for the manufacture of so many of the objects we live by, to realize how great a part wood played in the lives of our forebears. The forest was the chief source of building and manufacturing materials, and often of energy. Moreover, among the thinking reading public the idea of the forest as the controlling factor of a stable water supply had spread and taken hold. The "hanging sponge" theory put forth by Colvin was already generally accepted, that heavily forested watersheds governed the flow of water to the lowlands, retarding its rush and tempering floods. It is a fact that mountainous regions tend to receive more rain and snow during the year than adjacent lowlands do, since the prevailing winds must rise on encountering the mountains; as the rising air cools it forms clouds, which in turn release their moisture. In recent years the Adirondacks' mean annual precipitation amounted to between forty-four and fifty-two inches, their adjacent lowlands thirty-six to forty inches.

Foresters and other scientists have argued for years about the precise effect of forests on climate. Nineteenth-century doctrine had it that once the forests and their wet soils disappeared, a region's air became warmer and drier and there was less rainfall, thus hastening its conversion to a desert. In those Bible-reading days most people were familiar with the topography of the Near East. That they were painfully aware the Garden of Eden had withered into desert only increased their uneasiness about the future of their own land as the lumbermen moved unchecked across it. Scientific fashions changed and, while there was agreement that forests slowed the velocity of wind and the melting of snow cover, there was for a time some doubt that they had much impact on the total precipitation or the mean temperature. Today the pendulum seems to be swinging back to the nineteenth-century view. Evidence shows that mountain forests are particularly effective in combing the moisture out of the clouds and fogs in which they are habitually draped. Moisture adheres to any objects it encounters, as people who walk through dense fogs know from experience. The droplets of moisture that form fogs and mists are often too small to fall, but on encountering objects such as trees, especially the dense mesh of evergreens, they stick to the twigs and leaves (or needles), coalescing and growing until they are large enough to fall as rain. Studies in the Green Mountains have revealed that the forests "comb" between five and thirty inches of rain a year from the passing clouds. H. W. Vogelmann of the University of Vermont wrote in 1976:

> Were it not for mountain forests, this additional moisture would never be available. It augments stream flows and percolates into the soil, eventually adding to groundwater supplies at lower elevations.

> Mountains are thus important aquifer recharge areas. Not only do they cause more rain to fall by forcing air upward, where it cools and releases its moisture, but their forests also collect fog moisture. Considering the importance of maintaining adequate water supplies today, it is essential to keep our high mountain ecosystems intact.

Vogelmann's investigations in parts of Mexico's Sierra Madre Oriental demonstrate the insidious climatic changes that have occurred there since the rain forests were removed from the western slopes. Although moisture-laden fog still rolls over the mountains and across the denuded slopes, it drops none of its rain and the once fertile lands on the slopes and the adjacent plateau have become barren.

A century ago Verplanck Colvin's "hanging sponge" theory was the decisive element in the eventual preservation of the Adirondack forests. As a contemporary book on the subject phrased it, "the forest waters the farm." Without the spongy forest floor, composed of mosses or dead leaves and other natural debris, the water would simply rush unchecked across the denuded land and descend in damaging floods to the lowlands; and, once the water had rushed off, there would be none withheld to maintain a flow in the rivers during the dry seasons. Moreover, the rushing water would gully the land, sweeping the topsoil with it. The soils would pile up as sediment, clogging streams and rivers. On the eroded hillsides there would not be sufficient soil for the vegetation to take root. A state report described conditions in New York in the 1880s:

> Streams once used for driving logs cannot be used for that purpose now; they are too shallow in summer, while at other times the water rises and falls too quickly to be of use. Rivers that once furnished ample water-power for mills and factories have failed, and the expense of substituting steam has been incurred. Rivers that once were forded with difficulty in summer, can now be waded by children, while some of the smaller creeks and trout streams dry up completely, leaving nothing but a bed of stones.

In this case, modern foresters and hydrologists no longer place quite the emphasis they once did on the forests' power to control floods. The rich, sponge-like humus soils underlying forests do indeed store large amounts of rainwater and even some of the water from snowmelt. But their storage capacity is limited, often dependent on the depth of the soil itself. Because the soils of many forests are comparatively wet and shallow, they cannot absorb heavy rains or sudden thaws. The water sinks into the soil, setting up a powerful subsurface flow as the excess water seeks an outlet in gullies and stream beds. For example, the highest flood ever recorded on the Black River in the western Adirondacks occurred in April 1938, when temperatures soared into the middle seventies for five straight days after a long cold spell and thawed the winter's accumulation of deep snow. The abundantly forested watershed was unable to cope with the sudden melt. Long periods of rain, especially those covering large watersheds, also are likely to overburden a forest's capacity to store water. As a modern scientist wrote:

> The great floods that inundate the principal valleys are caused by general and protracted storms, covering wide areas and precipitating great depths of water. Although the rates of rainfall are usually low, the volume is enormous. As a result of such storms, the soils become saturated and finally can retain no more water. Under these conditions, every small stream over thousands of square miles flows at or above bank-full stage for many days. The tremendous volumes of water moving down through the tributaries pass into the valley of the main stream, filling it like a great trough into which water is poured from both sides. Runoff causing floods like these is, of course, affected but little by treatment of the land.

If the late-nineteenth-century campaign to preserve what was left of the forests was sometimes based on mildly exaggerated claims of their value, the campaigners were nevertheless on the side of the angels. Forest soils do play a part in preventing floods and stabilizing stream flow. Without healthy soils in important watersheds the periodic floods would cause even greater damage. This calamity is seen in areas where the soil has been abused or indiscriminate cutting practices disturb the forest floor. In careless cutting operations, for example, skid roads and loading sites may cover as much as 40 percent of the logging area, compacting the soils or stripping them down to their mineral base; erosion and gullying begin, heavy rains sweep away more of the spongy humus, and the forest loses its storage capacity. Fires, too, often burn away the humus as well as the trees, leaving thin mineral soils in which new growth cannot take root. As a forester wrote in 1964:

> There is little doubt that complete forest destruction . . . does great harm. . . . But a distinction should be made between clear-cutting steep lands, followed by conversion to pasture or hillside crops, and clearing without serious soil compaction followed by regrowth. As long as the forest floor remains intact, most of the beneficial effect of the forest, hydrologically speaking, may still be present.

But sound cutting practices, though carried out in Europe, were almost unknown in the United States in the early 1880s. The pressure to cut the forests wholesale was enormous. The increasing demand for paper, coupled with the cost of manufacturing it from rags, had driven paper prices higher each year. New processes had suddenly made it feasible to manufacture paper economically from wood pulp, and such species as poplar and spruce were in demand. In 1866 a treaty of reciprocity with Canada, permitting the importation of lumber into the United States without tariff payments, had expired. Critics called the new tariff "a bounty on forest destruction" because the price of lumber and pulpwood immediately rose, with the attendant rush to get in on the profits. It is not surprising, then, that newspapers and periodicals (dependent in part for *their* profits on a steady supply of cheap paper) often led the campaign for the preservation of American forests. The press became an important factor in the movement to establish a forest preserve in the Adirondacks.

"It is not the axe but the fire-brand that destroys the forest," William J. Stillman wrote in *The Nation*. Indeed, the people who had a commercial or an aesthetic interest in forests began to view the increasing fires with great concern. Lumbermen crudely cut their swath through the forests, leaving behind limbs and other brush too small to be of value. Drying out, this litter soon became a hazard, and lightning or a carelessly abandoned campfire could spark the forest into an inferno. A state report in 1885 described some of the other ways in which forest fires began. People known as "bee hunters" often cut down trees where hives were found, then set fire to them to drive out the bees; if there was no source of water nearby, the bee hunters simply went on to other areas, leaving behind a smoldering tree, "and a few pounds of honey will be obtained at the expense of many acres of valuable timber." Bands of timber thieves (often called "the Grenadiers") roamed the woods stealing timber from the state and often from each other, then set fire to the area to hide the traces of their cutting. And finally, the report noted, "in New York State at least, more fires are traced to railroads than any other source."

The railroad was an object of both pride and anxiety for nineteenth-century Americans. It was a technological marvel revolutionizing civilization, exciting even Thoreau as he sat in reverie at Walden Pond, the locomotive's whistle penetrating his woods "like the scream of a hawk." This iron monster often intruded a jarring note into his idyll, for it was sometimes "a bloated pest," but it also had the potential of pointing the way toward a brighter world:

> . . . when I hear the iron horse make the hills echo with his snort like thunder, shaking the earth with his feet, and breathing fire and smoke from his nostrils (what kind of winged horse or fiery dragon they will put into the new mythology I don't know), it seems as if the earth had got a race now worthy to inhabit it. If all were as it seems, and men made the elements their servants for noble ends!

But eventually there came to be some doubt whether men were putting this machine to noble ends. Like so many other technological marvels introduced into our society, the railroad's benefits were often tempered by its side effects. The fire that Thoreau saw spouting from its nostrils continued to burn once it touched the countryside. Railroad blazes were by no means confined to the forests. Burning cinders or smoldering ashes from the steam engines touched off many prairie fires in the West, where local laws tried to control the damage. In 1874 Colorado required its railroads during the dry season to "plough as a fire guard a continuous strip of not less than six feet in width" on each side of their tracks, and another one at the boundary of their rights-of-way.

The danger was even greater in heavily forested regions, especially where dry brush lined the route. (In wood-hungry Europe this was not much of a problem, the people taking care to clean up the faggots and other woody litter from cutting operations for use in their homes.) Now railroads were straddling the Adirondacks and even penetrating the mountains. Dr. Thomas C. Durant, who had taken over the old Sacketts Harbor and Saratoga Railroad Company and reorganized it as the Adirondack Company, pushed it to North Creek in the heart of the mountains in 1871, where it delivered tourists and took away ore from the iron mines. Other lines followed it into the region. A new incentive was the timber itself. While softwoods (pines, spruce) were usually floated out of the mountains on streams, hardwoods are not suitable for floating as they tend to grow waterlogged and sink. There was a rush for new railroad franchises in the Adirondacks.

And wherever the fire-breathing steam engines went they left a trail of fire in their wake. There were no safeguards, such as wire mesh over the stacks, to control the emissions, while clinkers often dropped from the speeding trains onto the tracks. The authorities had little understanding of the nature of the problem or even, in some quarters, of the terrain in which the fires spread. William Stillman recalled that, at a meeting of state officials in Saratoga to deal with the hazard, someone suggested sending out mounted patrols to watch for fires in the Adirondacks. "In a country through most of which a deer had difficulty in running," Stillman marveled, "and travel is entirely by boats, this suggestion of a mounted police is indescribably funny, and only illustrates the impossibility of any person unfamiliar with the region giving or utilizing counsel."

The railroads intended to expand their holdings in the Adirondacks. Durant's line had plans to push through the mountains another hundred miles to Ogdensburg near the Canadian border. Many newspapers, jealous guardians of the forest by then, sent up a hue and cry. The Utica *Morning Herald* denounced this expansion of the railroad "in connection with gigantic schemes for stripping the timber from the half million acres contiguous to its route and owned by the company. Its prospectus, recently issued under the name and authority of State Engineer Seymour, is filled with glittering talk about a rich agricultural country, which is thus to be opened up for settlement—talk which everybody at all familiar with the characteristics of this region knows to be nonsense." The newspaper demanded an investigation by the Legislature, and suggested that the state seize the railroad's land "for the public good" under the right of eminent domain. Durant's railroad never got any farther, but others eventually did.

The railroad's impact on the forest was not limited to fire and the stripping of the land. American railroads used nearly sixty million wooden ties in construction and repair each year, only two of which as a rule could be cut from a single tree. Thus thirty million trees a year were consumed by railroads. (In Europe the railroads generally used iron ties.) But it was in another direction—as oppressors of the New York City business community—that railroads were to play their most important role in the creation of an Adirondack forest preserve.

CHAPTER XII

The City Intervenes

The Erie Canal undoubtedly helped to make New York the "Empire State." One of the less populous states at the time of the Revolution, it became the largest by 1820, in part because of its principal city's superb harbor. The harbor, its value magnified by the Hudson River and the great canal which connected it to the opening West, spurred the city's expansion, and it passed the half-million mark in population by 1850. A potential check on the city's unbounded growth, however, was ice, which closed the canal during the winter. The railroads took advantage of nature in this respect, carrying the bulk of the city's goods during the cold months and, as their power and confidence increased, trying to gain a monopoly by binding the merchants to year-round contracts. Once the railroads secured a grip on the westbound traffic, they could fix their shipping rates accordingly, and with some justification the New York business interests feared their rapacity. It was vital that the water levels be maintained in the canal, and anything that affected the canal's source of water threatened the city's future as well.

Another potential check on the city's growth was a clean and ample water supply. The Hudson, which flowed past its shore, was badly polluted, and the city fathers were already looking to the Adirondacks as the most likely replacement. Indeed, in 1873 Verplanck Colvin suggested an aqueduct be built from the mountains to New York City (a proposal that never came to pass, since more convenient sources of supply were found, chiefly in the Delaware River). In any event, the lumbermen and railroad magnates came to be seen as twin threats to the city's economic well-being, and the Adirondacks a key to its survival.

By the 1880s forest preserves were becoming a reality. Communal forests designated by several European cities provided a model. In 1882 an act of the Massachusetts Legislature authorized local voters or city councils to establish municipal forests; towns could accept gifts of land or even condemn land for the purpose. To maintain the forests, individual towns were given the power to make appropriations and hire local forest "keepers," while the state Board of Agriculture became a Board of Forestry as well.

In that same year destructive and well-publicized floods on the Mississippi River made New Yorkers aware that flood protection in their own state was urgent. What better place to begin than with the forests? And in 1883 New York itself was gripped by a severe drought, the waters in its principal rivers, the Hudson, Mohawk, and Black, falling to uncomfortably low levels. The threat of fire increased. "The matter is reduced to a simple business issue," noted the New York *Tribune*. "Is the [Hudson] river worth to the City and the state as much as it will cost to save the woods? This is the most important economic question which the coming legislature will be called to answer." The same editorial writer asked the state Chamber of Commerce to help solve this problem, "which might be more important to the future welfare of the State than all other questions combined."

At that time the president of the state Chamber of Commerce was a tall, bewhiskered man of imposing presence named Morris K. Jesup. Though the family name had dropped an "s" during the intervening century, he was a great-grandson of that Ebenezer Jessup who had been keenly interested in the Totten and Crossfield purchase in pre–Revolutionary War days. Jesup, born into a big, pious, and largely destitute family in Connecticut, left school at twelve to work as an errand boy. Ironically, he owed his rise in the world in a sense to the railroads. For a while he worked for a manufacturer of locomotives, then struck out on his own, at first selling railroad supplies and later railroad securities, a very lucrative trade in those days, for he soon became a multimillionaire and retired. From that time on he remained a power in charitable and other nonprofit organizations. He was a founder of the YMCA. The New York Society for the Suppression of Vice was formed at his house. In 1881 he became the third president of the American

Museum of Natural History and served in that position for twenty-seven years. When the Audubon Society of New York State was founded in 1897, he became its president too. "He did not understand any of the details of science—in fact, it was all a sealed book to him—yet he had intense faith in the results," his successor as president of the American Museum once wrote of him, and it is for his benefactions that Jesup is chiefly remembered. Although he was a "tenacious supporter" of Anthony Comstock in his campaign against indecency, Jesup did not have a closed mind; while strictly observing the Sabbath himself, he opened the museum to the public on Sundays because he knew that it was the only day on which most people were able to visit it.

One of Jesup's most enduring benefactions was his gift to the museum of a collection of specimens "of all the woods of our country, that are or may be used for architectural or building purposes, or in the manufactures—as gums, resins, and dyewoods." The collection, called "North American Woods," consisted of four hundred species on which Jesup spent about a hundred thousand dollars.* As a businessman, his interest in forestry was chiefly economic, but during the crisis in the Adirondacks he was all on the side of preservation. "He held a position very common in those days—strong for what he called Forestry, but equally strong against cutting any trees," the noted scientific forester Gifford Pinchot wrote rather disapprovingly many years later. But like the other businessmen and scientists who joined him in the campaign to preserve the Adirondacks, Jesup's chief purpose was to stop the destruction. It was left for later generations to decide what to do with the forest after it had been saved.

The Chamber of Commerce's interest in forests was not entirely new. During the 1870s there was some concern that the cutting of forest lands to build a railroad to Sandy Hook, New Jersey, might upset the stability of the peninsula there, causing it to be eroded away with destructive effects on New York Harbor, but the fears were determined to be unfounded. Late in the fall of 1883

* According to the museum's historian, Geoffrey Hellman, Jesup gave that institution alone more than four hundred and fifty thousand dollars during his lifetime, a million dollars in trust upon his death, and, through his wife's will, another five million dollars upon her death.

there were more solid fears about the Adirondacks. An editorial in the November 30 New York *Sun* sounded an urgent note:

> The *Morning Herald* of Utica is advocating with great force and urgency the preservation of the Adirondack forests. It very properly points out that the greatest and most immediate danger to these forests is found in the attitude of the Adirondack Railroad Company. The State long ago granted a right of way through the very heart of the forest to this corporation or to one of its predecessors. This was an exceedingly short-sighted and stupid piece of business. If it is desirable to exterminate a forest, the quickest, the most certain and the least expensive method to adopt is to build a railroad through it. Wherever a railroad penetrates the forest, the forest disappears.

On December 6, Jesup addressed a meeting of the state Chamber of Commerce and brought up the subject of the Adirondacks. He said that forest destruction was already seriously reducing the flow of the state's important waterways and that "the effects of the diminution of water upon the Hudson is already so great that navigation above Troy is rendered almost impossible in dry seasons." Extensive cutting and fires were certain to follow in the railroad's path through the wilderness. And he proposed a solution:

> A wise and comprehensive state policy will seize upon the whole forest region, perhaps 4,000,000 acres in excess of the present State holding, and keep it for all time as a great forest preserve, and in this way insure abundant water to the Hudson and the Canal. This can be done by the exercise of the right of eminent domain by the Governor, with the sanction of the legislature. The money that this would cost the State, great as the sum would be, would be returned in improved and more permanent agriculture and a better water supply.

The other members supported Jesup's proposal and the Chamber of Commerce appointed a committee of seven men to study the problem further, invite other associations and individuals to participate, and ultimately approach the Legislature to get the necessary laws passed. The committee, chaired by Jesup, went right to work. A week later Charles S. Sargent, professor of arboriculture at Harvard, spoke to the committee at its invitation and briefed the members on why the forests must be protected. Although he was an advocate of scientific forestry, Sargent did not have a very high opinion of either the competence or the scruples of the lumbermen then operating in the Adirondacks and believed a policy of preservation was the only practical one. One of the committee members, while agreeing that the state should buy up the forests, thought the Chamber of Commerce should make it plain to the public that the proposal to buy up the lands was not simply a get-rich scheme by landholders. The rest of the committee agreed and decided to secure public support by circulating a proposal for signatures throughout the city and the state. The New York *Tribune* reported on the meeting with favor, commenting that the proposal "ought to have a hundred thousand signers before it leaves Manhattan Island. Our lawmakers should be made to understand that the businessmen of the City are in earnest, and that they are not inclined to sit still and see the waterways of our inland commerce destroyed."

The enthusiasm for buying the forests was mainly restricted to the city and its environs, but there it burned consistently and sometimes fervidly. In the spring of 1884 a mass meeting was held at New York's Chickering Hall. Sponsored by a committee of prominent citizens, it was presided over by Mayor Ebson and enlivened by Gilmore's Band and the Union Glee Club. But as a discussion of the Chamber of Commerce's proposal got under way in the Legislature, the battle lines were formed. Theodore Roosevelt, then a young assemblyman, supported the Chamber's bill with a vigorous speech about how forest destruction had blighted southern France and warned that "we are preparing our land for a similar fate." But there was much opposition from upstate. At a hearing before the Senate Committee on Forest Lands, lumbermen called the proposal a "swindle" by landowners. The Ogdensburg *Journal* feared a lockup of forest resources (a cry to be heard time and again during the next century from local interests whenever a plan was afoot to preserve some parcels of land for parks or wilderness). Even Governor Grover Cleveland was against buying land for preservation; he seemed to share a commonly expressed belief that the land would eventually revert to the state for taxes in any case. This view was disputed by a preservationist who wrote to the New York *Tribune:*

> In a measure this is true, but the rapidity of the process depends wholly upon how rapidly the forests are cut off. The valuable timbered lands of this region are never abandoned. It is only after they have been rendered valueless for commercial purposes, transformed into treeless wastes of parched earth and rock, that they are acquired by the state.

Early in 1884 the Senate committee decided against buying the land (though the Chamber of Commerce had lowered its sights, reducing the proposed purchase from four to one million acres). However, the Legislature appropriated $5,000 to hire a committee of experts to "investigate and report a system of forest preservation." The committee was headed by Harvard's Sargent. One of the difficulties in looking into the tangle of state and privately owned forest lands in the Adirondacks was that it was just that—a tangle of vague boundaries overrun by timber hunters who often didn't know or care on whose land they were cutting. Even county lines were subject to dispute. In his attempts to unravel the mystery, Verplanck Colvin found many of the century-old boundary markers obliterated by time and weather. According to one of his biographers, he became so skillful in finding old blaze marks on rotting tree trunks "that he could kick one apart and point out the original blaze." That he was inexhaustible in the pursuit of his goal of surveying the Adirondacks is undeniable, and he went on year after year, pushing himself and his men, piling up his records and his facts. It is rather sad, then, that his most lasting achievements were as a propagandist rather than as a scientist. Donaldson writes:

> The years have shown his work as a whole to be of uneven scientific value. The resurvey of many of his lines has proved them to be inaccurate. Much of the great mass of material which he collected, owing to the lack of any systematic filing, tabulation or indexing, was made useless to his successors. His office in Albany, indeed, looked more like the dressing-room of a sporting club than the repository of valuable records. These, if there at all, were apt to be buried beneath a picturesque profusion of snow-shoes, moccasins and pack-baskets.*

* State surveyors of our time who have studied Colvin's field books are far more supportive of his work.

A further irony was that as the years went by Colvin turned away from the bright image of the Adirondack wilderness that had sustained him in his prime. He grew embittered, grumbling that his expenses were withheld or never paid him at all, and that politicians in league with the lumber interests belittled his work. He left state government in 1900, taking many of his disordered records with him, and concocted a plan to push a railroad through the heart of his beloved Adirondacks. Nothing ever came of the plan. At some point he "tumbled down the stairs of his wits" (as John Ruskin once said of himself), and during his last years he became a pathetic figure, walking the streets of Albany and muttering to himself, perhaps living over in a dream the exhilarating days when he climbed alone to wilderness summits where no man had ever been before him.

But in early 1885 Colvin was still an effective propagandist on behalf of an Adirondack preserve. He was going strong while Morris K. Jesup, having had a taste of the political machinery at work, was retreating from the battle in disillusion. The Chamber of Commerce withdrew most of its active, if not moral, support, but several other important business associations jumped wholeheartedly into the campaign, most prominent among them the New York Board of Trade and Transportation and the Constitution Club, an organization of businessmen in Brooklyn (then a large city in its own right). As Donaldson wrote in 1921, "the Board of Trade saw in the watersheds a mighty asset of the Empire State, and it has persistently followed the policy of protecting them, as being essential to the commercial, industrial, and transportation interests of the commonwealth."

On Washington's Birthday of that year the Board of Trade and Transportation invited Colvin to deliver a speech at its annual banquet. Rising in response to the board president's toast to "the Adirondacks—the land of magnificent mountains and lovely lakes, the source of the Hudson River, the feeder of our canals," Colvin launched into his own panegyric, pointing out to his audience that "the ice that tinkles in your goblets, and the pure water which upholds the ice, are both fresh from the head-waters of the Hudson." Always the visionary, Colvin went on to say he hoped to see great ships sail up the Hudson someday and then, to avoid the bridges, roads, and cities along the Erie Canal, be lifted by locks to Lake Champlain and enter the "new northwest passage," skirting the northern Adirondacks to the St. Lawrence and on to Lake Ontario and the West. This ship canal route, he warned, like the Erie Canal, would be threatened by the destruction of the Adirondack watershed. And, on a personal note, he admitted that, like all other surveyors, he felt a special kinship with Washington, who had surveyed the forests of the Appalachians. "The child who marked the tree with his hatchet in his father's garden was probably already in his daydreams a surveyor in the wilderness," he said. Colvin had a great knack for holding an audience.

Meanwhile, in Brooklyn the Constitution Club was preparing a report of its own, which echoed others in the fear that the great arteries of transport were being destroyed by reckless cutting, and then it forged ahead into other areas. "Your attention is called to artificial flooding for log driving, done always in the season of swollen streams," the report said. "For this end, the waters of lakes and streams, raised sometimes as high as 12 feet, cover the adjacent lands for three and even for six miles. It is scarcely possible to comprehend the force of such vast masses of water when set free." The report speculated that thousands of tons of boulders and earth, torn from the banks and beds of streams, swept into the Hudson and down to New York Harbor, gradually filling it up over the years and reducing its value as the world's greatest port; moreover, rocks and sandbars were suddenly cropping up in the Hudson itself, impeding navigation.

The Constitution Club's report also went into a matter that was of great public interest at the time and played no little part in the eventual establishment of the preserve. This was the issue of public health, and was based in part on erroneous concepts. It was not recognized at the time that malaria is a parasitic disease usually transmitted by mosquito bites. It was thought to occur because of "miasmatic vapors," or, as the club's report phrased it:

> Malaria is a poison not cognizable by the senses, nor can it be detected by chemical tests. It is known only by its effects upon the system. Marshes are prolific sources of the subtle poison, especially in a certain stage of the drying process under a hot sun. Also

> grounds alternately flooded and drained, parts of which are covered with low and dense brushwood or with seeds and grass, and vegetable matter susceptible to decay. . . . The character of the [Adirondack] streams which before sparkled with health-giving power, is changed by the malignant and deadly matter which now fills the atmosphere with intermittent and remittent fevers and diphtheria.

It was also believed that trees filtered and purified the miasmatic exhalations that arose from marshes.

Meanwhile, the Sargent Committee continued to prepare its own report for the Legislature. It held hearings to take testimony from interested parties during the summer of 1884. (The lumbermen contended that they were only "pruning the woods" and that all the trouble was caused by hunters and fishermen who left their campfires burning.) The committee filed its report early in 1885. It was a scathing indictment of the timber thieves, the lumbermen, and the railroads who were reducing "this region to an unproductive and dangerous desert." It estimated that state land as now amounting to three quarters of a million acres, most of it badly depleted of its forest cover and returned to the state in lieu of taxes, though even some original state lands were denuded by timber thieves. While the committee said that "private ownership means—sooner or later—forest destruction," it believed the acquisition of those private lands to be impractical. Instead, it proposed means for protecting the state lands from fire, thievery, and overcutting and recommended the establishment of a Forest Commission.

The Board of Trade and Transportation tried to reintroduce the old Chamber of Commerce bill to buy forest lands. But the Legislature would have none of it; in fact, it was not very enthusiastic about implementing the Sargent Committee's proposals. Opposition was strenuous, as usual. Dr. Hough discussed that opposition, and in passing made some remarks that shed light on the original plans for the Forest Preserve:

> In the recent discussions upon the subject of reservations in our State Legislature, the strongest opposition was experienced in the counties partly included in the wilderness. Influential men and committees appeared in Albany to obstruct and delay, and, if possible, to wholly prevent any conservative legislation whatever, as if

> their property was endangered and their interests threatened with ruin if the projects demanded by a great public interest became laws. . . . This opposition, I believe, would be changed to firm support if the true end and aim of forestry were rightly understood. It is *not* the object of forestry, at least in this country, to maintain the woodlands as a shelter for game and as a region of pleasure resort to those who can afford the time and means for this kind of enjoyment. . . . Our taxpayers would never tolerate such an object of expense, and it is to be regretted that the word "park" has ever been used in this connection, because it leads to the erroneous idea that expenses are to be increased for the enjoyment of those who have time or money to spend in sporting or in woodland life.
>
> We regard the principal and by far the most important end of forestry to be the growth of timber for the supply of man.

With the "Sargent Bill" bogged down in the Legislature, the Board of Trade and Transportation stepped in and used its expertise in Albany to break down the opposition. Frank S. Gardner, the Board of Trade's secretary and an experienced lobbyist, helped to draft a bill and set up a conference of interested people, including Sargent himself and several friendly legislators. Jesup provided his office as a meeting place. There the wording of a bill, satisfactory to the forest preservation faction, was agreed upon. Who drafted what has come to be called the "Forever Wild" clause seems to be one of history's secrets, though guesses have ranged from Bernard Fernow (of whom more will be said later) to Sargent.

Years of rhetoric and agitation were about to produce their first tangible result. Both officials and legislators in Albany were by now aware that something had to be done to enable them to manage the block of land that each year increased as individual plots reverted back to the state, and the preservationists' bill passed both houses of the Legislature with little opposition. Governor David B. Hill signed it into law on May 15, 1885. This legislation established a state Forest Preserve and a three-member Forest Commission. (California had beaten New York to the punch, ten weeks earlier having become the first state to establish a Forest Commission.) The law also provided for a forest warden and forest inspectors, set penalties for the deliberate burning of state land, and required the railroads to cut and remove brush and other flammable material along their rights-of-way twice a year and equip their locomotives with steel wire and similar devices to prevent sparks from escaping from ashpans or smokestacks. The law's two more memorable provisions were:

Section 7: "All the lands now owned, or which may hereafter be acquired by the State of New York, within the counties of Clinton, excepting the Towns of Altona and Dannemora,* Essex, Franklin, Fulton, Hamilton, Herkimer, Lewis, Saratoga, St. Lawrence, Warren, Washington, Greene, Ulster, and Sullivan,† shall constitute and be known as the Forest Preserve."

Section 8: "The lands now or hereafter constituting the Forest Preserve shall be forever kept as wild forest lands. They shall not be sold, nor shall they be leased or taken by any person or corporation, public or private."

The state at this time owned a total of 681,374 acres in the Adirondacks in widely scattered parcels, and another 33,893 acres in the Catskills. The groundwork, even some of the phrasing, had been laid for the unique instrument of the Adirondacks' preservation that would be devised in the next decade.

* The Legislature had already set aside state lands within Altona and Dannemora for the use of the Clinton and Dannemora state prisons.

† State lands within Greene, Ulster, and Sullivan counties made up a section of the Forest Preserve in the Catskills.

CHAPTER XIII

Looting the Parks

The creation of a Forest Preserve in the Adirondacks met with a mixed response. New York City's commercial interests were gratified, at least for the time being. So were rusticators, and those who catered to them. Said a man in Saranac Lake:

> The people in this region will second every effort of the Forest Commission. The whole business of the village is built up on the patronage of summer boarders or tourists, and it is getting so now that people from New York and Boston come here and stay the year round. This winter there are a number of such people stopping in the place, some of whom have built fine residences for themselves. The woods attract them, and so it stands us in hand to do what we can to keep the forests as they are, or better them. In order to do this, timber and stealing and firing must be stopped.

But even among the most upstanding local citizens there was some uneasiness at the prospect of the state solidifying its holdings in the central Adirondacks. "People are opposed to the State buying the land and paying no taxes on it," a surveyor in Hamilton County told the Forest Commission. In this case, the state moved vigorously with a piece of unprecedented legislation, passing a law in 1886 that provided for all lands then or thereafter included in the Forest Preserve to be "assessed and taxed at a like valuation and at a like rate as those at which similar lands of individuals within such counties are assessed and taxed." This provision, which continues in effect down to the present time, is unique in the United States* and

* Except that the United States Forest Service makes stumpage payments to localities where trees are cut on Forest Service land.

has done much to muffle the resentment that often surfaces elsewhere when large tracts of land are acquired for public purposes and therefore kept off the local tax rolls.

Not even imagination and initiative were able to clear up some of the other problems inherent in the new Forest Preserve. The Forest Commission itself became a center of controversy because one of its three members, Theodore B. Basselin of Lewis County, was a prominent lumberman. (The two other members appointed by Governor Hill were from New York City—Townsend Cox, a broker, and Sherman Knevals, a lawyer.) Because the law creating the preserve had not specified how the timber should be managed, the commissioners (perhaps influenced by Basselin) came to see it not simply as a "reserve" whose chief function was to mitigate water shortages, but as a source of managed timber. They were supported in this view by the Legislature in 1887, which passed a law authorizing the commission to sell "separate small parcels or tracts wholly detached from the main portions of the Forest Preserve and bounded on every side by lands not owned by the state," to exchange those tracts for others that adjoined larger portions of the preserve, and to sell the timber on the "small" tracts. Consequently the commission sold cutting rights to individuals and companies (Basselin, running one of the largest cutting operations in the Adirondacks, apparently benefited from this), and left the commission open to serious charges; one such small tract on which the commission sold timber amounted to 3,673 acres. The commission also wanted the Legislature to grant it the right to lease campsites within the preserve, on the grounds that the renters would take an interest in the land around them and help to prevent both fires and timber thievery. This plan ran into immediate opposition (the magazine *Garden and Forest*, which was edited and published by Olmsted and Sargent, thought it comparable to permitting people to fence off parts of Central Park for themselves) and the Legislature let the matter drop.

The new commission made a serious and, for a time, successful attempt to reduce fires within the preserve, but it had much less success with timber thieves. The natives often considered the cutting of a tree on state land as much their right as killing a buck or taking a few trout there, and they resented the restrictions imposed on them by the new law. Such sentiments were not confined to the Adirondacks. In the West the public domain was already fair game, with a great deal of capital and ingenuity invested in trying to outwit the federal government. A lumberman on the West Coast, S. A. D. Puter, who became known to the press eventually as "the King of the Oregon Land Fraud Ring," was a master in circumventing government regulations to acquire rich timberland. When he was finally convicted of various misdeeds, he whiled away his time in jail dictating his memoirs to a former employee of the General Land Office, who happened to be in there with him. In his bulky book, which he called *Looters of the Public Domain*, Puter spoke of the men for and with whom he had worked:

> Thousands upon thousands of acres, which included the very cream of the timber claims in Oregon and Washington, were secured by Eastern lumbermen and capitalists, the majority of whom came from Wisconsin, Michigan, and Minnesota, and nearly all of these claims, to my certain knowledge, were fraudulently obtained. As to the special agents sent out by the government, they were picked up, each in turn, as they appeared on the scene, and with the capitalists and locators standing hand in hand, it was an easy matter, with the aid of these agents, to baffle the Government in its attempts to secure evidence.

Corruption became so widespread that Charles S. Sargent suggested that the government's forested lands be entrusted to the care of the U.S. Army and that forestry be taught at West Point. This notion, in fact, was in keeping with tradition in the West, where military men, from Captain Meriwether Lewis to Major John Wesley Powell, contributed so much to the natural sciences during the nineteenth century. The Army, which carried out weather forecasting as well as important geological and topographical surveys, remained an important scientific arm of the government until the final "pacification" of the Indians.

In the Adirondacks the rascals did not even attempt to lay claim, fraudulent or otherwise, to the land. They simply made off with the trees. For a while the new law had little effect on these men. When a visiting reporter asked a local man about state laws, he replied (as one of his modern counterparts in the Adirondacks might): "They ain't enforced at all. The laws were made by men who don't know what we need here. Give us some laws that we can take care of and we'll put them through."

The local people, thinking alike, seldom reported timber thievery to the authorities, or testified in court if the culprits were caught. In 1889 *The New York Times* sent a reporter to the area and a lumberman explained to him how he made a profit on taking trees from state lands.

> When the State Forester comes around, as he does in the spring, he counts the number of stumps which have been cut on the state land, and he tells us how many trees we have felled. He has the privilege of charging, under the State Law, five times the value of each market (one thousand board feet) felled for such a violation. But when he does this he must be convinced that the cutting was done maliciously. Well, of course, we do not cut these trees maliciously. We are not responsible if the State fails to run strings around their lots. We can't always tell which is State and which is our timber. So the Forester inquires what the market price is of logs we cut, and we pay him, and everybody is satisfied.

At other times the thieves paid nothing. Where the state lands were poorly marked marauders simply went in and cut the timber, sometimes leaving fires behind to mask their disturbance of the forest. Often the local wardens were paid to look the other way. In the event of a serious effort to try to stop the thievery, the gangs (like mountain bootleggers) established a system of signals, sounding warning notes on the horns at sawmills. When the state apprehended a culprit in the act, it was difficult to obtain a conviction in that region, where, as a reporter put it, "every man is a lumber man"; the Forest Commission sometimes petitioned for a change of venue.

And so as time went on it began to appear that simply calling the state lands a "preserve" was doing very little to preserve them. The press constantly described the destruction that went on in the Adirondacks. In 1887 the Syracuse *Standard* made an impassioned appeal for stricter legislation, saying that "never has the destruction of the North Woods proceeded more rapidly than this year," and, going beyond economics, ventured the opinion that "the people can as safely despise religion and education as despise the educating and religious power of great scenery."

Such sentiments were no longer confined to a few preservationists and sportsmen. As the country progressed the effects of technology and commerce began to burden the landscape and weigh on the minds of millions of people. Blight spread to the unlikeliest places. Not many years before, Charles Baudelaire saw corruption mingling with beauty around him in France and noted the peculiarly modern ring to it: "As a new example, as fresh victims of the inexorable moral laws, we shall perish by that which we have believed to be our means of existence. So far will machinery have Americanized us, so far will Progress have atrophied in us all that is spiritual." And only a few years in the future anyone looking for the handwriting on the wall might have discerned it on England's white cliffs of Dover, their pristine face bearing during the 1890s a large sign saluting "Carter's Little Liver Pills." Harvard's Professor Charles Eliot Norton, contemplating the "strange, hideous, barbaric spectacle which the rush to Oklahoma has presented during these last weeks," expressed his sense of a national malaise in 1889:

> Never has the waste of what should be the permanent, inexhaustible fund of a nation's prosperity been exhibited on so wide a field as in our own country during the last twenty years. We have been living like spendthrifts, flinging away treasures slowly accumulated during the past without consideration of the rights and interests of future generations or recognition of our responsibilities toward them. We have used the goods of Nature as if we were sole and absolute owners of them. We have behaved like fradulent trustees. A people can only justify its claim to be called civilized by so using the free gifts which it has received from Nature and its own predecessors as to transmit them undiminished and improved to its successors.

All land in the United States, whether under the ostensible protection of a governmental unit or not, seemed ripe for exploitation. Within fifteen years three great new parks had come into existence in the United States—Central Park, nominally under a city's jurisdiction, Yosemite under a state's, and Yellowstone, removed from the public domain yet remaining under federal supervision. But developments soon occurred at each park that dismayed its original advocates.

Of them all, and contrary even to Olmsted's earlier fears, Central Park fared best for a time at the hands of the public. In 1857 the Republican State Legislature took control of the park away from the Democratic city government and put it in the care of an independent Board of Commissioners; although New York's decorous Mayor Fernando Wood had actively resisted suggestions to reduce the size of the proposed park and was a cut above the average Tammany leader ("No one," the New York *Herald* once said, "ever saw him put his feet on the desk or spit on the carpet"), there was considerable suspicion about the corrupt environment in which he operated. It wasn't until 1870, when the Legislature reorganized the city's government, that a Department of Public Parks was created in the city. Meanwhile, the new Board of Commissioners hired a special police force of fifty men called "park-keepers" to preserve the plantings and other aspects of Olmsted's creation. People flocked to the park, behaved on the whole quite admirably (despite some public drunkenness), and contributed a Currier & Ives conviviality to the formal background. A report made by the commissioners in 1863 describes a winter scene in the park, where the artificial lake had suddenly prompted a new fad in ice skating:

> The movements of a throng of skaters, on a clear day, chasing each other in a gleeful mood over the crystal ceiling of the imprisoned lake, the fur-clad inmates of a thousand gay vehicles coursing along the silver snow to the music of bells, the dusty foliage of fir and pine on the adjacent heights, wrapped with wreaths of fleecy white; leafless branches strung with a fairy network of icy pearls, frail but gorgeous as it glistens and flashes with a thousand hues in every glance of the sunlight, form in our midst a winter scene unmatched by that of any capital or country of modern times, because it is obtainable only in a climate, amid an extent of population of wealth and liberality, such as peculiarly characterizes this Queen City of the Western Hemisphere.

This New York conviviality (not more amazing to the modern reader than the commissioners' prose) apparently was matched on summer Saturday afternoons during the public band concerts. (Remember that during the summer of this report, the torn country experienced the agonies of Vicksburg and Gettysburg, and New York itself was plunged into a bloodbath by the draft riots.) The commissioners grew lyrical:

> Few landscapes present more attractive features than that of the park on a music day. Thousands of brilliant equipages throng the drives. The waters of the lake are studded with gaily-colored pleasure boats, appearing now and then in striking contrast with the green foliage that fringes its banks; the waterfowl float proudly over its surface; children play on the lawns, throngs of visitors from diverse climes move among the trees, whose leaves, fanned with the soft lays of the music, wave silent approval; all seems full of life and enjoyment; and as some familiar strain breathes a sweet influence around, the whole appears like some enchanted scene.

Olmsted, who had returned to join his partner, Calvert Vaux, at Central Park after the Civil War, lasted until the notorious Tweed Ring took over the city in 1870. During his absence, the efficiency of the "park-keepers" declined (according to Olmsted, the force became "an asylum for aggravated cases of hernia, varicose veins, rheumatism, partial blindness, and other infirmities compelling sedentary occupations"), while incompetent "gardeners" dug up his precious shrubs, mutilated the trees, and tamed parts of the rugged landscape to banality. Olmsted and Vaux, out under Tweed, came back to make restorations, but the city's politics eventually discouraged the sensitive Olmsted and in 1878 he resigned for good. From afar he viewed with distaste the invasion of the park by a variety of constructions for which there was no place in his immaculate design. As the heart of the city swept northward (in 1874 the center of its population reached Union Square at Fourteenth Street), the park drew more visitors while its land came under greater demands for alternate uses. There was no plan in the park's administration, and the whims (or worse) of city officials opened the door to a variety of abuses. Trees were removed so that strollers in the park might view the homes and hotels *outside the park*. The zoo was built; the art museum built and expanded. The invasion of statuary began, wherein wealthy men and women finance a specious immortality for themselves by paying sculptors to reproduce their likenesses or their ideals in stone; as a result, the park has sometimes been called "Central Park Memorial Cemetery." There were plans made (and occasionally even legislation passed) to put a world's fair, a circus, a trotting speedway, and churches within the park, though on each of these occasions a vigilant public defeated the proposal. The park, in fact, survived pretty well intact into the twentieth century, when the lack of binding deterrents caused the floodgates to open and the park to be in large part spoiled by discordant incursions.

Incursions of another sort afflicted Yosemite. From the time the valley was taken from the public domain and handed to the state in 1864, it came under unceasing pressure. The California Legislature provided barely enough money to pay the commissioners' expenses and the salary of a "guardian" for the valley. For the rest, the commissioners had to turn to private funds. Under the terms of the act, the commissioners might grant leases for a ten-year period, and this they did, which enabled private interests to put up a hotel and other buildings within the park. Others constructed entrance roads, with the provision that they could collect tolls. Soon a substantial part of the valley floor was cluttered with fences to hold horses, or meadows where hay was grown to feed them. Just outside the park the miners, lumbermen, cattlemen, and sheepmen were making inroads, threatening the integrity of the park itself.

Fortunately there appeared on the scene an indomitable wilderness lover named John Muir. He had been born in Scotland but grew up in the Minnesota backwoods, and finally set off on a series of wanderings on foot and by boat that led him in 1868 to California. "All the world was before me and every day was a holiday, so it did not seem important to which of the world's wildernesses I first should wander," he wrote later. "Arriving by the Panama steamer, I stopped one day in San Francisco, and then inquired for the nearest way out of town. 'But where do you want to go?' asked the man to whom I had applied for this important information. 'To any place that is wild,' I said."

And Muir was on his way into his lifelong journey in the Sierra. He worked for a time in a sawmill (one that cut only "windfalls," a friend of his assures us) and later married and became a fruit farmer. But his true vocation was wandering in the mountains.

"In the wilderness Muir looked like John the Baptist as portrayed by Donatello and other Renaissance sculptors," Robert Underwood Johnson of the *Century* magazine once wrote.

> He was spare of frame, full-bearded, hardy, keen of eye and visage, and on the march eager of movement. It was difficult for an untrained walker to keep up with him as he leaped from rock to rock as surely as a mountain goat, or skimmed along the surface of the ground—a trick of easy locomotion learned from the Indians. If he ever became tired, nobody knew it. He delighted in gentle badinage at the expense of the tenderfoot. . . . Though never lonely, he was not at all a professional recluse; he loved companions and craved good talk.

Muir approached the mountains, his "wilderness temples," with a religious awe. He wrote of them the same way: "Meadows grassed and lilied head-high, spangled river reaches, and currentless pools, cascades countless and untamable in form and whiteness, groves that heaven all the valley!" And again: "Climb the mountains and get their good tidings. Nature's peace will flow into you as the sunshine into the trees. The winds will blow their freshness into you, and the storms their energy, while cares will drop off like autumn leaves." Yet with his own brand of pantheism Muir combined keen observation and the scientific method. Geologists who studied Yosemite at the time thought the valley was created by a cataclysmic convulsion that had pulled its bottom deep into the earth. "The bottom never fell out of anything God made!" Muir roared, and proceeded with the careful studies that helped to establish the theory that the valley had been scoured out by glaciers and erosion.

Knowing the mountains in great detail, he came to be profoundly concerned about what was going on in Yosemite. When he visited the valley with Robert Underwood Johnson in 1889, he was shocked at the intrusion of hayfields, fences, piles of tin cans, tree stumps everywhere, and a saloon to go with the hotel; there were plans to dress up the famous falls in colored lights. The two men decided to wage a campaign, writing and lobbying, to preserve the wilderness around Yosemite. Muir contributed articles to the *Century* and other publications. He hoped for the return of the valley to the federal government and the formation of a large national park, but he held out little hope for so drastic a move. "A man may not appreciate his wife," he said, "but let her daddie try to take her back." Muir's chief target became the sheepmen and their animals —"hoofed locusts," he called the latter, which he thought were even more destructive than the lumbermen in the mountainous watershed. Fueled by Muir's articles, a public clamor arose to provide greater protection for Yosemite. In 1890 this movement focused on a plan to create a large federal reservation around the valley. The Department of the Interior investigated the conditions at Yosemite and issued a report that supported the charges against the state's administration. Timber had been cut indiscriminately, the valley fenced with barbed wire and planted to grass and grains, most of the wild flowers grazed over or plowed under. Of the land included in the grant to the state but lying outside the valley, the Secretary of the Interior charged:

> This seems to have been abandoned to sheep herders and their flocks. The rare grasses and herbage have been eaten to the bare dirt. . . . These acts of spoliation and trespass have been permitted for a number of years and seem to have become a part of the settled policy of management. . . . For the purpose of realizing the largest possible revenue obtainable from the valley there has, it is claimed, been permitted a largely indiscriminate devastation of the magnificent forest growth and luxuriant grasses that many years alone can repair.

The movement to protect the valley's watershed gained momentum in Congress. Muir wrote that if the reservation was not made a reality, the great forests of the Sierra "will vanish like snow in summer." It was widely speculated that the Southern Pacific Railroad, with its keen interest in transporting tourists to scenic attractions, played an important role behind the scenes in pushing the legislation through Congress. On October 1, 1890, a law was signed by President Benjamin Harrison setting aside 1,512 square miles as a "Yosemite forest reservation." The state's grant in the valley was now surrounded by a huge tract of land under the supervision of the Secretary of the Interior. In 1892 Muir founded the

Sierra Club as a private organization that would become a self-proclaimed watchdog over the new forest reservation. He served as the club's president for the rest of his life and took an active part in all the battles that lay ahead. With the Sierra Club in the vanguard (and Muir's good friend Edward H. Harriman, president of the Union Pacific Railroad, in the background), the California Legislature agreed to re-cede Yosemite Valley to the federal government in 1905; a year later, Congress accepted the recession, and the valley took its rightful place at the heart of Yosemite National Park.

Meanwhile, there were the old problems. The Department of the Interior had neither the funds nor the manpower to police Yosemite or its larger park at Yellowstone, where poachers continued to slaughter the game and curio seekers to attack the bizarre rock formations around the geysers and carry them away by the cartload. At both parks, in the romantic tradition of the Old West, the United States Cavalry came to the rescue. After an appeal by the Secretary of the Interior in 1886, the War Department dispatched Troop M, First United States Cavalry, "to perform the duties in the Yellowstone National Park that recently devolved upon the superintendent of the park and his assistants." Acting on that precedent, in 1890 the Interior Department appealed to the War Department for the protection of Yosemite and other new parks (Sequoia and General Grant parks, the latter now a part of Kings Canyon National Park) under its jurisdiction in California. With some prodding by President Harrison, the War Department agreed, and detachments arrived in 1891. Captain A. E. Wood, the first acting superintendent of Yosemite, sent word to every stockman in the area to keep his herds out of the park:

> This Yosemite Park is to be a park throughout all time—it is not a temporary arrangement. The time will be when the United States will be possessed of the title to all the lands within its boundaries [referring to the private inholdings that still existed] and in the meantime it would be better if the citizens living near the Park would make arrangements to conform to the new condition of things, thus avoiding the consequence of a violation of the law.

Poachers at Yellowstone and sheep herders at Yosemite continued to be a minor plague for years to come. But the cavalry on the whole did a commendable job, giving the parks protection they would not have had under ordinary conditions and helping to preserve their "wonders" until Congress created a formal system of parks in 1916. At that time many of the old cavalrymen went right on protecting the parks, this time as park rangers.

CHAPTER XIV

An Adirondack Park

The preservation of Yellowstone and Yosemite had set a precedent, and the idea of a great Forest Preserve was given further impetus by the affirmative action taken on such a large scale in New York in 1885. Men of wisdom were beginning to look to science, as distinct from technology, as a solution to some of the most severe problems in dealing with natural resources. The federal government had created a Division of Forestry within the Department of Agriculture in 1881. The division's first chief was Bernhard Eduard Fernow, a German who had practiced forestry in Europe for a number of years before marrying an American woman and settling in this country as its first "forestry consultant." Dedicated and capable, he brought with him European ideas about scientific forest management.

"It is not the control of the Government over private property," he wrote in a Department of Agriculture publication in 1886, "it is not the exercise of eminent domain, it is not police regulation or restrictions that have produced desirable effects upon private forestry abroad, but simply the example of a systematic and successful management of its own forests, and the opportunity offered by the government to the private owner of availing himself of the advice and guidance of well-qualified forestry officials."

Fernow busied himself in Washington with statistics on forests and forest products, though he was diverted for a time by his experiments in rainmaking. A series of tumultuous explosions over Washington resulted, sending him back to his statistics. Later he wrote a bulletin on the value of forests in preserving water supplies which was instrumental in gaining support for the government's forest programs in the thirsty West.

By the 1890s new concepts were taking hold. A landmark in conservation legislation was slipped through Congress in 1891 by what has sometimes been called a fluke. Fernow had been talking up his ideas to Secretary of the Interior John W. Noble, whose department controlled the government's forested lands. Noble went to President Benjamin Harrison and suggested he set aside a part of the public domain as forest reserves.

There did not exist a presidential authority for such an act, but Harrison was interested. (He was, a little later, to build a camp in the Adirondacks, on Second Lake near Old Forge.) With Congress nearing the end of its session and its members eager to adjourn, he permitted Noble to draft a rider to a bill dealing with the revision of land laws which was soon scheduled for a vote. To congressmen who objected to giving the President such powers, Noble hinted that Harrison might veto the entire bill if the rider was not included. The bill went through intact. The General Land Law Revision Act of 1891 gave the President the authority to create forest reserves from the public domain by proclamation. Harrison almost immediately set aside fifteen reserves totaling thirteen million acres, most of which were on the Pacific slope. Among them was a large tract of sequoias, trees often cut though their brittle wood made poor lumber. (A later Secretary of the Interior, Ray Lyman Wilbur, once remarked that talking about the majestic sequoias in terms of board feet was like talking about German soldiers in terms of lard.) Congress had provided neither funds nor a management plan for the reserves, but despite cries of a "lockup" of natural resources in the West, they were there to be acted upon at the opportune moment, less than a decade away.

In the 1890s a portent of future action might have been detected by close observers as familiar Adirondacks topics once more came to the surface. There was a renewed clamor against the railroads as destroyers of the forest. There were attacks in the press on the lumbermen and on what many critics viewed as a too compliant Forest Commission. *The New York Times* once more was pointing out not only the natural glories of the Adirondack forests but also their status as the "great sanatorium of the Northern States." As

Edward Trudeau's work became widely recognized, other doctors were convinced of the benefits of a mountain cure. Many invalids, indeed, did return from the mountains, cured and eager to live an active life once more, though others died at Saranac Lake and were laid to rest in what a dying patient called "Trudeau's Garden." In the early 1890s groups of doctors actively supported and testified for some further legislation that would preserve this great regional "sanatorium." One prominent doctor, however, while supporting the legislation, looked with dismay on its proponents' use of evocative but murky phrases such as "balsamic influences, health-giving emanations and aromized atmospheres."

Allied with the doctors were a growing number of sportsmen. A perusal of *Forest and Stream* during the late 1890s and early 1900s reveals that hunters and fishermen were coming to realize that game and fish depended on a healthy environment—a flourishing forest—as well as on laws to curb the "game hogs." Sportsmen were growing into conservationists; they took the lead at the time in founding a variety of conservation organizations—from the Boone and Crockett Club to various Audubon Societies.

It was not until 1890 that the Legislature appropriated any money with which the Forest Commission could buy land within the Forest Preserve counties. In that year it gave the commission $25,000 and stipulated that the highest price to be paid was $1.50 an acre for the land; looking to the future, the Legislature added the phrase "as shall be available for the purpose of a State Park." For that matter, the commission was already looking forward to gathering the scattered preserve holdings into a park in "one grand domain." Governor Hill, who had put forth such a proposal in his annual message earlier in the year, was disappointed by the Legislature's niggardliness, but he was not happy with the commission's initiative and performance, either. As if to support the governor's doubts, the commission revealed a confusion of aims in its year-end report. It published a map of the Adirondacks and set a historic precedent by circling the proposed area of a state park with a "Blue Line." The Blue Line has ever since been synonymous with the park's area; for a long time, in fact, the Blue Line's reality exceeded that of the park itself, which had little unity or direction. But it was not clear from the report what plans the commission had for the area.

It seemed to say that to be effective the commission must obtain by purchase all of the land within the Blue Line, and at other times that it didn't really matter; and it seemed to hesitate at advocating that timber be cut for revenue on the state lands.

In any case, there was a growing sense of urgency that a further step be taken to protect the Adirondacks. The concept of a Forest Preserve was a convenient umbrella under which to gather and manage all of the forested lands owned by the state in the mountainous counties, including the Catskills. The concept of a park, on the other hand, gave the state a defined region into which to concentrate its holdings in the Adirondacks. Now, with talk of a state park in that region, prices had risen to at least five dollars an acre for forested land, making a mockery of the Legislature's appropriation for buying available tracts. Newly competing for the large acreage were wealthy individuals and clubs, the most notable of the latter being an organization of five hundred socially prominent men (most of whom were from New York City) called the Adirondack League Club. In 1890 the club bought 104,000 acres of prime forest and twenty-five lakes for $4.75 an acre in the southwestern Adirondacks. Perhaps thirty other such clubs of wealthy men from the East Coast and the Midwest bought large tracts in the area, posted their property, and reserved the fishing and hunting for themselves. Sportsmen's groups and politicians were quick to point out that between the lumbermen's depredations and the clubs' restrictions, the "little man" might soon be shut out of the Adirondacks altogether.

Organizations such as the New York State Association for Fish and Game, the New York State Forestry Association (whose president was the indefatigable Morris K. Jesup), and the Adirondack Park Association (whose moving force was the doctors concerned with the treatment of pulmonary diseases) began pushing for a bill in the Legislature in 1890. The last-named group's message was especially important to the cause because it was suspected that the public would not support a park thought of simply as a playground in which the rich could "enjoy the spell of a romantic woods life." In fact, the doctors wrote their own bill to create a park; introduced to the Legislature, it was considered a rival to that submitted by Governor Hill and the sportsmen and forestry groups. There were fears that the governor's bill would benefit mainly the lumbermen and the politicians, for it proposed a new commission and a plan to exchange public lands owned by the state outside the Blue Line for private lands within it. *The New York Times* grumbled that the lumbermen were the power behind Hill's plan: "They have sought in every possible way to secure such of the State lands as lie along streams or lakes which are extremely valuable, in exchange for tracts not directly drained, which if cut, would, because of their location, make the lumber worthless because of the impossibility of getting it to market."

Upstate the governor's plan was preferred, sometimes with passion. An editorial writer in the Warrensburg *News* wrote:

> This whole idea of shutting so many hundred thousand acres of valuable timber lands which has and does constitute one of the chief sources of industry and commerce in the state for the enjoyment of a few wealthy politicians and summer tourists would be a serious mistake. . . . When we consider the amount of employment afforded by the lumber industry, the thousands of saw mills, tanneries, pulp and paper mills and factories of all kinds giving labor to hundreds of thousands of poor people and that all this is to be stopped to afford a deer park and fishing ground for a few wealthy pleasure-seekers to air their smoke-dried anatomies is an injustice, the boldness of which is astonishing.

The park's proponents had been talking of putting together an area of two million acres or more. In 1891, when the Forest Commission published its report on the proposed park, the Blue Line included a part of most Forest Preserve counties in the Adirondacks with the exception of a large portion of forest in Herkimer County. The New York *Tribune* was quick to notice that "Forest Commissioner Basselin draws supplies for his lumber mill from this omitted portion of Herkimer County, and it is therefore suspected, with good reason, that his personal business has interfered with the faithful execution of his duties as Forest Commissioner." And the New York *Herald* suggested that the Forest Commission's motto, "Protect the Forests," should be extended to read "from Theodore B. Basselin." In the same year a legislative committee, reflecting the Legislature's concern about the spreading attacks on the commission, found that the commission had not made its first exchange of lands (under the 1887 act) until 1890, and even then the exchange happened to involve a company controlled by one of Basselin's partners.

The effort to create a park finally succeeded the following year, and on May 2, 1892, Governor Roswell P. Flower signed the Adirondack Park Enabling Act. The new law defined the park:

> All lands now owned, or which may hereafter be acquired by the State within . . . the county of Hamilton; the towns of Newcomb, Minerva, Schroon, North Hudson, Keene, North Elba, St. Armand, and Wilmington, in the county of Essex; the towns of Harrietstown, Santa Clara, Altamont, Waverly, and Brighton, in the county of Franklin; the town of Wilmurt in the county of Herkimer; the towns of Hopkinton, Colton, Clifton, and Fine, in the county of St. Lawrence; and the towns of Johnsburg, Stony Creek, and Thurman, in the county of Warren . . . shall constitute the Adirondack Park.

The act did not refer to private lands. The area within the Blue Line consisted of 2,807,760 acres, of which 551,093 belonged to the state. The state lands within the Blue Line, according to the act, were to be "forever reserved . . . for the free use of all the people," but they were by no means inviolate—the Forest Commission had the right to sell state lands in parts of the park and lease lands for camps and cottages. The new legislation, however, repealed the 1887 law which permitted the exchange of "small" parcels of land. Governor Flower noted that "all revenues from the sale of the so-called 'outside' lands will be devoted to the purchase of new lands better adapted for the purposes of a forest preserve. Eventually, the State preserve ought to pay the expense of its maintenance from the judicious sale of timber and the leasing, at moderate rentals, of small parcels of land to individuals for the establishment of summer homes."

Governor Flower and the Legislature were not yet finished putting the state into the business of running a profitable venture in the Adirondacks. In 1893 a bill, proposed by Flower, was passed creating a new five-member Forest Commission (the controversial Mr. Basselin departing) and authorizing it to sell timber from any part of the Forest Preserve, including the park. With the inclusion of the islands in Lake George the park's boundaries were redefined. Curiously, the downstate press was not strenuous in its opposition to the bill, though Verplanck Colvin fulminated against it and the New York Board of Trade and Transportation and the Brooklyn Constitution Club sent members to Governor Flower to persuade him not to sign it into law. Flower, however, signed this "cutting bill" and at the beginning of 1894 jubilantly announced that the commission had sold "spruce stumpage" on 17,468 acres, bringing the state an estimated $53,400. He said:

> If from so small a portion of the Forest Preserve, so considerable a revenue is received without injury to the forest, we can reasonably look forward to the time when the Forest Preserve will not only be a great conservator of our water courses and the restorer of health, but will contribute a large part of the money required for the support of State government.

Seldom has a state official displayed such baseless optimism, or seen his hopes confounded in so brief a time. The legal practice of forestry in the preserve was cut short by the dramatic events that took place in Albany later that year.

CHAPTER XV

Forever Wild

Drought gripped parts of the East in 1893, and the dry weather continued through the summer of 1894. Forest fires raged in a number of states, particularly in Pennsylvania and New York, recalling the disastrous fires of a decade earlier. In New York City business leaders continued to fret about watersheds and the inimical effects their destruction would have on the city's transportation, drinking supplies, and fire protection. The Adirondacks were not spared during this dry season, and smoke from their smoldering forests hung like a vague threat over the upper Hudson.

Opposition to the 1893 "cutting law" was spreading, even to the unlikeliest places. Some of the large clubs in the Adirondacks were unhappy about the sloppy cutting practices on state lands that adjoined their own. Among them was the Adirondack League Club, each of whose members had bought shares in the club and its property. This, the largest of the private preserves, provided its members not only with exclusive hunting and fishing rights but also with dividends from the proceeds of timber sales, which actually increased the value of the shares; large-scale fires on state lands threatened such investments. More surprisingly, the government's chief forester and prime exponent of scientific forestry, Bernhard Fernow, criticized the Forest Commission's cutting practices as revealed in the 1893 legislation; he charged that the commission had no rational plan for cutting or selling the timber rights, and that its restriction of cutting to certain sizes of trees was not always the best policy. Fernow's criticism of the commission was supported by the state engineer and surveyor, Campbell W. Adams, who thought the cutting practices it specified were destroying new growth and that it was not getting what it should from the timber rights it sold. Referring to the commission, *Garden and Forest* said, "It would seem that the time has already come when the Park ought to be preserved from its preservers."

The time had certainly come. A convention had been called at Albany in 1894 to revise the state Constitution, particularly as it pertained to the judiciary. When the convention opened on May 5, 1894, the Republican majority elected as president one of its own, a liberal member of the party named Joseph H. Choate. There were no plans to discuss forestry during its proceedings. But the New York Board of Trade and Transportation, frustrated by what it considered a series of failures over the years to preserve the forests of the Adirondacks, saw a chance to settle the matter once and for all. The Board of Trade had maintained an active Forestry Committee for some years, and in this convention year had also created a Special Committee on Constitutional Amendments. The two committees collaborated on the draft of an amendment to the Constitution that would place the Forest Preserve under its ironclad protection; the proposed amendment prohibited the sale of preserve lands, as well as the timber on them. The committee members then took their draft to David McClure, a leader of the New York City bar and a Democratic delegate to the convention. McClure agreed to sponsor the amendment.

The convention had already been in session for more than three months when McClure presented his amendment on July 31. The following day, in support of his proposal, McClure asked the convention to appoint a committee to investigate the importance of the Adirondack forests and to determine if a clause on the preserve ought to be inserted in the proposed Constitution. While he did not ask to be named to the committee, Choate graciously appointed a five-member Committee on Forest Preserves with McClure as its chairman. Choate said in later years that the 1893 law authorizing the Forest Commission to sell timber had convinced the convention delegates that the preserve could only be saved by "some unpassable constitutional barrier."

Roger Thompson, a park historian, has pointed out that "a constitutional convention is in fact the one time when interest groups sit as legislators." When the McClure Committee opened hearings on the proposed amendment a number of interest groups gathered in the capital in a rare display of unanimity. Verplanck Colvin came to testify on behalf of preservation. So did John H. Washburn, the president of the New York Board of Underwriters. (The board's statement disclosed that fire insurance policies then covered property in New York City worth "two thousand millions of dollars," reason enough for the insurance companies to worry about a dependable water supply for the future.) Sportsmen, physicians, and businessmen extolled the benefits of the forest from their own points of view. The beauty and grandeur of the mountains also seemed to be on people's minds.

But while there was talk of "forever wild," it is clear that some of the proponents of a protective clause did not believe that a ban on cutting would be needed *forever*. As the New York *Tribune* said in an editorial: "On the whole, we are inclined to think that there is less danger of irretrievable loss in the rigid prohibition of the proposed amendment than in leaving the forests entirely at the mercy of Legislatures and Commissions." Those preservationists who were also foresters were in favor of prohibition until another state Constitutional Convention might be called in twenty years or so, at which time it was hoped that both spreading enlightenment and refined forestry techniques might once again make the preserves available for commercial exploitation.

On September 8, McClure was ready to argue the worth of his amendment to the convention. He said that he had only lately come to see its great importance.

"It has surprised me with an ever-increasing surprise that this matter of all the questions affecting the people of the State should have been left to so late a day and be the subject of almost accidental action at last," he went on. "As I look at it now, Mr. Chairman, it seems to be almost the great and important subject, which at the inception of this Convention demanded prompt relief and action in the interest of the people of this State."

In arguing that the state forests should not be sold, McClure referred to a fact that arouses in moderns a pining for "the good old days"; in short, the state was not in debt and didn't need the money.

"In 1893 three millions were raised by taxation of dead men's estates and nearly two millions by taxation of corporations," he said. "By these extraordinary means, in part, this State is in this grand financial condition."

Then he went on to say, somewhat inaccurately, that because the Legislature had seen fit to allocate only a paltry sum to the Forest Commission, it was forced to sell timber from the preserve to pay the salaries of its wardens. (The commission, on the contrary, got money for salaries from the Legislature and put the proceeds of timber sales into a special fund to buy more land.) And he listed the familiar reasons why the preserve should be held intact: to protect the watershed so there would be a stable water supply for drinking, fire fighting, and the canals (in this connection McClure spoke of the railroad monopoly "that is grinding when there is not competition"); to provide a "great resort for the people of this State"; and to prevent the erosion of the land (he even managed to evoke the deserts of Africa and Asia).

While no one spoke against the amendments, there were several questions from delegates that McClure fielded well, helping to give posterity a clearer idea of exactly what the convention had in mind when it considered the Forest Preserve.

Did the amendment prevent the Legislature from authorizing a railroad or a highway through the preserve, even in cases of demonstrated public need? "I think so," McClure answered. "The scope of the matter is to prevent its being taken by any corporation, public or private."

Was a further amendment necessary to define the limits of the area to which the amendment referred? "But this constitutional amendment refers to the forest preserve as now fixed by law. The law is contained in the Statute of 1893."

Did the drafters of the amendment believe its language would effectively prevent any Legislature in the future from reducing the preserve's extent? "We do, sir. We carefully considered that."

While there were many sound reasons for establishing an inviolable Forest Preserve, it is clear that the amendment's primary function was to protect the water supply on which the state, particularly *downstate*, was dependent. The amendment was conceived and brought before the convention by the New York Board of Trade and Transportation and those who worked in cooperation with it. The conservation of timber, of fish and game, of an atmosphere notable for its "restorative" powers on body and spirits, of a storehouse of sublime natural treasures—all were important in the argument, yet they were secondary to the repeated emphasis on the preservation of a vital watershed.

It is ironic, then, that almost at the last minute the amendment was altered in such a way that it went to the people bearing the seeds of the water users' defeat in the years ahead. The amendment as it was prepared by the McClure Committee said of the Forest Preserve lands: "They shall not be leased, sold, or exchanged, or be taken by any corporation, public or private, nor shall the timber thereon be sold or removed." Judge William P. Goodelle, a delegate-at-large from Syracuse, rose to suggest a change in its wording:

"I refer to that system which has been for some years carried on by our State in destroying our forests, in piling up great burdens upon the State for that purpose, by reason of building dams and reservoirs which they have constructed in certain regions of the Adirondacks."

Goodelle, speaking from personal knowledge, told how dams were often built, at state expense, on the region's beautiful rivers to raise the water level and float logs to the sawmills. As a consequence, water backed up into the forest, flooding thousands of acres, so that dead trees stood in a "vast sea." He spoke in particular of a dam that the state put across the Beaver River for the benefit of a logger whom Goodelle intimated was the former forest commissioner Theodore Basselin. He therefore recommended that the concluding phrase of the clause, "nor shall the timber thereon be sold or removed," be amended to read: "Nor shall the timber thereon be sold, removed or destroyed."

The additional word greatly expanded the amendment's scope and, as we shall see, had an enormous bearing on future controversies in the Adirondacks. Goodelle's change was accepted. It was more than a month afterward, late in the evening on Thursday, September 13, when the convention in its waning hours got around to voting on the Forest Preserve amendment. Perhaps by then some interested lumbermen had begun to realize its full impact. At any rate, one of the delegates attempted to stifle action on the amendment by making a motion to adjourn. The motion was defeated, as were several last-minute proposed changes, including one that would have legalized a number of leases within the preserve which the Forest Commission had authorized at an earlier date. The convention rejected the amendments and, in a show of accord that has never been repeated in any matter having to do with the Adirondacks, approved the clause 112–0.

Thus the clause, Article VII, Section 7, became a part of the new Constitution that was submitted to the voters of the state later that fall. It read: "The lands of the State, now owned or hereafter acquired, constituting the Forest Preserve as now fixed by law, shall be forever kept as wild forest lands. They shall not be leased, sold or exchanged, or be taken by any corporation, public or private, nor shall the timber thereon be sold, removed or destroyed." The "Forever Wild" language was carried over from the 1885 legislation that created the Forest Preserve.

Only two sentences made up Article VII, Section 7, but they set an example that remains unique, giving the state-owned portion of the Adirondack Park (and certain state lands in the Catskills) protection that cannot be undone by any agency or Legislature. Only the people of New York, voting in a statewide election, can make exception to the blanket of prohibition that was thrown over the Forest Preserve in 1894. (The referendum must be preceded by the approval of the proposed amendments in two successive sessions of the Legislature.) Whether it took the Forest Preserve completely out of the realm of politics, as its proponents had hoped, remains a matter of interpretation. Roger Thompson, speaking for the forestry profession, which was thus forever barred from practicing its science on those lands, expressed the dissenting view when he wrote that the clause, "while ostensibly a move to take the preserve 'out of politics,' succeeded in practice in placing the preserve within the politics of the recreational interest group." The remainder of this history then, is mainly an account of how Article VII, Section 7, and its successor, have fared as a trophy fought over by various "interest groups."

The people of New York approved the new Constitution in November by a vote of 410,697 to 327,402 (a result attributed by some of the Forest Preserve's friends, but without substantial evidence, to the popularity of what came to be called the Constitution's "Forever Wild" clause), and it went into effect on January 1, 1895.

As its proponents pointed out, the constitutional protection came not a moment too soon. In late summer while the convention was still in session, the state's comptroller, James A. Roberts, accused the Forest Commission of skulduggery in its dealings with lumbermen, particularly by faking land sales, permitting the "buyer" to cut the timber, and then canceling the sale of the land. While the disclosure may have helped to sway a few fence-straddling delegates at the convention, no criminal charges were brought against the departing commissioners.

Before completely fading away, the commission had one more dubious card up its collective sleeve. The Delaware and Hudson Railroad had bought Dr. Thomas C. Durant's Adirondack Railroad in 1889, hoping to extend its tracks from North Creek to Long Lake and beyond to take advantage of the tourist trade that frequented the lakes of the central Adirondacks. Because part of the route led across state land, the railroad (its chairman was James Roosevelt, father of Franklin Delano Roosevelt) approached the Forest Commission to obtain a right-of-way. The request was vigorously opposed by a number of individuals who resented the intrusion of another railroad in the Adirondacks and, it was rumored, by the New York Central Railroad, which did not want a rival line competing for its Adirondack business. Moreover, it was late December 1894, and time was running out for the Delaware and Hudson because the new Constitution was about to go into effect.

Horace G. Young, the railroad's vice-president and general manager, knew that three of the five commission members favored granting the right-of-way. With the other two members away for the Christmas holidays, the pliable majority called a commission meeting in a private room of the Delavan House in Albany on December 27 for the purpose of approving the application. One of the three members was in Plattsburgh. To secure the necessary quorum, the railroad officials dispatched a locomotive and car to Plattsburgh to fetch the commissioner, then returned him to his home immediately after the vote. When word of the meeting and its circumstances became known, the railroad's opponents secured an injunction against the commission. Several days later the Constitution went into force, and the Delaware and Hudson's plans evaporated. Article VII, Section 7, began its life with no strings attached.

CHAPTER XVI

The Forester

Gifford Pinchot did not invent "conservation," and perhaps he did not even invent the word as it is used in the popular sense. (He wrote that he could not recall whether he or an associate, Overton Price, had first used the word to describe the Theodore Roosevelt administration's policy toward natural resources, though he usually possessed a remarkable memory about his own accomplishments.) But Pinchot was certainly the new movement's outstanding publicist and one of the first Americans to apply its tenets on a large scale. It is ironic that he did much of his original forestry work in the Adirondacks just when a large part of that region was being closed "forever" to scientific forestry. Pinchot was at the center of the storm as the battles that would shape the conservation movement during the twentieth century got under way.

Like his great friend Roosevelt, Gifford Pinchot was born of wealthy parents and attended the appropriate school—in Pinchot's case, Yale. His father, James M. Pinchot, was a New York merchant who encouraged his early interest in forestry, which certainly was influenced in college by his reading of George Perkins Marsh's *Man and Nature*. Since there were no forestry schools in the United States (Pinchot's parents later established the Yale Forest School, endowing it with $300,000), the young man went to study the science during 1889–90 in France and Germany, where the people had had to live within their natural resources for generations. When Pinchot returned to the United States, he was full of ideas about transforming American forestry from its current course of "cut out and get out" to a systematic practice under which the dwindling forests might become eternally renewable, providing stable profits for the industry and a stable timber supply for the nation.

Among the elder Pinchot's friends was Frederick Law Olmsted. About this time Olmsted was engaged by George W. Vanderbilt, a grandson of Commodore Cornelius Vanderbilt, to design his new estate in the Appalachians near Asheville, North Carolina. (Vanderbilt called his place Biltmore, a word put together from "Bildt," the Dutch town from which the family took its name, and "more," an obsolete English word for moor, or rolling, upland country.) Having heard of the young man and his enthusiasm, Olmsted arranged for Pinchot to come to Biltmore and put his theories into practice. Later Pinchot described the raw material on which he went to work:

> Up to the time of its purchase by Mr. Vanderbilt, this forest was owned by a number of different individuals, who treated it in the usual farmer's way. They cut all the timber that was salable either for saw logs, fence rails or cord wood, and turned the cattle into the forest to graze, often burning the woods over for the sake of the pasturage. The evil results of such a course are sufficiently obvious, and the woodland—never in its best days very good—grew steadily worse.

Pinchot shooed away the cattle and cut only trees that shaded the smaller ones' growth. The results were impressive. In a very short time he presented Vanderbilt with a healthy forest and a profitable addition to the Vanderbilt holdings. Much gratified, Vanderbilt recommended the young man to his brother-in-law, William Seward Webb, already the owner of what was probably the largest expanse of privately held land in the Adirondacks (perhaps 175,000 acres) and the builder of one of its showplace "camps."

Webb's career had somewhat paralleled that of another physician–financier–railroad builder, Thomas Clark Durant. After attending Columbia College, he studied medicine in Paris and Vienna and then graduated from the College of Physicians and Surgeons in New York, where he established a private practice. His marriage to Lila Vanderbilt in 1881 apparently convinced him that medicine was not his vocation. Although he came from an old New York family, that city's high society did not consider doctoring a fit profession for one of its own, being neither respectable nor lucrative enough by its standards, and he was persuaded to plunge into Wall Street instead. Railroads offered as quick a way as any in those days to gain both wealth and power, and soon Webb went the approved route, gathering the trappings of the mighty through his blossoming executive talents. One of his projects was the Adirondack and St. Lawrence Railway Company, under whose aegis he bought 115,000 acres of private Adirondack lands on which to build a line from Herkimer to Malone; partly through a Canadian company of his, he extended the line to Montreal. His railroad and its trunk lines opened the Adirondacks to thousand of tourists.

Webb was a maker and a shaker, a tall, regal man with light hair and a George V mustache and beard. A railroad historian has recorded one of his triumphs:

> Early in 1892, when the line from Malone had reached Loon Lake Station, he [Webb] wired Chief Engineer Roberts that he had agreed to build a temporary spur to the Loon Lake Hotel so that President Benjamin Harrison could take his invalid wife to that resort. It must be ready the next day. Roberts swore that it could not be done, and immediately started doing it. He graded and laid a mile of track in twenty-four hours, and when the Presidential special arrived the road was ready for it.

Besides his railroad lands and other holdings in the Adirondacks, Webb owned perhaps 40,000 forested acres in Hamilton County which he named Ne-ha-sa-ne Park. A wire fence, nine feet high, enclosed 8,000 of Webb's acres, on which (like Edward Hubbard Litchfield) he propagated large game animals in the hope of re-establishing them in the Adirondacks. Among them were the white-tailed deer (sadly depleted in the region but already beginning a comeback under the new game laws), moose, and elk. The experiment was not generally successful, for poachers immediately took most of the animals Webb liberated.

The focus of his estate was Ne-ha-sa-ne Lodge, overlooking Lake Lila, with Mount Lila in the background. The long, low building, gabled, and rimmed by verandas where guests might rock away the evening or dream in a hammock, was in keeping with an age when luxurious camps were commonplace. Eight chimneys surmounted the whole. A striped awning, raised to shade one of the porches, relieved the somber shingled façade, while flower beds and a manicured lawn rambled through curving drives to the shore. The great room of the lodge was a riot of taxidermy. A black bear stood at the left of the massive boulders that framed the fireplace and a mountain lion stalked its mantelpiece, while shaggy antlered heads, plaqued and lacquered fish, and stuffed birds up to the size of owls and swans stared glassily out at the guests from their perches in eternity.

Having seen Gifford Pinchot's work at Biltmore, Webb summoned him to Ne-ha-sa-ne.

"October of 1892 found me there making an examination with a view to the practice of sound forest management," Pinchot wrote later. "I carried my pack through many enchanting miles of autumn forest, put in a gorgeous week, and as a result was able to make Dr. Webb a report which led before long to forestry on many Adirondack acres."

Although Pinchot found chiefly a typical northern hardwood forest of maple, birch, and beech, there was a considerable stand of spruce, which was commercially the most important tree on the estate. As at Biltmore, the older trees often overshadowed the younger ones, holding back their growth, "and so made it possible to cut and yet increase the annual production of wood from year to year." This Pinchot did, devising a plan which promised a "sustained yield" from the forest, while cutting to favor the propagation of the valuable spruce and so increasing the land's real value. "We had to make forestry pay, and pay it did," Pinchot wrote.

Perhaps of even more immediate interest to Pinchot was a study of the spruce forest which Webb financed on his land in 1896–97. Pinchot published his pioneer study under the title *The Adirondack Spruce*, a little book of 150 pages, "with rounded corners to slip in your pocket," which served as a working plan for lumbermen and landowners. Despite its tables of growth, volume, and yield, enabling the forest manager to predict the composition of his forest in ten, twenty, or thirty years (depending on what types of trees he cut in the present), the book was "strictly American" in that the simple text was tailored to readers in a land where resource management was utterly alien.

"It dealt with the forest strictly as a factory of wood," Pinchot wrote later, "a factory that must be kept going for the benefit of the owner. Lumbering must keep it in order and speed it up instead of leaving it a dismantled wreck."

Like Webb's large game animals, the forestry innovations at Ne-ha-sa-ne overflowed to neighboring lands. The new scientific measures were taken up on the adjoining estate of William C. Whitney, a wealthy lawyer-politician-sportsman, and are carried on there today by his descendants. Perhaps Pinchot's most satisfying convert, however, was Pat Moynihan, the rough-and-ready leader of a famous Adirondack lumbering family. There were, it was true, moments of backsliding on Moynihan's part, during one of which a scientific forester named Gene Bruce, according to Pinchot, "beat him up severely as an inducement to follow the rules."

But more lasting trouble was already brewing in the Adirondacks, where the water users' victory seemed to have been certified by the state Constitution. On April 25, 1895, the Legislature consolidated the Fisheries Commission, the Game Commission, and the Forest Commission into a new agency called, so as not to slight anyone, the Fisheries, Game and Forest Commission, giving it the "care, custody, control and superintendence of the Forest Preserve." This entity now assumed the power to buy lands inside the Blue Line for inclusion within the Forest Preserve, as well as the authority to lay out roads and paths there.

The chief avenues of transport already in existence through the preserve became a source of trouble. These, of course, were the waterways which the Legislature had years before decided were "public highways" for the transportation of logs. Webb used the Beaver River as a highway on which to raft the logs cut on a large section of his land. As early as 1849 the state had diverted the upper reaches of the Beaver River from its natural course toward the Black River valley so that it might supplement the dropping water levels in the Erie Canal. This diversion naturally robbed the Black River of some of its traditional flow. By the 1880s, as factories at Watertown and elsewhere along the Black River needed more water to turn their waterwheels and generate power, the state decided to build a dam and reservoir on the Beaver River at Stillwater in Herkimer County. The reservoir's function was to provide a steady flow of water down the Beaver River and into the Black River at all times of the year.

In this case, the eighteen-foot-high dam at Stillwater not only backed up the Beaver River twenty miles to flood a large part of Webb's forest, but also cut off his "highway" to market. Webb sued the state for $184,350 in damages. At length, in 1896, the state reached an agreement with Webb by which it bought the 75,000 acres he contended had been damaged for a price that amounted to $600,000. This sum, which averaged about eight dollars an acre, was a third higher than the going price for Adirondack forest land; some eyebrows were raised, but chicanery was never established. In any event, the "Webb purchase" remains the largest single piece of land the state has ever bought for the Forest Preserve.

Meanwhile, Pinchot, now becoming nationally known for his scientific approach to forestry, was breasting a hostile tide of sentiment as New Yorkers turned against forestry of any kind on state lands. Easterners generally distrusted the idea of cutting on public land, which they believed led to both fraud and devastation. As we have already seen, a rider to the General Land Law Revision Act of 1891, submitted to Congress late in the session by President Harrison and passed hurriedly with little discussion, had given the President the authority to create forest reserves from the public domain by proclamation.

But the presidential proclamations served as a very fragile barrier against the lumbermen. Congress, hostile to the idea, provided no funds for their management. At first many Westerners looked favorably on the reserves, seeing them as sources of water for irrigation, power, and (in California) flood control. Soon grumbling was heard among other Westerners, who looked upon the federal action as a "lockup" of their natural resources. When President Grover Cleveland established some more reserves, there was a move in Congress to rescind the orders of both Harrison and Cleveland (and impeach the latter!). When this move was beaten back, a western congressman cried out in frustration: "Why should we be everlastingly and eternally harassed and annoyed and bedeviled by these scientific gentlemen from Harvard?"

No one even knew the condition of the forests that had been set aside. In 1896 the National Academy of Sciences (at the request of Secretary of the Interior Hoke Smith) appointed a National Forestry Commission to survey the existing reserves and recommend a forest policy for the federal government. Charles Sargent, the Harvard botanist, became the commission's chairman and Pinchot, though not a member of the Academy, its secretary. Congress appropriated $35,000 for expenses, and the commission members headed westward, where they were joined by John Muir, the "Grand Old Tramp" of the Sierra, who served the commission as a guide and sort of ex officio member.

Although he was only thirty-one years old, Pinchot was able to hold his own with his distinguished colleagues on the commission. No one could have mistaken him for anything but a "comer." Tall and lean, with sharp blue eyes and a patrician nose, he easily assumed an attitude of authority if not of leadership. He could ride and shoot, fell easily in with the others, and had considerable endurance in the field; for all his comfortable background there was a hint of the Spartan and the Puritan about him (later he became an outspoken prohibitionist).

On this trip the men who emerged as the leaders of the two conflicting wings of the American conservation movement came together and shared a brief moment of intimacy. All of the commission members knew about Muir—his wanderings in the Sierra, the almost religious reverence with which he spoke of his forested "temples"—but Pinchot grew closest of all to the older man. The party made a pilgrimage to the rim of the Grand Canyon. Pinchot and Muir drank in the spectacle, pointed out to each other awesome sights, and when Pinchot tried to kill a tarantula they had come upon, Muir restrained him with the admonition that the insect "had as much right there as we did." When the rest of the party returned to the hotel, Muir and Pinchot stole away with the remains of their lunch and made their beds for the night in cedar boughs among a thick stand of trees. Pinchot listened raptly to Muir's tales by the fire until midnight.

"It was such an evening as I never had before or since," Pinchot wrote years afterward. "That night it froze, but the fire kept us from freezing. In the early morning we sneaked back like guilty schoolboys, well knowing that we must reckon with the other members of the Commission, who probably imagined we had fallen over a cliff. They had done just that, and they told us what they thought of us with clarity and conviction."

But starry eyes turned steely in the meeting rooms and it was soon apparent that Pinchot's admiration for Muir did not carry all the way to the matter of the wilderness temples; for Pinchot, the forests remained "wood factories." It is true that both men recognized the "multiple use" concept of forests, but Muir held that their value in providing wood and water ranked below their function as a source of refreshment for body and soul. Pinchot put their utilitarian value at the head of the list. He also disagreed with Sargent's long-held belief that the Army ought to stand guard against the lumbermen in the forest preserves as it did against the poachers and timber thieves in the national parks. The side of Pinchot that was publicist and politician (later in life he served twice as governor of Pennsylvania and even harbored presidential ambitions) fused with the scientist to take a dissident stand. He believed that the reserves should be managed to provide a steady supply of timber, rather than locked up. To do otherwise, he thought, would only serve to antagonize still further the Westerners who were fed up with eastern do-gooders and thus threatened the very existence of the preserves. The two factions agreed in their report only in the urgent recommendation that new reserves be created before the timber companies completely destroyed the nation's forests.

Pinchot was to win the battle on the national level. He lobbied in Congress and told his side of the story to government officials and the interested public. He believed the forests should be used, and perpetually renewed, through wise cutting practices. When, in 1897, he was appointed a "confidential forest agent" by the Secretary of the Interior, he toured the country, keeping an eye on the preserves and carrying on his crusade. One of his principal goals was to win over the disgruntled Westerners who might use their political pressure in the Interior Department (which originally had control over the preserves) to have the forests put up for grabs again before management practices could go into effect. In Seattle he was confronted by sheepmen who were alarmed about a lockup of federal lands. Eager to placate them, Pinchot said he saw no harm in letting sheep graze in the preserves (he was later to reverse himself and find sheep to be a menace in the western forests just as he had advised against letting cattle into those at Biltmore).

Unfortunately for Pinchot, Muir had arrived in Seattle just at that time on his way home from Alaska. When Muir read about Pinchot's remarks in the newspapers, he was enraged; sheep were an obsession with the older man, and he agreed with another Westerner who once remarked that "he could not see a sheep without wishing to kick it." During the day he encountered Pinchot in the lobby of his hotel talking to a group of newspapermen.

"Are you quoted correctly here?" Muir asked, extending the paper but not his hand.

With reporters standing nearby, Pinchot had no alternative but to own up to his quoted remarks.

"Then I want nothing more to do with you," Muir said, and stalked out.

A friendship split, and so did the American conservation movement. The two men would meet again in an even more bitter battle—preservationist versus utilitarian—over the Hetch Hetchy Valley in Yosemite, but meanwhile Pinchot was to define an important aspect of the nation's conservation goals for decades to come. In 1898 he became chief of the Forestry Division in the U.S. Department of Agriculture. It was a little like becoming admiral of the Swiss Navy, for the forests were under Interior's, not Agriculture's, control. But Pinchot built up his staff of experts, refined his theories and methods, and bided his time. Before long he was invited to advise Governor Theodore Roosevelt about New York's state forests.

"I laid before the governor my plan for a single-headed New York Forest Commission instead of the spineless, many-headed commission of those days, and he approved it entirely," Pinchot wrote later (though Roosevelt was unable to accomplish that reform during the two-year term allotted to New York governors at the time). "TR and I did a little wrestling, at which he beat me; and some boxing, during which I had the honor of knocking the future President of the United States off his very sturdy pins."

Pinchot had hitched his wagon to a star, and the future President would secure him the forest reserves he wanted so badly in the Department of Agriculture. As Chief Forester and a presidential adviser more powerful than any cabinet member, Pinchot set conservation policy during Roosevelt's two terms and established his ideas about forestry almost everywhere but in the National Parks and the New York Forest Preserve.

As a footnote to the story, Vice President Roosevelt became President while hurrying down the slopes of Mount Marcy during the predawn hours of September 14, 1901. An anarchist, Leon Czolgosz, had shot President McKinley in Buffalo a week earlier, but doctors assured Roosevelt he would recover. Roosevelt went climbing in the Adirondacks, and was on the slope of Mount Marcy when a guide reached him with the news that McKinley had taken a turn for the worse. A special train was on its way to North Creek to take the potential President out of the wilderness. In pitch blackness, down the bumpy mountain roads, Roosevelt hurried to the station in a buckboard driven by an Adirondack guide named Mike Cronin. When they reached the station at 4:39 A.M., Roosevelt received the news that he was President of the United States.

Legend has it that later in life Cronin made a career of retelling the story of that hazardous dash and giving away sets of the "original" horseshoes (to the number of 400) to all interested parties. The matter of the horseshoes, Cronin's granddaughter recently assured the magazine *Adirondack Life*, is "absolutely and completely false."

CHAPTER XVII

Golf and Game

As Gifford Pinchot's gospel of scientific forestry began to take hold among government agencies as well as in the American lumber industry, the New York Forest Preserve itself remained, in theory, if not in fact, a bastion of "wilderness." It did so in the face of some second thoughts about the Forever Wild policy. As early as 1895 there was introduced into both houses of the Legislature an amendment that would have undone Article VII, Section 7; it proposed to allow the sale and exchange of Forest Preserve lands and the lease of five-acre sites for camps and cottages. By law the two houses had to pass the proposal in successive years, which they did. But the next step was to present it to the people in the form of a statewide referendum, and on November 3, 1896, New Yorkers crushed the proposal by a vote of 710,505 to 321,486. As *Forest and Stream* said, the people were voting not only for themselves but for future generations as well:

"This was a spirit which animated tens of thousands of voters the other day who have never seen the Adirondacks nor expect to see them. The vote was a vote of sentiment which is gaining every year . . . and which is not to be overcome by specious schemes of lumbermen and permanent camp-site grabbers."

Forever Wild obviously had acquired a constituency. It was, as a defender of the Forest Preserve said a few years later, "the greatest vote ever cast in the state of New York on any amendment ever presented to the people." On the national level, preservationists of the time were hard-pressed to make any progress in Congress, where the notorious "Uncle Joe" Cannon ruled the House Appropriations Committee from 1897 to 1903 with the ironclad rule: "Not one cent for scenery." But we have already seen the variety of New York individuals and interest groups that flocked to the defense of the northern wilderness in the years leading up to the Constitutional Convention, and it may be instructive to note how that constituency was beefed up during the years 1894–1915 when the voters were given an opportunity to vote on a new Constitution.

William Seward Webb's Adirondack and St. Lawrence Railroad, which was planned not simply to take lumber out of the woods but to get vacationers into them, had permitted many of those downstate voters their first taste of the north woods—a land which for most of them had been merely an old rumor to which the tales of their betters, returning bronzed and refreshed from their wilderness sojourns, gave substance. Harold H. Hochschild, in his *Township 34*, described its effect:

> In opening new areas to recreation seekers, Dr. Webb performed a great public service, as the Durants had done earlier. In 1892 much of the Adirondacks was still inaccessible except to those who could afford the time to penetrate the forest by coach, by guide-boat or on foot. The day of the automobile and of the shallow-draft motorboat was still to dawn. Webb's railroad did not leave the forest unscarred, but it so shortened the time of transit to many points in the woods and on the lakes that new scores of thousands of city-dwellers could enjoy them every summer.

And within a few years the automobile began penetrating the wilderness, again easing the entry of thousands. Hochschild, the historian of the central Adirondacks, was himself a pioneer, riding in the first motorcar (a 1905 Winton) to reach the Blue Mountain Lake region; this daring escapade was carried out in the company of two other college boys in August 1906, the party leaving Williamstown, Massachusetts, and, guided by a U.S. Geological Survey map, reaching Blue Mountain Lake two days, a broken spring, and five flat tires later. Most of the astonished mountain people they encountered had never seen an automobile before. The difficulties of ascending the hills beyond North River were recalled years later by one of Hochschild's colleagues:

> On the first hill, the road was so bad that we had to take everything out of the car. After we got the car to the top, we had to make several trips by foot to bring up the baggage. On another hill we had to back the car to the top. The gasoline tank, which was under the front seat, fed gasoline to the carburetor by gravity. The grade was so steep that the tank could not feed while the car was going forward.

The automobile, which soon was to bring the great national parks to the West within reach of Everyman, is often looked upon as a prime villain in the story of America's conservation movement. We forget the new world it opened for those people of all ages, suddenly thrust into natural glories they had never dreamed of, who returned home with a resolve to vote for parks and other conservation measures they would not have supported without a first-hand experience. Probably no one was better equipped to describe this experience than Henry James, a writer who had spent his active life prowling two continents in search of "impressions," and then felt old age closing the countryside to him. In a letter written in 1905 to his brother, William (an old Adirondack devotee), he expressed his delight in the motorcar (specifically his friend Edith Wharton's) and how it had opened up the countryside for him once more:

> The potent way it deals with a country large enough for it not to *rudoyer* [treat roughly], but to rope in, in big, free hauls, a huge netful of impressions at once—this came to me beautifully, convincing me that if I were rich I shouldn't hesitate to take up with it. A great transformer of life and of the future!

Henry James saw a golden future, but he did not detect another Henry, who would soon remove the automobile from the exclusive clutch of the rich, sending shiny little Fords into all the backwaters of America. Meanwhile, the rich were staking out their claims to the Adirondacks and providing the wilderness with powerful voices at the seats of power. Among them was the Adirondack League Club, whose membership watched with suspicion any developments on the adjoining Forest Preserve lands that might endanger its own investment.

As civilization encroached on the Adirondacks it opened opportunities for those transient vacationers who wanted something a little more comfortable than Paul Smith's rusticity. They found it at the Lake Placid Club, which was organized in the 1890s by one of those talented and obsessed men who leave behind them mixed reactions. Melvil Dewey was a librarian who developed the Dewey Decimal System of book classification and founded schools for training librarians at Columbia University in New York and at the New York State Library in Albany. From libraries his energies overflowed to spelling reform, which he also tried to simplify. On the whole he was not successful in this crusade, though bits and pieces of accomplishment remain, particularly in his own first name and in such woodsy relicts as the Adirondack Loj. (When he dropped the final "ue" from "catalogue," a wag asked why he didn't proceed logically and perform a similar operation on "glue.") Dewey carried his personal quirks into the management of the exclusive Lake Placid Club, which he ran according to what he thought were the highest standards, including the exclusion of both liquor and extensive portions of humanity. One of the club's brochures spelled it out:

> No one will be received as member or guest against whom there is physical, moral, social or race objection, or who would be unwelcome to even a small minority. This excludes absolutely all consumptives, or rather invalids, whose presence might injure health or modify others' freedom or enjoyment. This invariable rule is rigidly enforced; it is found impracticable to make exceptions to Jews or others excluded, even when of unusual personal qualifications.

Dewey's racial predilections brought about his forcible retirement from the New York State Library in 1906, but he went on running the Lake Placid Club in his own way until his death in 1931. In the meantime he continued to make Lake Placid a summer retreat and a winter sports attraction for those who could measure up to his standards.

Golf was becoming one of the attractions in Lake Placid as well as elsewhere in the Adirondacks. Ned Buntline's old stamping grounds at Eagle Nest on Blue Mountain Lake were turned into a golf course by William West Durant in 1900, and the famous Scottish professional Harry Vardon came to give an exhibition. This sport, too, was still almost the exclusive domain of the rich and the powerful. (During the early years of this century, when the editor of a New York newspaper asked Francis Albertanti, his sports editor, to print some golf news, Albertanti refused. "But there are many wealthy and influential men interested in golf," the editor persisted. Albertanti, a true plebeian, closed the conversation with the logical reply: "Then let them print it on the *financial* page.")

All of the above, wealthy and influential, were as yet unorganized in the defense of the forest's integrity. Some friends of Warren Higley, the president of the Adirondack League Club, suggested to him late in 1901 that there ought to be a group devoted exclusively to that aim. (A colleague once described Higley in a letter to Donaldson: "Judge Higley had a good voice, was fine looking, knew something about the Adirondacks and forestry, but had *no* brains.") Apparently, the original plan was to form an association of clubs and the owners of large estates, but as Higley and his friends talked about it they came to the conclusion that a membership of individuals would provide the organization with a broader base of support. The Association for the Protection of the Adirondacks came into being on January 3, 1902, and soon had over a thousand members, all men who were seriously concerned with the forest's future. The association earned a reputation as the "watchdog" of the Adirondacks, and during its early years numbered among its trustees J. Pierpont Morgan, Henry Phipps, Dr. Edward L. Trudeau, Henry Fairfield Osborn, Harry Payne Whitney, Alfred G. Vanderbilt, Louis Marshall, William G. Rockefeller, Adolph Lewisohn, Ogden Mills Reid, Samuel H. Ordway, and David McClure. It also earned a reputation as a rich man's club, devoted solely to selfish interests (to this day the association holds its meetings in the Wall Street area), but this estimate is hardly fair. The association has struggled persistently and often tenaciously to live up to its name.

The chief lure of the north woods remained, for many Americans whether wealthy or not, its big game. Government in one guise or another finally stepped in at the end of the century to save what was left. Probably the most important step was taken by the United States Supreme Court in 1896, when it ruled that game was the property of the state. The question was asked by a man named Geer, who had been arrested in New London, Connecticut, charged with having in his possession, with the intent of shipping them out of the state, "certain woodcock, ruffed grouse, and quail," in violation of a state law. When a local judge fined Geer, he appealed on the grounds that he had shot the birds in season and had the right to ship them out of the state. In *Geer* v. *Connecticut*, the Supreme Court was asked to decide the question: Does the state have the power "to regulate the killing of game within her borders so as to confine its use to the limits of the State and forbid its transmission outside of the State?" The Court noted that the common law of England "based property in game upon the principle of common ownership, and therefore treated it as subject to governmental authority." This right was vested in the King, as well as in colonial governments, and thus it passed to the states after independence.

The state was now on firmer footing in its dealing with "game hogs." Since deer were still declining in the Adirondacks, the Legislature in 1897 passed an anti-hounding law, which was supported in particular by the owners of large preserves who believed the hounds were running game off their land. Hounds remained a menace to deer for some years after the law was passed, not only in the case of those who were employed illegally for that purpose by their masters, but also because dogs ran wild in the woods all year round, chasing deer in packs. John B. Burnham, an active New York conservationist, recalled that after the law was passed, "we set to work ridding the Adirondacks of the dogs, and it was a thrilling and dangerous job."

As deer began to recover in the Adirondacks, the state bought some of the surplus from local trappers, as well as from those in Maine (for prices of up to twenty-five dollars an animal), and restocked the Catskills, where the herds had been devastated. While this program was a success, the stocking of other large game animals was not. The owners of several of the large preserves unsuccessfully tried their hand at reintroducing moose and elk to the Adirondacks, as we have seen, but the most ambitious plan was conceived by a young man named Harry V. Radford.

Radford was heir to the mantle worn by the Reverend Murray, and indeed during his brief life was called "Adirondack" Radford by those unknowns who bestow such epithets. As a high school boy in New York City, he became impassioned about the beauties of the great forest to the north, and at the age of eighteen even put out a magazine called *Woods and Waters* in celebration of them. He formed the Association for Restoring the Moose to the Adirondacks, with a membership fee of one dollar and a cluster of eighteen influential politicians who served as vice-presidents. The Legislature appropriated $5,000 to collect a herd of moose (imported to the state from the Northwest). Liberated, the bewildered animals were shot by enthusiastic locals or wandered off into oblivion. A few years later Radford himself wandered off to Canada to kill a wood buffalo "for scientific purposes" and never returned. An investigation by the Bathurst Inlet Patrol of the Royal Canadian Mounted Police revealed that after killing the buffalo, Radford went on to the Arctic with a friend named Street; on the ice at Bathurst Inlet he got into a dispute with an Eskimo guide and struck him with a dog whip, whereupon the Eskimo and his friends stabbed the two white men to death. Their bodies drifted away into the Arctic mists.

Brief though his part was, Harry Radford added to the story of the mountains, helping to bring in the vacationists, camp owners, sportsmen, and their friends. These people made up the park's constituency. There remained that vague phrase Forever Wild, and soon the constituency would be called upon as the state debated what to *do* with this vast area.

CHAPTER XVIII

Taking the Forester out of the Forest

The defense of the Forest Preserve was complicated in the new century by the intrusion of two elements, both of them pledged not to the destruction of America's natural resources but to their wise use. The first of these was the growing band of scientific foresters and the second the very group, in a sense, that had been chiefly responsible for the passage of the Forever Wild amendment—the water users.

In 1897 the State Legislature responded to the Adirondacks' new constituency by appropriating a million dollars and providing for a Forest Preserve Board, to which it granted the authority to condemn land for inclusion in the preserve. Many lumbermen and the owners of large preserves (including W. Seward Webb) were against this proposal, but it was by no means an innovation to acquire land in this way for parks and other public purposes; just two years before, for instance, the United States government had exercised its right of condemnation in taking land owned by a railroad company when it created the military park at Gettysburg. There was some thought at the time that eventually the state would be able to acquire all of the land within the Blue Line. But though the Legislature continued to appropriate smaller amounts of money for land purchase during the next few years, it soon became apparent that full public ownership of the park was out of the question. As a report published by the Forest Preserve Board said in 1900: "Under condemnation, the owner of the Forest Land would undoubtedly include in the claim for damages, the loss of his mills and other idle plants, which would become worthless when his supply of raw material is thus cut off. Hence to the cost of the lands must be added the millions of dollars invested in mills and plants dependent on these lands, property which must be bought as well as the forest." By then the state owned 1,230,889 acres in the Adirondacks. Even after the Forest Preserve Board was abolished, the right of condemnation was given to the Forest Commission to use as needed.

As the state acquired more land, the pressure increased to put it to use. William F. Fox, a believer in Gifford Pinchot's tenets, was a proponent of scientific forestry on the Forest Preserve, and similar beliefs were spreading among many leaders in the state government. Governor Frank A. Black, in his message to the Legislature in 1898, ventured the belief that at some time in the future the Forever Wild clause would be relaxed. "The time will come when the State will sell timber to the lumbermen, spruce to the pulp mills, reap a large revenue for itself, and still retain the woods," he said. To prepare the state for that eventuality and to diminish the chance that the woodsmen would revert to their destructive old techniques, the Legislature that year established the New York State College of Forestry at Cornell University, the state's land grant institution. The Legislature directed the college to educate its students "in the principles and practices of scientific forestry," and the Forest Preserve Board to buy 30,000 acres on which the faculty and students could carry out the principles and practice.

The board members were not very enthusiastic about the scheme. In the first place, money to buy the college land came out of the board's fund for acquiring Forest Preserve land. (The Legislature later appropriated money to pay back the board.) Besides, though there was some technical language in the Legislature's directive to the effect that the land was part of the Forest Preserve "except as may be inconsistent with the provisions of this act," and was to be given back "to the People" by Cornell in thirty years, there is doubt whether the act was in compliance with the Constitution. Any land bought by the state within the Blue Line automatically became a part of the Forest Preserve, and the bill simply made it legal to cut trees on the land. At any rate, nobody seems to have made a fuss about this particular aspect of the scheme at the time; the College of Forestry went into business.

The school's first step was to hire a director, and what seemed to be the best choice eventually proved to be a fatal one. Bernhard Fernow, as we have noted, was the first scientist skilled in European forestry to work in America. He was born and schooled in Prussia, and possessed many of those characteristics given to the movie version of Prussians ("Very *inter-resting*, Governor Roosevelt!"): a strong will, methodical attention to detail, and boundless arrogance. He had served as the chief of the Division of Forestry for some years, where he made many enemies among Washington bureaucrats, and was replaced by Pinchot, who didn't like Fernow, when he came to the Adirondacks. The members of the Forest Preserve Board, not eager to spend much on the college's land, acquired 30,000 acres east of the village of Tupper Lake that had already been heavily logged by the Santa Clara Lumber Company. The Spanish-American War was to stimulate a tremendous interest in newspapers, doubling the demand for newsprint and thus for spruce pulpwood within a few years, but spruce was practically absent from the land Fernow was given to work with. The remaining hardwoods seemed chiefly suited for making barrel staves. A further handicap, Fernow discovered, was that he could not get the wood to market because the land was largely hemmed in by the inviolate Forest Preserve. Expected to prove that scientific forestry could be made a paying proposition, Fernow found himself almost literally in a cul-de-sac.

Yet the Prussian forester's arrogance was matched by his self-confidence, and he tried to come to grips with the challenge. He found a downstate firm, the Brooklyn Cooperage Company, which agreed to put up two plants near the College of Forestry and produce staves and wood alcohol from the hardwood, while Fernow established a nursery to begin raising spruce on a long-term plan. The experiment was doomed from the outset. According to the agreement signed between Cornell and the cooperage firm, which naturally wanted to pay off the investment in its plants as soon as possible, Fernow had to deliver twice as much wood as he had planned on each year, thus defeating his aim to operate the forest on a sustained-yield basis. The Association for the Protection of the Adirondacks and other groups of preservationists and landowners grew fearful, about both the aggressive cutting practices and the danger of fire. Fernow did nothing to mollify them.

"We must repeat again that forestry is a technical art, wholly utilitarian, and not, except incidentally, concerned in esthetic aspects of the woods," Fernow wrote in the college's report for 1901. "It is engaged in utilizing the soil for the production of wood crops, and thereby of the highest revenue obtainable."

At first, state legislators and officials were generally enthusiastic about the prospect of introducing scientific forestry to the Forest Preserve, and had even gone so far as to make a contract with Pinchot's Division of Forestry in Washington to draw up a plan for cutting certain areas of the preserve; apparently many people believed the day was not far distant when it would be opened to forest "management." If so, they reckoned without Fernow's ability to alienate those whom he ought to have been most eager to propitiate. According to Marvin W. Kranz (in *Pioneering in Conservation*), he insulted some of the owners of the largest nearby estates; when fires broke out on the college's land and spread to Adolph Lewisohn's estate, that gentleman approached Fernow to complain and was promptly given a "brush-off." Beset by financial problems, Fernow demanded, rather than requested, additional help for the college from the Legislature. It was not a surprise, then, when a legislative committee visited the college in 1902 and its members noted: "We deeply regret that our careful investigation of the experiment leaves us unable to approve what has been done and obliged to condemn both present and prospective results."

The end came the next year. Excessively hot and dry weather in early spring set the stage. Railroad locomotives, bulky shadows racing through the night, eerily accompanied by a shower of sparks, touched off the fiercest fires in years and cast a pall over the forest. The Forest, Fish and Game Commission's report for 1903 told the grim story:

> In the latter part of April forest fires broke out with alarming frequency along the lines of the New York Central, the Chateaugay, the New York and Ottawa, and the Saranac and Lake Placid Railroads. At first the firewardens extinguished these railroad fires wherever they appeared, but the locomotives continued to throw sparks and start fresh ones faster than the men could attend to them. The dead leaves, bushes, undergrowth, stumps, logs and leafless

> trees . . . were such that incipient fires sprang up in the wake of nearly every train. . . . On the nineteen miles of Raquette Lake Railway, running through the State forest from Clearwater to Durant, no fires occurred, because in granting a charter for this road the Legislature stipulated that the locomotives must use petroleum for fuel.

The coal-burning locomotives were equipped, according to state law, with spark arresters, but they were ineffectual. Pea-sized sparks escaped through the 5⁄16-inch wire mesh installed on the engine boilers and flew up the stacks; the railroad men contended that they could not get up a full head of steam when the boilers were fitted with a finer mesh.

"The officials of the Saranac and Lake Placid Railroad made no apparent effort to lessen the danger from their trains, and manifested a surprising indifference when notified of the destruction caused by the locomotives," the commission charged. "The great fire which at one time threatened the hotels at Lake Placid, and burned over an area of several square miles, was started by a locomotive on that road."

The state listed the causes of 377 of the fires that it investigated. One hundred and twenty-one were started by locomotives, eighty-eight by farmers burning over their land (many of them were arrested and convicted), forty-seven by sport fishermen, twenty-three by smokers, seven by hunters, and one each by a "lunatic," by a man smoking out a hedgehog, and by lightning; the others were spawned by the wind, which carried flames from one area to another. Despite the inevitability of new fires breaking out every day, the state fire wardens were not permitted to hire men to patrol susceptible areas; they could hire a crew only after a fire had broken out! The owners of the large preserves, on the other hand, assigned men to patrol the tracks that ran through their land. The estate of William Rockefeller, a brother of John D. Rockefeller, Sr., suffered extensive damage, forty thousand acres going up in smoke when a New York and Ottawa locomotive set fire to several miles of right-of-way.

Nearly a half million acres were burned in the Adirondacks. On many parts of the Forest Preserve itself the standing trees were killed by the intense heat, but, though it was still in marketable condition, the attorney general gave an opinion that the Forever Wild clause prohibited the timber from being sold. This instance was the first of many that have stirred controversy when timber interests felt the state was "wasting" timber already doomed by fire or storm damage. Whatever disgruntlement the attorney general's decision caused in this case was more than offset by the fact that many of the hardest-hit areas in the Adirondacks were those which had been lumbered, the flames being fed by the litter left by woodsmen.

The lesson was clear to preservationists all over the state: the Forest Preserve was to be protected against the woodsman, under whatever guise he appeared. The preserve's constituency put added pressure on Governor Benjamin B. Odell. He vetoed the 1903 legislative appropriation for the State College of Forestry, and it promptly closed, having barely survived to its fifth birthday, while the cooperage firm pursued a legal case against the state. The great experiment not only failed to prove that scientific forestry could pay on state lands but it seemed to have played its part in the holocaust of that year. The profession has not recovered in New York to this day, but the sanctity of "wilderness" was confirmed. As Roger Thompson has written: "Practicing forestry in New York is analogous to attempting to practice medicine in a society which endorses Christian Science as an ethic."

Adding to the value that the public saw in the constitutional clause was the low reputation of the men who were entrusted with the Forest Preserve's administration. The evolution of the commission itself during those years reflected the uncertainty those with an interest in the preserve felt about its administration. The five-member body created by the Legislature in 1895 was called the Fisheries, Game and Forest Commission, but in 1900, in deference to the importance of the preserve in state politics, the name was changed to the Forest, Fish and Game Commission. Meanwhile, Governor Roosevelt had been more concerned during his two years in office (1899–1900) with the makeup of the commission itself. Although he was not able to carry out his idea of limiting the forests' administration to a single strong commissioner, he tried to find a chairman who would act in that relationship vis-à-vis the other four members. He picked Major W. Austin Wadsworth, president of the Boone and Crockett Club, the organization of sportsmen and conservationists with which Roosevelt had been intimately connected since its formation. In his choice he was embarrassed nearly as quickly as some Presidents and presidential candidates of recent times have been by their own selections for appointment to high office. The press was quick to point out that Wadsworth had been convicted several years before for violating state game laws. Roosevelt and his chairman were fortunate to survive their critics' howl of protest.

"I wish to Heaven he had done anything else, save committing murder for instance, rather than shooting that quail," the governor wrote wistfully to a friend.

But once Roosevelt left the scene for Washington, there emerged darker allegations against the appointments of both his predecessors and successors. A well-known sportsman named Timothy L. Woodruff had served as lieutenant governor as well as on the Forest Preserve Board under Governor Frank S. Black (1897–98), and on the Forest, Fish and Game Commission under Governor Benjamin B. Odell (1901–03). It seems that Woodruff was adept at feathering his own nest while serving the public. As a member of the Forest Preserve Board he was active in the state's purchase of 24,000 acres from William West Durant, though a choice one-thousand-acre section around Lake Kora in the middle of the plot was left out of the transaction. In 1898 Woodruff himself turned up as the owner of that section, with "an elegantly appointed lodge . . . a most luxurious forest affair" (as the Albany *Sunday Press* described it), where he entertained not only the other members of the Forest Preserve Board but Governor Black. Woodruff, off and on through those years, was reported to have kept a pack of hounds with which he buttressed his reputation as a deer slayer.

The situation did not improve in 1903, when the commission got its single head, DeWitt C. Middleton. Although there was dissatisfaction with his administration of the Forest Preserve, many of the facts did not come out until some years later. A report by the Moreland Commission (which is any commission appointed by the governor of New York to investigate a part of the state government) in 1910 enlarged on Middleton's dealings with local lumber companies and his deference to the railroads even after their implication in the great fires. The report on Middleton's administration read, in part:

> Timber stealing had reached enormous proportions and was notoriously permitted with the knowledge and acquiescence of the Forest, Fish and Game authorities; great areas of forest land had been devastated by fires caused largely by the negligent operation of railroads in the Adirondack region; suits involving title to large tracts of land in the Forest Preserve had been compromised under terms most disadvantageous to the State's interest; and the entire operation of the Forest, Fish and Game Commission was the target of severe criticism.

As late as 1915, a state attorney general was referring to the operations of Middleton and his assistants. Apparently after the fires of 1903, and against the opinion of the attorney general then in office about cutting dead timber on the Forest Preserve, Middleton had connived to let timbermen salvage what they could. The 1915 report noted:

> Assuming that the State authorities had no power under the constitution to sell the trees in question, the J. & J. Rogers Company, by its agents and contractors, deliberately committed a trespass upon the state lands with the knowledge of state officials, who were on the ground, and after a certain quantity of timber had been cut, measured and removed, the contractor went with a state official before a justice of the peace and confessed judgment for the amount of the agreed price of the timber. Many of these so-called judgments were void, exceeding in amount the sum of five hundred dollars, which was the limit of the court's jurisdiction. The money was paid over to the State official, who was a party to the transaction. He pocketed one-half of the money and the remainder went into the state treasury.

James S. Whipple, clerk of the State Senate, succeeded Middleton in 1905, partly on the recommendation of the Association for the Preservation of the Adirondacks, but he too came under fire from the Moreland Commission because of his suspicious entanglements with leading Adirondack lumbermen. It was not until 1908, during his tenure, that the state began to catch up with some of the culprits, however small a part they played in the forest chicanery. In that year two state game protectors, employed by the commission, were indicted in Herkimer for extorting $7,750 from a lumberman in return for their connivance in the cutting of two thousand cords of spruce on the preserve. The lumberman tidily kept their signed receipts for the money, and those receipts were later used as evidence. There was a suspicion, supported by the testimony of one of the defendants, that part of the money reached "higher-ups" in Albany, perhaps Commissioner Whipple himself, but the press later reported that those allegations were not prosecuted very vigorously by the authorities. Conservationists expressed themselves as satisfied when one of the state employees went to prison for a year.

Through all these years there were frequent calls, reflected or perhaps stimulated by the Forest Commission's annual reports, to relax the provisions of the Forever Wild clause. As Governor Charles Evans Hughes said in 1909: "The time must shortly come when, no longer having reason to fear the grasp of the selfish hand and having settled the inviolability of the public interest in our priceless forest possessions, we shall make possible their scientific protection and their proper utilization for the public benefit." In other words, the Forest Preserve ought to be managed in the public's interest. But the attempts to amend the Constitution invariably met opposition in the Legislature and died there. Despite plans to secure Gifford Pinchot's help in getting a forestry amendment, it was the water users, rather than the foresters, who were to make the first crack in the Forever Wild clause.

CHAPTER XIX

The Constitution Ascendant

Hetch Hetchy, that grating and faintly convulsive name (John Muir preferred to call it the Tuolumne Yosemite), resounds as loudly in the history of conservation as Valley Forge, the Alamo, and Gettysburg in this country's more inclusive history. The Hetch Hetchy Valley lies in the Sierra less than twenty miles north of Yosemite Valley, and within the borders of Yosemite National Park itself. When Muir first knew it, the Tuolumne River flowed through the three-and-a-half-mile valley; he called it a "wonderfully exact counterpart of the great Yosemite, not only in its crystal river and sublime rocks and waterfalls, but in the gardens, groves, and meadows of its flowery, park-like floor." He could rejoice that the valley and its waterfalls (including one with the lovely name Tueeulala, which brought the cliffs alive with "sun-illumined fabrics") were forever inviolate as a part of the national park.

But the old man reckoned without the laws of the land. In 1901, at the urging of some California legislators, Congress passed the Right of Way Act, which has been succinctly described by John Ise in his study of our national parks: "The act was in most respects perfectly tailored for looters of the parks, for it authorized the Interior Secretary to grant rights of way through government reservations of all kinds . . . for practically any sort of business that might want a right of way including 'the supplying of water for domestic, public, or any other beneficial uses.' "

At the time the justification for the act seemed unclear, but it later developed that only a year earlier the officials of San Francisco had secretly decided that the Hetch Hetchy Valley, which lay one hundred and fifty miles from the city, would solve all of their water problems. The water carried through the valley by Muir's "crystal river" was sweet and pure. The valley's "flowery, park-like floor" was flat and suggested an ideal bottom for a reservoir, and its "sublime rocks" formed steep cliffs narrowing at one end into a slit that would be convenient and relatively cheap to dam. The city's engineers made a study of the valley, an unauthorized step for which they were later criticized by Secretary of the Interior Ethan A. Hitchcock. But no matter. By their study and the later enabling act, they were in a position to satisfy the demands of San Francisco citizens that the city be released from the yoke of a local private water company.

The city applied for permission to build a reservoir in Hetch Hetchy, from which it could draw water for drinking, electricity, and fire fighting; the great fire of 1906 was an added inducement to the request. Hitchcock turned it down, as not being in the public interest, but his days in President Roosevelt's administration were numbered. He was out of tune with the views of Gifford Pinchot, who had just used his enormous influence in the Administration to raid Interior for the forest reserves, where they had lodged since the 1890s, bringing them to the Department of Agriculture; there, elevated to chief of the newly created U.S. Forest Service, Pinchot functioned both as custodian of the reserves, which (since he disliked the connotation) he renamed the national forests, and as Roosevelt's chief adviser in conservation matters. He held the "aesthetic conservationists" and their non-utilitarian national parks in disdain, but he and the capable men he had gathered around him in the Forest Service were very much interested in the development of the West's water resources, among them the river at Hetch Hetchy. In 1906 Hitchcock was succeeded at Interior by James R. Garfield, Pinchot's close friend and a son of the former President. Muir's friend and supporter, the editor Robert Underwood Johnson, later wrote of Pinchot:

> He felt it more important to get the support of the Pacific slope and other Western sentiment for his general conservation policies than that the recreational, hygienic, and aesthetic uses of the na-

> tional parks be preserved. He therefore contributed his great influence to the commercialization of the Valley and but for him I believe the scheme would never have succeeded.

Egged on by Pinchot, San Francisco renewed its application to build a reservoir in Hetch Hetchy and the new Secretary of the Interior believed the application was now, indeed, in the public interest. Muir and his supporters jumped into the battle, and held the line for seven more years, lobbying Presidents and congressmen, filling the pages of periodicals with encomiums to Hetch Hetchy, and pointing out that there were alternate sources of water in the Sierra at a cost little above that of invading the national park. San Francisco and Pinchot stuck to their guns, but Garfield's initial approval was later reversed when Roosevelt (who was lukewarm about the reservoir, despite Pinchot's enthusiasm) was succeeded by William Howard Taft; Taft replaced Garfield with a new Interior Secretary, Richard Achilles Ballinger, and when Pinchot (whom Taft distrusted, considering the forester "a socialist and a spiritualist") later got embroiled in a dispute with Ballinger, Taft fired him, too.

The battle went on, pitting conservationist against conservationist, and nearly wrecking the Sierra Club itself because of internal divisions over Hetch Hetchy. "This playing at politics saps the very foundations of righteousness," Muir grumbled. Conservationists such as Pinchot, Senator George W. Norris, and Representative William Kent (an old friend of Muir's) saw Hetch Hetchy as a chance to deal the private power interests a staggering blow, and pushed ahead. Pinchot carried on the propaganda and lobbying war from his own organization, the National Conservation Association. Muir, nearing the end of his life, fought gamely in his hortatory fashion: "Dam Hetch Hetchy! As well dam for water tanks the people's cathedrals and churches, for no holier temple has ever been consecrated by the heart of man." In the 1912 election he voted for Taft against his old friend Roosevelt (and Pinchot), but Woodrow Wilson's victory sealed Hetch Hetchy's fate. Franklin K. Lane, Wilson's Secretary of the Interior, approved the city's application for a reservoir there, and the House of Representatives concurred.

During its final stages the struggle spilled over into the Senate.

The battle was strenuous, sometimes acrimonious. Senator James A. Reed of Missouri, who never could understand what conservationists of any stripe were talking about, observed that the passion of the contenders seemed to escalate in proportion to their distance from the controversial site, so that "when we get as far east as New England the opposition has become a frenzy." A confrontation during a Senate committee hearing between Senator Norris (the man eventually responsible for the Tennessee Valley Authority project) and Robert Underwood Johnson is worth quoting in detail because it illustrates the conservation dilemma which also came to the fore among men of goodwill in the Adirondacks. (Johnson later contended that he and other Muir supporters were treated like "criminals in the box," and that the committee report distorted his testimony.)

NORRIS: Mr. Johnson, I want to ask you a few questions. Just at the close of your remarks you made the statement that this bill was anti-conservation.

JOHNSON: Not at all.

NORRIS: What is the object of the argument that you have been making? I realize that men may disagree as to even the meaning of conservation, but I had always supposed that the utilization, for instance, of water power was one of the fundamental principles of conservation. Why are not the people who are in favor of the building of this dam and the use of this water power and the rest of the water itself entitled just as much to the designation of conservationist as those who are opposed to that and who desire to keep the park undisturbed?.

JOHNSON: I will tell you, sir. You must go back to the object for which the park was made; the purpose for which it was created. I read you the report of the Committee on Public Lands in regard to that, and I say to you gentlemen that there should be a distinction drawn between the forest reserves and the national parks. The forest reserves were made for the purpose—

NORRIS: I am not talking about the forest reserves. I am talking about this particular bill. While I concede there is a chance for argument perhaps on both sides of it, I am trying to get your idea as to what conservation is.

JOHNSON: Conservation is maintaining the natural resources of the government for the use of the people; for the highest use that each one may properly have. I do not think the best use of Niagara would be the running of electric works.

NORRIS: Possibly so; but that question is not involved here today.

JOHNSON: The Almighty put it there to be looked at.

NORRIS: There is not a reclamation project in the country, Mr. Johnson, which has ever been undertaken by the government but that it destroys some of the beauty of nature somewhere.

JOHNSON: The point I make, Senator, is not that we shall not do it; but that we should consider the character that the reservation was made for.

NORRIS: What would be a reasonable construction of that?

JOHNSON: I say you are paying a colossal price for San Francisco's water.

The Senate passed the bill in 1913 and Hetch Hetchy was destroyed. Fortunately, perhaps, John Muir did not live to see the dammed waters creep up over those cliffs across which the streams once had fallen like silver scarves. He died the next year. Though the dam was built, World War I and other developments slowed the pace of construction, and when the pipes were opened at last in the 1930s the city had no means of distributing the water and sold out to the Pacific Gas and Electric Company—the very result that Pinchot, Norris, and the other utilitarian conservationists had hoped to avoid by destroying the valley. Today, while nearby Yosemite is visited almost to destruction, Hetch Hetchy, which might have relieved the tourist pressure, is comparatively neglected, its litter of stumps and barren rocks ceaselessly covered and laid bare again as the water rises and falls according to the city's needs. Robert K. Cutter has described the reality of Hetch Hetchy in the *Sierra Club Bulletin*:

> Before it was flooded, the flowing water and the valley vegetation cooled it and the trees gave shade and relief from the heat reflected from the granite walls. Now, with the grass and trees all gone, there is nothing but a narrow body of monotonous water with an ugly shore line (typical of all reservoirs where the water level shifts) surrounded by stark stone walls. It is hot and uninviting. The falls, as seen through trees from the floor of the valley, were beautiful, but now, with the setting gone, they are about as interesting as the spillway over the dam.

The controversy began on a less heroic scale in the Adirondacks. Here and there through the years disputes had broken out about dams that flooded forest land (as in the Webb case). In 1908 Paul Smith, the hotel man, built a dam to provide power for the Saranac Lake area, and the water backed up to flood several hundred acres of the Forest Preserve. The Association for the Protection of the Adirondacks lodged a protest, but Smith, king of all he surveyed, simply went on with his project and won a subsequent court case.

But it was apparent that more ambitious power projects would be proposed for the Adirondacks, with its wealth of swift-running streams. As Roger Thompson wrote:

> . . . the Adirondack region contains over three-quarters of the available power on the interior streams of the state . . . the reservoir sites offered in the Adirondacks have been more attractive than elsewhere in the state because of the relative lack of other developments, the transplanting or replacing of which would increase reservoir costs. . . . A pairing of the work-horse St. Lawrence River for primary power with a complex of readily controlled Adirondack streams for secondary power, is an idea of which both the public and private power development proponents have dreamed.

In 1902, after a series of destructive floods, the Legislature created a Water Storage Commission, which recommended building reservoirs around the state. And in 1906 the Legislature, reflecting the rising national interest in the conservation of water resources promoted by Roosevelt, Pinchot, and their followers in Washington, created the Water Supply Commission. The new agency began to devise plans for the development of the state's water resources "under State ownership, control and maintenance for the public use and benefit, and for the increase of revenue." The monopolies were already under fire from the Roosevelt administration's trustbusters, and there was great hostility among the country's progressives toward the private utility companies. It was not simply a feeling that private interests were amassing fortunes by exploiting natural resources (such as rivers and waterfalls) that ought to belong to the public. The progressives believed that state and federal governments are able to develop power more efficiently, being equipped with powers of condemnation as well as the ability to carry out long-range plans and fairly apportion the available resources. Not having to demand an immediate return on its investment, the government is more likely to build dams that will stand up.

In 1906 the first serious move was made to alter the Constitution so that parts of the Forest Preserve could be flooded for the purpose of storing water. Joining the government's utilitarian conservationists in a campaign for constitutional revision was the powerful Empire State Forest Products Association; the pulp and paper industry, for instance, depended, more than ever before, on water to power its factories. With increasing frequency these interests assured the people and their legislators that the power made and stored in the Forest Preserve would bring benefits to all, that no harm would be done by the dam builders, who would simply flood out some "unsightly" and "worthless" swampy lands. Sometimes the proposals were passed by the Legislature (as in 1906) but later died there (as in 1907). The Association for the Protection of the Adirondacks had become a rallying point for the preservationists. Perhaps among all the people actively concerned with the inviolability of the Forest Preserve during those years, one man stands out as a "voice of conscience." He was the lawyer, conservationist, reformer, and leader of the American Jewish Committee, Louis Marshall.

Marshall, whose parents were German-Jewish immigrants, was born in Syracuse in 1856. He was a prodigious scholar, largely self-taught in languages, who sailed through Columbia Law School in a single year and was admitted to the bar in 1878. He practiced in Syracuse for a number of years and then moved to New York in 1894 where he lived until his death in 1929.

Marshall became a leader in every field he entered—law, Zionism, conservation, labor relations, education, and the rights of immigrants and minorities. He was nearly thirty years old when he first became acquainted with the Adirondacks, and acquired a summer residence on Lower Saranac Lake in 1898. Trees became one of his passions, and when he was away from the Adirondacks he satisfied that passion by walking almost daily through Central

Park. It is worth quoting from a letter of Marshall's to Francis D. Gallatin, New York City Commissioner of Parks, in 1921 to illustrate not only his interest but also his particular knowledge of forestry. He wrote Gallatin of the importance of the park to the city and congratulated him on his efforts to restore the park, ravaged by hoodlums and politicians, to its former beauty. And then:

> I am very glad indeed to note the extent to which you are planting the beautiful ginkgo trees and oaks and elms. Permit me to suggest the desirability of replanting trees of the rarer species which have added greatly to the interest of those who have studied silviculture in the park. First of all let me refer to the Siberian elm. There is one near the Morse monument, close to the entrance at 5th Avenue and 72nd St. It is growing old and has been subjected to tree surgery, but still remains vigorous. Its leaves do not appear until late in May and do not depart until about the middle of December. It is a joy to the eye and to the soul. There are very few of these trees now in our parks. The addition of a number of them would be a boon. Then there is the Kentucky coffee-tree, the sassafras, the Paulownia imperialis, the Indian bean tree (just now in bloom and most beautiful and effective), the bald cypress, the red, black and willow oaks, the European cut-leaved beech, the Chinese golden larch, the red and paper mulberry, the Chinese cork-tree, the Wordmann silver fir, and the persimmon trees. Above all let me suggest the planting of the silver bell trees. Until the severe frosts of three years ago played havoc with them there was a double row of these trees on the path leading to the West 72nd St. entrance between the Webster statue and the mall. They overhung the path forming sort of an arbor and in the spring of the year the blossoms were glorious, which was a constant delight to those who had occasion to walk through that charming section.
>
> There should also be an effort made to plant more tulip, cottonwood, sweetgum and honey locusts in various sections of the park. These trees are impressive. Those of the species that are now in the park are getting old, some of them have passed beyond the stage of maturity, and we must therefore prepare against the day when the present giants have gone. I am anxious that my children and grandchildren shall have the same opportunity for enjoyment in beholding these noble trees that I have had. I also recommend the planting of

some copper beeches and osage orange trees. In fact it would add greatly to the educational value of the park if the effort were made to plant every possible variety of tree that can grow in this climate.

Marshall served as a delegate to the Constitutional Convention of 1894 and assisted David McClure in his campaign to secure passage of the Forever Wild clause. From then on, the welfare of the Forest Preserve was always before his eye. By letter and personal contact he goaded state officials in Albany to make the needed reforms to guard against fires, timber stealing, and threats to the Forever Wild clause. "I almost feel that a lynching is justifiable when a person sets fire to the forest and burns what has taken centuries to produce," this staunch foe of lynching once said, and went on to brand the locomotives then in use as "instruments of arson." When serious fires again broke out in the Adirondacks in 1908, he wrote to Commissioner Whipple with specific observations:

"The men who were designated to deal with these fires did so by sitting in a boat in the [Saranac] river, watching the flames as they drove muskrats, mink, and other animals out of their holes, availing themselves of the opportunity to shoot the game which was thus driven out. The fires did not concern them in any other way."

It was the complaints of men such as Marshall, John G. Agar, and others who belonged to the Association for the Protection of the Adirondacks that brought about the needed reforms, especially in fire prevention. At last the state began to hire men to follow the trains, picking up the clinkers that dropped from the locomotives and extinguishing the fires touched off by sparks. In fact, patrols became a general part of the state's fire prevention effort, while the first fire towers, built of wood, were erected on several peaks in 1909. Marshall was by no means against the practice of forestry itself. In fact, for many years after the demise of the forestry college at Cornell he kept up a campaign to have a similar college, with sounder planning and funding, established at Syracuse University, where he was a trustee. At last in 1911 the state established the New York State College of Forestry at Syracuse, with Marshall serving as the president of its board of trustees until his death eighteen years later. The institution has survived and even grown into the largest in the United States, but its opening did not soften the preservationists' view of the profession. When the lumber industry continued its efforts to open the preserve to cutting, blaming "uninformed" New York City residents and their Tammany Hall leaders for the waste of good wood, the anti-forestry view was effectively stated in 1914 by the chairman of the Committee on Forests of the New York Board of Transportation:

> The preservation of a forest in a state of nature is abhorrent to the scientific forester, for nature is the best of all foresters and leaves no room for the services of the artificial kind. Hence, it is that the hand of every so-called scientific forester is raised to strike down the nature policy of the State of New York which has delivered our woods from the axe and from destruction. It is, therefore, not difficult to see in the propaganda against our present Article VII, section 7, the hand of the so-called scientific forester who is envious of his only competitor—Nature; for he enters the contest as the agent of his employers, the lumbermen.

The forestry college at Syracuse has continued to turn out skilled foresters, most of whom have emigrated from the state to find woodlands where they may practice their profession.

While the struggle over flooding the preserve for waterpower projects was never very far beneath the surface, the first major confrontation in the Adirondacks was delayed until the year of Hetch Hetchy—1913. In the meantime there were some meaningful changes. The Moreland Commission report of 1910 had destroyed the reputation of the Forest, Fish and Game Commission and forced the resignation of Commissioner Whipple. The next year the Legislature reorganized the commission—consolidating within it a number of agencies dealing with the forests, fish and game, and water supply.

In 1912 the Legislature clarified the area of the Adirondack Park and defined it as "all lands located within the following described boundaries." Thus for the first time the private lands within the Blue Line were officially included in the park. The seeds were sown then for the bitter disputes of the 1970s, though the state paid little heed to those private lands in the intervening years; in fact, the only attempt to treat the park's public and private lands as a unified whole occurred in 1924, when the Legislature gave the Conservation Commission the authority to regulate off-premise billboards and other signs everywhere in the park to keep it "open, clean and in good order for the welfare of society."

Another event of 1912 was of more immediate import. Past Legislatures had appropriated money to buy twenty-five acres at Lake George to commemorate the Revolutionary War battle there and to make certain improvements on the site. Since the Forever Wild clause intimated that all land bought by the state within the Forest Preserve counties was automatically included in the preserve, there were questions about the constitutionality of those appropriations. Attorney General Carmody issued an opinion early in 1912 that the improvements were not in violation of the Constitution, the land "having been acquired by the State under a law authorizing its purchase for a definite and proper governmental purpose inconsistent with its use as a wild forest land."

This opinion, though never challenged, seemed to permit a crack in the monolithic Forever Wild clause. Yet it set forth the specific conditions under which the state could make improvements on land acquired within the Forest Preserve counties; as we shall see, the Conservation Department, when it used this opinion to justify its improvements on other parts of the preserve during the 1930s, was undoubtedly in violation of the Constitution.

It was the public (or that portion of it which was free, male, and twenty-one, women not then having the privilege of the vote) who approved the Forever Wild clause in 1894, and it was appropriate that the public should make the first alteration in the clause. The confrontation, when it came, dissolved in compromise. In 1911 a constitutional amendment was introduced in the Legislature to allow 3 percent of the total acreage in the Forest Preserve to be flooded for reservoirs, the water being diverted for drinking supplies, canals, and flood control. The amendment passed both houses that year, and again in 1913. The men and organizations who had fought for the forest's preservation in great part because of its future usefulness in stabilizing the state's water supply, could not very well argue now against this reasonable proposal, especially when the reservoirs would not be turned over to private interests.

The Association for the Protection of the Adirondacks, the New York Board of Trade, the Chamber of Commerce, and other organizations threw their support to the so-called Burd Amendment, which was approved by the electorate on November 4, 1913, by a vote of 486,264 to 187,290.

The spirit of détente seemed to carry over to 1915, when the state held its first Constitutional Convention since 1894. Among the papers collected by the Conservation Commission to guide the delegates on their vote on forest issues was one prepared in 1914 by John G. Agar, the president of the Association for the Protection of the Adirondacks, in which he suggested that the time had come to let the state cut mature timber on the preserve and earn the attendant revenues. He also recommended the leasing of campsites on the preserve, and permitting water storage there by both the state *and* private power companies.

Other delegates, buttressed by an attorney general's opinion, did not believe that a change in the Constitution was even necessary because the state already had the power to take many of these steps within the preserve. The attorney general had based his opinion on the word "kept" in the clause—that the state lands "shall be forever kept as wild forest lands"—which implied that the state was able to cut dead or diseased trees, lease campsites, and build roads for fire control.

The lumber interests were well represented at the convention and introduced an amendment that would have permitted the Conservation Commission to classify lands into two categories—one on mountaintops and along streams and lakes, and the second to include "all the other lands of the State within the forest preserve." The first class of lands was to be protected as before, but the Conservation Commission could "provide for the sale and removal of timber" ruled mature or "detrimental to forest growth" on the second class, the timber to be removed "by scientific forestry."

In one of the most eloquent speeches of the convention Louis Marshall, serving on the Conservation Committee, arose to fight this proposal. He pointed out that if cutting were permitted on the preserve, the state itself would not do the job, but would enter into contracts with lumber companies, the very firms employing the men who proposed this amendment. He went on to review some of the past depredations of those lumbermen, including the fiasco on lands administered by the State College of Forestry at Cornell, when "this tremendous tract of thirty thousand acres was to be cut down flat from one end of it to the other, in order that the scientific foresters might start a new forest which might mature a hundred years from the time that that contract was entered into. That is scientific forestry." Marshall recalled the deliberation of the delegates at the 1894 convention, the resounding defeat of the proposed amendment in 1896, and the fears that the denudation of the mountains would eventually affect the state's river flow and subterranean water supplies.

> It has been suggested in the Committee that those are trees which are diseased, but I am informed by the Dean of the College of Forestry [at Syracuse University] that under such a contract, or under such a term, eight per cent of all the trees in the Adirondacks would be cut down. What would you have left after you have adopted a provision of this character? Nothing but a howling wilderness. Not a wilderness of trees—wild forest trees—but of stumps, enough to make one's heart sick to behold them.

The lumbermen's proposal was defeated. However, the convention added certain other amendments to the Forever Wild clause before it sent the revised Constitution to the voters, among them provisions to allow the Conservation Commission to build fire trails, remove dead trees, and authorize a highway from Saranac Lake to Long Lake and Old Forge. The exercise was academic. In November 1915, the voters rejected the new Constitution for a variety of reasons by 910,462 to 400,423. The Forest Preserve, in any case, remained under the protection of the old Constitution and would not go the way of Hetch Hetchy.

It was a good year for the protectors of the forest. Even the Legislature's motherly protective instincts seemed to revive, and it passed a law against sending up unpiloted hot-air balloons over the Forest Preserve counties.

CHAPTER XX

A Wilderness Philosophy

The 1915 constitutional referendum effectively killed any serious plan to introduce lumbering on the Forest Preserve. The water resource interests were quiet for a while, too, satisfied in the Adirondacks by the amendment of 1913 which allowed them to flood up to 3 percent of the preserve. Even fire was partially tamed by the railroad's enforced cooperation and the state's employment of year-round forest rangers who replaced the seasonal wardens of earlier days. For the immediate future the conflicts were restricted to piecemeal assaults on the preserve, confined in their scope perhaps, but nonetheless intensely waged and often going to the heart of the fundamental constitutional question.

Outwardly all was calm. The new Conservation Commissioner, George D. Pratt, shared many views of the preservationists, having been president of the Camp Fire Club of America, and in later years he became the treasurer of the Association for the Protection of the Adirondacks. With Pratt's arrival, the era of general recreation began in the park; this era saw the development of hiking trails, lean-tos, and, in 1922, the founding of the Adirondack Mountain Club, in which Pratt himself became very much involved. Probably the commission's 1915 report expressed this approach to its job when it spoke of the Forest Preserve as a play area whose value was "beyond computation," and took pains to "emphasize its belief in the tremendous importance of the aesthetic and recreational advantages derived from conservation."

At the same time a new element, which may fairly be characterized as "the Schenectady force," was making itself felt in the Adirondacks. Its leader was John S. Apperson, a bachelor and an engineer who specialized in patents for the General Electric Company in that city in upstate New York. Apperson was originally a Virginian, but he came to the Adirondacks early in this century to view a canoe race and fell in love with the northern mountains. He was an enthusiastic hiker and sportsman. He gave up hunting after a while, though, his last kill being a deer he had tracked through the mountains for three days, sleeping in the open at night and finally catching up to the animal and dispatching it with a single shot. His favorite part of the mountains was on their fringe at Lake George. There he had a cabin to which he retreated when he was not involved in some passionate struggle to defend the Forever Wild clause.

"Lake George is my wife," Apperson once said, "and its islands are my children."

When he learned that a developer was going to build a hotel on Dome Island, the highest island in Lake George and often called its "centerpiece," he bought the island to preserve it, and later gave it to the Nature Conservancy. He named his boat *Article VII, Section 7*, after the Forever Wild clause.*

Apperson pursued his devotion methodically, like the engineer he was, disdaining sentimentalism and vague rhetoric for hard facts. Before he wrote a stinging letter to a state official or presented a statement at a public hearing, he spent days going over the site of the controversy, grasping details of law and topography that often put the "experts" to rout. Not even poor Verplanck Colvin, incredibly still wandering the streets of Albany in those days (he lived on until 1920), knew the specific "trouble spots" in the Adirondacks any better than Apperson did. "He told us never to talk about any problem area before we had gone and stood on the spot," a colleague of his once said.

Apperson, though in a sense he was always his own organization, became an ally of Commissioner Pratt and the Association for the Protection of the Adirondacks in 1916 when the Legislature approved the issue of ten million dollars in bonds to buy land for

* This boat is now in the Adirondack Museum collection.

state parks. Three quarters of this sum was to be used specifically for adding acreage to the Forest Preserve. Because the bond issue needed public approval, conservationists waged a spirited campaign to ensure its passage. Apperson believed with the association that the most important acquisitions would be the mountaintops and steep slopes, which were especially vulnerable to erosion and were being cut on private land at an alarming rate. The Adirondacks' grandest sights were being converted into wastelands of slash and stumps.

Just a few years before, the federal government had stepped boldly into the business of buying forests in the face of the penny pinchers and delicate constitutional questions. It accomplished this feat chiefly through the legislative wiles of Representative John Wingate Weeks of Massachusetts (who served afterward as Secretary of War under Presidents Harding and Coolidge) and the promotional wizardry of Gifford Pinchot, working through his National Conservation Association. The object of the Weeks Bill was to protect eastern forests and watersheds on non-government land from the lumbermen. Weeks secured its passage in 1911 by assuring his colleagues in Congress that its major purpose was the protection of navigable streams, always a goal dear to the heart of logrolling legislators. The system of large eastern national forests, including that in the White Mountains, may be traced to this bill.

A campaign of public education, similar to Pinchot's, worked in New York. In November 1916, the voters approved the bond issue, 650,349 to 499,853, and the Conservation Commission started to buy land. According to the commission's reports in succeeding years, the program went nicely, but it proceeded only in company with bitter internal division. The boat rocker was Warwick S. Carpenter, the secretary of the commission, who soon found an outspoken ally in John Apperson. Writing to Apperson years later, Carpenter recalled the dispute that cost him his job and commented:

"When anyone says today [1962] that government officials should be given wide lattitude [*sic*] in administration of the forest preserve probably the only way to prove that this could be disastrous is by showing that it did not work at the time of the first bond issue."

Adirondack Railway Station, North Creek, New York, 1888

Keeseville, New York, early in this century

Camp Pine Knot, Raquette Lake

Fort William Henry Hotel, Lake George, New York

Above and directly below, Prospect House,
Blue Mountain Lake, New York

Steamboat Towahloondah, in operation between 1882 and 1908,
at the Prospect House Landing

W. Seward Webb

Dr. Edward Livingston Trudeau

Facing page, clockwise from upper left:
Edward Zane Carroll Judson (Ned Buntline), Orson "Old Mountain" Phelps,
Dr. Thomas Clark Durant, Paul Smith, and (center) Verplanck Colvin

William West Durant

Tubercular patients at Dr. Trudeau's sanatorium, 1890s

The "Big Boom" on the Hudson River above Glens Falls at the turn of the century

An outing of the Horicon Sketching Club on Lake George, 1882

Hunters and their catch, 1891

The Adirondack Museum in Blue Mountain Lake, New York, today

By 1919 Carpenter became aware that the commission's priorities in buying land did not coincide with its original promises. The plan to protect the steep slopes and mountaintops had apparently been dropped, for the commission waited until the lumber companies cut over those critical areas and only then stepped in to acquire the denuded remains. Carpenter got involved in a long correspondence about the matter with C. R. Pettis, the State Superintendent of Forests, who was mainly responsible for selecting the land to be purchased. The replies Pettis sent back, Carpenter thought, were vague and inadequate, and he enlisted Apperson's support. Apperson, a prolific letter writer, challenged Commissioner Pratt to do something about the situation, but Pratt assured him that everything was being handled in the best possible way. Still dissatisfied, Apperson visited the various mountaintops in question and wrote back to assure Pratt that everything was *not* being handled as it should be, and invited Pratt to inspect the sites with him. Again, neither Carpenter nor Apperson received much satisfaction for their pains.

In August 1920, Carpenter (no slouch as a letter writer himself) sent a twenty-eight-page memorandum to Pratt, reviewing the whole matter of land purchases and pointing out that there were no records either in the commission's files or anywhere else from which one could discover what had already been done and what plans had been made for the money still remaining from the bond issue.

Pratt was furious, not at the situation but at Carpenter's letter, which he felt could be "ruinous" to his administration. Although he probably knew his days with the commission were numbered, Carpenter tried to placate Pratt; he told Apperson later that he did not think badly of Pratt, only thought him "deluded." He told Pratt he would let him have all the copies of his letter, as well as the stenographer's notes, if that would make him feel any better. Pratt thought that would be the decent thing to do, so Carpenter turned over the copies and notes to him and they were never seen again.

The dispute had taken on another dimension late in 1920 over an area known as the Gore (or piece of land) Around Lake Colden. A year earlier the comissioners of the State Land Office had given the Conservation Commission the approval to buy this area near Mount Marcy, but discussions had dragged on with the MacIntyre

Iron Company, its owners, and the Tahawus Club, an organization made up of well-to-do men which leased certain rights on the property. The club opposed selling the lakes and the strip of land nearby because it wanted to go on using the area as part of its preserve. Apperson and Carpenter contended that the state ought to acquire the lakes. The Land Board scheduled a hearing on the matter in Albany, at which both sides assembled their firepower. Carpenter appeared with Apperson and his supporters from Schenectady, while the Tahawus Club people brought their battery of lawyers, the latter to no avail. The Land Board ruled that the Conservation Commission could take the lakes as well as the forested land. Afterward Carpenter said:

> The significance of this is that precedence was established that in land purchases lakes should be taken with the land, and that private clubs should not be entrenched on lakes to the exclusion of the public. A practical result of major importance was that free and full use of the beautiful country constituting the Gore Around Lake Colden was assured to the public.

But bitterness lingered among the clubmen, particularly because of Carpenter's remarks at the hearing, later amplified for the press, that the Tahawus Club simply wanted to keep people "out of that part of the woods." Judge Samuel Ordway, a member of the club and the secretary of the Association for the Protection of the Adirondacks, wrote to Commissioner Pratt, complaining about Carpenter and denying that the Tahawus Club was in any way inhospitable to the public. A long correspondence followed, mostly between Carpenter and Ordway, during which the assiduous Carpenter dug up a lot of past incriminating letters written by the judge and other club members that proved without a doubt they had systematically discouraged anyone but themselves from enjoying the lakes. Carpenter eventually extracted a very grudging and unsatisfactory apology from Ordway; Pratt fired him anyway in the spring of 1921, and followed him out of Albany shortly afterward when Governor Nathan L. Miller dismissed him as commissioner.

. . .

Carpenter may have been right about the disastrous consequences certain to follow upon any decision to give government officials wide latitude in the preserve's administration; certainly its self-appointed guardians since then have tended to agree with him. But all around the country, park administration was achieving a higher tone as trained officials and imaginative private citizens took a guiding hand in the nurture of parks that did not have the supposedly inviolable protection of a constitutional clause. We have noted Louis Marshall's nod of approbation toward the leadership of Central Park, though even there neglect continued toward the plantings, and the park lovers had to fight off a barrage of suggested "improvements," including plans (later fortunately abandoned) to build, during the years immediately following World War I, a large stadium, an airfield, underground parking lots, a swimming pool, a circus and running track, and towers for the city radio station. One incompatible "useful gift" was the Heckscher Playground, an offer the park's guardians apparently could not refuse. "Fences were put up and an extensive concrete wading pool installed," wrote the park's historians. "Bitterly attacked at the time, the donor nonetheless *forced* his way onto the greensward and firmly attached his name to the 'gift.' "

Until 1915 the national parks had been a stepchild of government. There were fourteen of them, abused, badly administered, protected only occasionally by the Army or by organizations such as John Muir's Sierra Club. Their revitalization can be attributed almost solely to a businessman named Stephen Tyng Mather, who made his money promoting and marketing borax. All his life he was subject to nervous breakdowns, and he had recuperated from several of them by hiking and climbing in the western mountains. The neglect he saw around him in the national parks prompted him to write a letter to his friend Franklin K. Lane, the Secretary of the Interior, in 1915. Lane recognized at once that the letter was not that of a crank or scold. It was a comprehensive report on what was wrong with the parks. According to Mather's biographer, Robert T. Shankland, Lane sent off a note in reply:

"Dear Steve," it read. "If you don't like the way the national parks are being run come on down to Washington and run them yourself."

Mather, wealthy and confident enough to accept that sort of challenge, went to Washington and set up an office in the Interior Department, authorized by Lane to administer the parks. There was considerable hostility in Congress to the notion of national parks. Easterners didn't see why they should appropriate money for them because they were all in the West, while Westerners looked on them as a means of "locking up" natural resources, a sentiment vividly expressed by Representative Martin Dies of Texas, who got so carried away that he confused Gifford Pinchot with the preservationists:

> I am not for reservations and parks. I would have the great timber and mineral and coal resources of this country opened to the people and I only want to say, Mr. Chairman, that your Pinchots and your conservationists are theorists who are not in my humble judgment making a propaganda in the interest of the American people. Let California have it and let Alaska open her coal mines. God Almighty has located the resources of this country in such a form so that his children will not use them in disproportion, and your Pinchots will not be able to controvert and circumvent the laws of God Almighty.

But Mather was a great promoter. He lobbied for the parks with Congress and with the public. He even turned World War I to his advantage, since people had no choice but to see America first; he courted major magazines like *The Saturday Evening Post* and *National Geographic*, and they, with other sections of the American press, helped him to get his story across to the people. The railroads, to whom the people turned for transportation, also became enthusiastic publicists for the parks. Over a thousand articles about the parks appeared in a three-year period, and Mather soon had the constituency which stimulated Congress to consider a bill creating a National Park Service. Many of those congressmen who had voted for the dam at Hetch Hetchy now assuaged their consciences by coming down on the side of the parks. Frederick Law Olmsted, Jr., wrote the legislation for the park bill, incorporating many of the ideas his father had pulled together for the old state park at Yosemite and formulating a policy that would make it difficult to devise another fiasco like Hetch Hetchy. One of the few conservationists who opposed the bill was Pinchot, who disliked the idea of national parks, wanted to see them put to use as national forests, and saw a National Park Service as a rival for the money and prestige he thought belonged to his old first love, the U.S. Forest Service. But the tide of events once more was against him. Congress passed the act creating the National Park Service in 1916, and Mather became its first director.

While railroads were still important to the great western parks, the automobile was becoming as important there as it was to the Adirondacks. A later Secretary of the Interior, Stewart L. Udall, has written:

> Strangely enough, one of Mather's chief concerns in those days was to get people to visit the parks. In persuading one investor to build a hotel in Yosemite Valley—a sober man who drew back in fear of empty rooms and little business—Mather said: "Why, look at those cars! There must be 200. Where's your imagination, man? Some day there'll be a thousand!" In 1965, hundreds of thousands of cars brought 1,635,400 visitors to Yosemite National Park.

It is ironic that the organized wilderness movement in the United States did not arise out of the National Park Service, which was the product of the aesthetic recreation movement, but out of the utilitarian Pinchot's Forest Service. The catalyst was an outdoorsman, hunter, and forester named Aldo Leopold. A graduate of the Yale Forest School in 1909, Leopold had spent years roaming the southwestern wilderness in New Mexico, where he was stationed with the Forest Service. The huge Gila wilderness area he fell in love with was not "virgin" land any more than the Adirondacks that Verplanck Colvin and Louis Marshall had treasured; it had been hunted, trapped, and grazed, while both Indians and a few homesteaders had called it home. But it was a thousand square miles of rugged mountainous country. Leopold camped in its fastnesses and hunted its big game ("I am glad I shall never be young without wild country to be young in," he wrote later in *A Sand County Almanac*. "Of what avail are forty freedoms without a blank spot on the map?") But the national forests were beginning to feel the same sort of pressure that was both the salvation and the bane of the national parks, as "recreationists" of all kinds swarmed over them. Until then, the wilderness of the Gila National Forest had been marred only by the ruts of an occasional wagon, but now, after World War I, there was a proposal to build roads into it to accommodate the automobile. Leopold was horrified. He certainly didn't want windshield tourists, whether they included Henry James or a druggist from Des Moines, roping in huge netfuls of impressions in his practically unspoiled wilderness. As he also wrote in *Sand County*: "Recreational development is a job not of building roads into lovely country, but of building receptivity into the still unlovely human mind."

Leopold formulated a counterproposal, based on the ideas of a young landscape architect in the Forest Service, Arthur H. Carhart. The Gila region was so rugged and isolated that it was considered of little economic value to lumbermen, farmers, or miners; only a few ranchers used it for grazing their cattle. In the *Journal of Forestry* in 1921, Leopold argued that there was room, and even a need, for wilderness preservation areas in the national forests. He questioned whether the Forest Service's policy in every case must be to push for development in the forests; or whether it should recognize "the principle of highest use," in which a few especially rugged and inaccessible regions were left that way for all time.

"Heretofore, we have been inclined to assume that our recreational development policy must be based on the desires and needs of the majority only," he wrote, and went on to argue that Americans were now in a position to set aside areas of wilderness for the minority who believed that in some cases this was the highest use to which a region could be put. "By wilderness, I mean a continuous stretch of country preserved in its natural state, open to lawful hunting and fishing, big enough to absorb a two weeks pack trip, and kept devoid of roads, artificial trails, cottages or the works of man." Having married the daughter of a rancher who had a permit to graze his cattle in the Gila National Forest, Leopold saw no reason then to include that aspect of commerce among his prohibitions, though later on he changed his mind.

Amazingly enough, his proposal bore fruit within the Forest Service, where the climate often favored innovation. For one thing, the service had been structured by Pinchot to grant considerable autonomy to the district forester in each of the several regions into which the forest system was divided. It was the district forester in New Mexico and Arizona who approved Leopold's plan to set aside 574,000 acres for wilderness use in the Gila National Forest.

Secondly, the men at headquarters in Washington saw no reason to veto that decision. Henry S. Graves, who followed Pinchot as chief of the Forest Service, did not share his old mentor's aversion to national parks and other manifestations of the aesthetic conservation movement, and even threw his support behind the National Park Act of 1916. Graves's successor, William B. Greeley, opened the national forests to a variety of recreational uses, not so much because he was convinced that this was a legitimate function of the forests, but because he was exercising political judgment; Steve Mather's grasping hand was trying to turn some of the national forests into national parks (he was successful in some cases, especially in creating Glacier and Rocky Mountain national parks) and he had enthusiastic public support. To hold on to his forests, Greeley aggressively promoted recreation within them, under the Forest Service's "multiple-use policy."

The Forest Service established wilderness areas in other forests besides that at Gila, agreeing not to build roads or issue recreation permits. However, those areas were by no means "forever wild." The service reserved the right to alter their designation if economic conditions changed and there was a demand for their use. James P. Gilligan, a historian of Forest Service policy, recounts a story about Greeley testifying at a congressional hearing, where the question of wilderness areas came up. A congressman leaned forward and shook his finger at Greeley.

"I know why you set up those wilderness areas, Greeley," he said. "Just to keep them out of Steve Mather's hands!"

As the idea took hold within the Forest Service (much to the disgruntlement of rigidly utilitarian foresters), Leopold began to formulate a philosophy of wilderness. If he was too practical a forester and outdoorsman to believe in a "pure" wilderness, he expected at least a measure of purity from the men and women who used those remote areas. He was outraged on one occasion when, in the wilderness region of the Superior National Forest, he came upon a party of canoeists using professional guides to tote their packs on a portage. "We objected to people in the wilderness who hired guides to carry packs," he wrote later. "We objected because they had bought their way instead of working their way into our wilderness." Leopold, the forester, hunter, and fisherman, was edging toward a land ethic, which he conceived primarily as a scientist, postulating the "rights" of the land as well as the animals and plants that lived on it. He wanted to create an "ecological conscience" in his fellow human beings, but for the moment his goal was to organize his ideas about wilderness. He did so in a series of articles, in one of which he wrote:

> Public wilderness areas are essentially a means for allowing the more virile and primitive forms of outdoor recreation to survive the receding economic fact of pioneering. These forms should survive because they likewise are an improvement on pioneering itself.
>
> There is little question that many of the attributes most distinctive of America and Americans are the impress of the wilderness and the life that accompanied it. If we have any such thing as an American culture (and I think we have), its distinguishing marks are a certain vigorous individualism combined with ability to organize, a certain intellectual curiosity bent to practical ends, a lack of subservience to stiff social forms, and an intolerance of drones, all of which are the distinctive characteristics of successful pioneers. These, if anything, are the indigenous part of our Americanism, the qualities that set it apart as a new rather than an imitative contribution to civilization. Many observers see these qualities not only bred into our people, but built into our institutions. Is it not a bit beside the point for us to be solicitous about preserving those institutions without giving so much as a thought to preserving the environment which produced them and which may now be one of our effective means of keeping them alive?

Leopold knew that wilderness areas in the national forests could be altered or even abolished by the decisions of district foresters responding to local economic pressures, and he foresaw the later conflicts that would arise over the "lockup" of natural resources. At the same time the national parks, under Mather, were embarked on a course of development—building roads, interpretive centers, lodges, trails, and other appurtenances—to accommodate the traveler who liked to go in comfort and, in fact, would not mind having somebody tote his bag for him, too. But the National Park Service did follow the Forest Service's lead in setting aside certain areas as wilderness, mostly for scientific purposes. In contrast to the degree of administrative decision or whim that determined the extent of wilderness in the national forests and parks, the New York Forest Preserve (despite Pratt's promotion of "recreation") remained a tough nut to crack.

CHAPTER XXI

Bobsleds and Truck Trails

During the middle 1970s the people of Lake Placid were somewhat bemused by a report prepared by a big-city firm to assess the impact of the coming 1980 Winter Olympic Games on their village. "Hosting the Olympic Games will have a tremendous psychological and social impact on this small community, which is unaccustomed to such publicity and visibility in large part because it is tucked away in the Adirondack Mountains." The local citizens properly pointed out in reply that their village was not virginal, in respect to either publicity or Olympic Games. Lake Placid had been a major resort even before it was the site of the 1932 Winter Olympics, an event that also triggered one of the shortest but most significant battles in the controversy over Forever Wild.

Bobsledding, a sport in which either two or four persons ride an open sled down a twisting, snow-packed course, was developed at St. Moritz, Switzerland, during the late nineteenth century. Because of the speed and danger associated with the sport, it soon became popular and it was added to the Winter Olympic Games for the first time in 1924. When the organizing committee began preparing the Lake Placid area for the 1932 games, they decided to include a bobsled run. (It is still the only such course in the Western Hemisphere.) Their plans were reasonable, but the way in which those most concerned with the course went about getting it was very curious.

Early in 1929 Assemblyman Fred Porter of Essex County, in

which Lake Placid lies, introduced a bill in the Legislature to allow the Conservation Department to build a bobsled run "on state lands in the Forest Preserve." Just a few weeks earlier, the Legislature had passed, and Governor Franklin D. Roosevelt had signed into law, a measure that authorized the construction of a course "on lands in which any necessary easement may be provided"; in other words, wherever the state could legally secure an easement to build, most probably on private land. The new statute, Chapter 417 of the Laws of 1929 (which was also signed by Roosevelt), clearly posed a challenge to the State Constitution.

The Association for the Protection of the Adirondacks picked up the challenge. The proposed course, one and a quarter miles long and six and a half feet wide, would require the removal of at least twenty-five hundred trees, far in excess of the "no cutting to any material degree" phrase usually adhered to by state officials within the Constitution's restrictions. During the years immediately preceding the 1929 statute, the Forest Preserve had taken, in the eyes of most preservationists, an unusual buffeting. The Conservation Department had embarked about 1927 on an extensive program to build or improve campsites in all parks of the preserve, clearing brush (and cutting a few trees) to install fireplaces, toilets, and fire lanes. There was some doubt about how far the department could proceed legally in this direction, particularly as the crush of tourists now demanded further "improvements." (The automobile was now a commonplace sight in the Adirondacks.) And in 1927 the Legislature passed a measure for the second time to amend the Constitution so that the state could build a highway from Wilmington to the top of Whiteface Mountain. The proponents of this highway, believing there should be at least one road by which non-hikers could drive to an Adirondack peak, slipped an irresistible plum into their pudding by specifying that the highway be designated a memorial to New Yorkers who had served in the Army or Navy during World War I. Preservationists fought the proposal as an alarming precedent, but the support for it from powerful patriotic and veterans' organizations such as the American Legion proved decisive. The voters passed the amendment and approved the highway by 1,082,864 to 602,395.

There were no such mitigating circumstances in the case of the bobsled run. The hoopla, speed, and danger associated with such a course were obviously incompatible with an area set aside primarily for "watershed protection." When the Conservation Department proposed to build the facility on a slope in the Sentinel Range, John G. Agar, president of the Association for the Protection of the Adirondacks, went to court to stop it. One of the arguments put forth by the proponents of the bobsled run was that the number of trees to be cut was insignificant in comparison to the great forest around them. Shortly before his death, Louis Marshall spoke out vigorously against this attempt by the Legislature to subvert the Constitution. He pointed to the construction of various highways in the preserve, including the Saranac Lake–Long Lake–Old Forge road and the Whiteface Mountain Highway, as proof that the approval of the people of New York was needed to authorize a disturbance of that extent.

"My experience tells me," he wrote to a friend, "that a latitudinarian interpretation, on the theory that the violation is unimportant and trivial, invariably leads to an effective neutralization of the constitutional provision so treated."

He also pointed out that the earlier law, authorizing the state to secure an easement for the bobsled run on private land, was a violation of other clauses of the Constitution, which prohibited state money or credit from being given to individuals or associations. "It is obvious that if the bobsleigh run is built on private land, it becomes the property of the owner of that land," he wrote. "Consequently the money expended for its construction by the State would be given to the owner of the land on which the bobsleigh run is located."

A court of the Appellate Division in Albany ruled against the proposed bobsled course in November 1929, deciding that the Forest Preserve "must always retain the character of a wilderness." The Conservation Department took the case to the Court of Appeals. There, on March 19, 1930, Judge Frederick C. Crane affirmed the ban on the bobsled course in an opinion that was the most comprehensive yet written on the Forever Wild clause. Crane pointed out that the clause's purpose, as shown in the record of the debates during the 1894 Constitutional Convention, was to prevent the cutting or destruction of the Forest Preserve's timber. "The Adirondack

Park was to be preserved, not destroyed," Crane wrote. This purpose implied that certain measures might be taken to protect the trees from fire and other hazards, and that facilities might be provided for the public's use, as long as they "did not call for the removal of timber to any material degree." But trees cannot be destroyed to provide space where people may take part in a sport, whether it is golf or bobsledding. The timber, Crane ruled, "cannot be cut or removed to construct a toboggan slide simply and solely for the reason that Section 7, Article VII of the Constitution says it cannot be done."

Thus the state turned to private acreage, building the bobsled run on land owned by the Lake Placid Club (from which the state received a long-term easement) on the side of Mount Van Hoevenberg. The state had entered the winter sports business, a reflection of the increasing pressures to open the preserve to recreation.* Leading the recreationists was Robert Moses, the great manipulator who was providing the state with an imposing edifice of parks and parkways, but who as chairman of the State Council of Parks was frustrated in the Adirondacks by Forever Wild. It was reportedly at his instigation that upstate legislators introduced a constitutional amendment (which became known as the "Closed Cabin Amendment") in 1930 that would have permitted the clearing of timber on the preserve to build a variety of "closed" structures such as lodges and other recreational facilities, to be operated by the Conservation Department (to which the commission's name was changed in 1927) or a special "public authority." Once again, the preservationists prepared for battle. The Association for the Protection of the Adirondacks and John S. Apperson's Schenectady troops came out in full force, telling their side of the story to the press, in pamphlets, and at meetings of sportsmen's and civic groups assembled all over the state. In the 1932 election, the voters buried the Closed Cabin Amendment by a better than two-to-one margin.

* It expanded on a more profitable basis in 1941, when the voters, by a margin of less than 10,000, approved an amendment to permit the construction of ski slopes on Forest Preserve land on Whiteface Mountain; the Conservation Department supported the amendment on grounds that the memorial highway to the top had already "ruined" the mountain for wilderness purposes, but it is said that the tide was really turned in the amendment's favor on election eve by a favorable word given it on his news broadcast by Lowell Thomas, a skiing enthusiast.

Many employees of the Conservation Department, and their supporters outside it, came to believe that it was "in thrall" to the preservationists, that it could fulfill its responsibilities to the people who wanted more campsites and recreation facilities only by stretching the law to the breaking point. The argument that the majority of people "wanted" the elaborate facilities, of course, could not be substantiated by the record, because most attempts to open the preserve to them and thus make an honest agency of the department were defeated at the polls. It became the policy of the successive Conservation Commissioners, therefore, to try the patience of the preservationists to the breaking point, and to compromise when cracks began to show.

The commissioners were not precisely weaving the justification for their work out of thin air. They relied to a great extent on state attorneys general who had given various opinions on what sort of alteration was permissible in the preserve. For instance, though they recalled the 1912 opinion about making improvements in the Lake George Battlefield Park (in which an attorney general had allowed improvements specifically because the land had not been acquired for Forest Preserve purposes), they could point to several opinions in which the principle had been laid down that improvements might be made where there was no "material degree" of cutting. They could also point to Judge Crane's decision in the bobsled case, in which he suggested the preserve was to be saved, not destroyed, and that therefore "all things necessary were permitted, such as measures to prevent forest fires, the repairs to roads and proper inspection, or the erection and maintenance of proper facilities for the use by the public, which did not call for the removal of timber to any material degree."

Ever since the development of campsites for the public in the preserve about 1920, the commissioners had justified the step in part because it would protect the forest from illegal and indiscriminate camping; the building of fireplaces for campers, for instance, was a fire protection measure. The cutting of dead trees for firewood was also accepted.

But the self-appointed guardians of the preserve were always looking over a commissioner's shoulder. Adding weight to their wishes were those of the governors during this period, then as now generally "downstaters" and thus responsive to the increasing wilderness sentiment on the steamy sidewalks of New York. Preservationists like Apperson forged strong ties with the men at the top.

"Appie was friendly with all the governors, especially with Al Smith," one of Apperson's old colleagues has said. "When Smith was first sent to Albany as a young assemblyman from the city, he wanted very much to get on a committee that would reflect his interest in city affairs. But the Speaker kept putting him off. Finally, after a lot of pestering, the Speaker said, 'All right, we've just assigned you to the committee on forests.' Smith was furious. He was all set to pack up and go home, and then he said to himself, 'Hey, what is this forest business all about? If I'm on the committee, I should find out something about them.' Well, he did, and he became a great supporter of the preserve. Appie could always go to him with a complaint or a suggestion and Smith would listen because he realized that Appie knew what he was talking about. Appie had the same relationship with Roosevelt, [Herbert H.] Lehman, and [Averell W.] Harriman when they were governor."

Many people on both sides of the controversy believed even the public campsites on the Forest Preserve were unconstitutional, but despite some abuses the preservationists were not eager to rock the boat over this issue. Some cutting went on in maintaining the campsites, but it was generally overlooked. One old-time resident of the Adirondacks recalls visiting a campsite on the preserve where workmen were cutting trees.

"I thought you couldn't cut trees on state land," he asked the foreman.

The foreman winked at him. "These trees are hazardous to the campers," he replied.

What is often overlooked is the impact of the invention of the bulldozer on American forests. Until then, road building in the woods was a difficult and expensive job, and heavily financed railroads were relied upon to carry out the logs where streams and rivers were absent. Around 1928, however, Edward P. Stamm, who was a manager of logging operations for Crown Zellerbach, devised a bulldozer attachment for the Caterpillar tractors that were used to skid logs out of the forest. With the new attachment, tractors were able to push dirt, large rocks, stumps, and other obstacles aside, and make road building in the woods almost a casual affair. The invention was of enormous importance to lumber companies in the West, of course, where waterways for floating logs out of the wilderness were often scarce. (It was also a boon to scientific forestry because, with railroads in use, the forest had to be clear-cut to make the building of a rail line economical; as bulldozers opened roads for trucks, the lumber companies were able to be more selective, cutting out pockets of the forest here and there as the maturity of the trees demanded.)

The ease with which roads could be carved from the forest also had an impact on the Adirondacks. The Conservation Department seized on the new development to open up "truck trails" in the preserve over which fire fighters and their equipment could reach remote trouble spots. Probably Lithgow Osborne, who was Conservation Commissioner throughout most of the 1930s, expected no difficulty when he began opening up the trails in 1935. He was a respected conservationist, taking seriously his responsibility to protect the Forest Preserve.

The year before, more than ten thousand acres of the Bay Pond tract in Franklin County had burned, the fire finally being brought under control by a unit of the Civilian Conservation Corps (CCC), stationed nearby. (The state attorney general had ruled that CCC camps could be built in the preserve during the Depression, provided the camps were not permanent and did not require any material tree cutting.) On the advice of his foresters, Osborne decided to build a series of dirt roads, using CCC labor, mostly along the route of old tote roads, into the preserve, so that trucks would have access to fires. "The truck trails are dead-end roads," Osborne said, "running nowhere from a communication point of view, and hence would fit into no conceivable state or county highway system." A few trees would have to be cut, of course, but he thought the number fell within the usual unofficial exemptions made on the Forest Preserve; nonetheless, to cover his flanks he secured the attorney general's approval. He also sounded out the Association for the Protection of the Adirondacks, fresh from its victories in the bobsled run and Closed Cabin Amendment uproars. He assured himself of no trouble from that quarter. The association was in a compromising mood, unwilling to risk its laurels in a case where the issues (and victory) did not seem at all clear. Aside from a few of its individual members, the association sat out the ensuing controversy.

John Apperson did not. Perceiving a threat to the preserve, he rushed into battle, supported by the coterie of Schenectady preservationists who formed the core of his Forest Preserve Association. Perhaps the most eloquent voice of all during the controversy was that of a comparative newcomer among the Forest Preserve's leading defenders, but by no means a newcomer to the Adirondacks themselves—Robert Marshall.

Bob Marshall, son of Louis Marshall, was the most charismatic figure in the modern wilderness movement—playing St. Paul to Aldo Leopold's Messiah, bright, articulate, and even eloquent in rallying the faithful, devoted to the cause almost to the point of fanaticism, and finally, in a sense, its martyr. He and his brother George had spent their boyhood summers at the brown-and-green-painted frame buildings that composed the Marshalls' Camp Knollwood on Lower Saranac Lake. They had read Colvin's reports with wonder and enthusiasm. In the company of an Adirondack guide, Herb Clark, Bob and George became the first people ever to climb forty of the forty-six Adirondack peaks over four thousand feet—and Bob was not yet out of his teens.

Marshall carried wilderness with him wherever he went. "As a boy I spent many hours in the heart of New York City, dreaming of Lewis and Clark and their glorious exploration into the unbroken wilderness which embraced three quarters of a continent," he once wrote. "Occasionally, my reveries ended in terrible depression and I would imagine that I had been born a century too late for genuine excitement."

His family's wealth gave him the opportunity to travel to all the places that he dreamed of, especially the vast wilderness of Alaska and northern Canada, but he was never a dilettante. He was graduated *magna cum laude* from the College of Forestry at Syracuse in 1924 and went on to earn his master's degree at Harvard and his doctorate in plant physiology at Johns Hopkins University. Like Leopold, Marshall chose the U.S. Forest Service for a career. There he became director of the Forestry Division in the Office of Indian

Affairs and later chief of the Division of Recreation and Lands. But even during his mature years the wilderness was never very far away. At his own expense he prepared an inventory map of all of the roadless areas of over 300,000 acres in the United States, with many of which he was personally familiar. According to Henry Clepper in his *Leaders of American Conservation*, Marshall took more than two hundred wilderness hikes of thirty miles in a day, fifty-one of forty miles, and several of up to seventy miles. It is said that rangers at isolated posts kept track of him by radio, marking his progress and speculating on when he would arrive on top of the next peak on his list. And yet all the while he was haunted by a vision of the American wilderness "melting away like the last snowbank on some south-facing mountainside during a hot afternoon in June."

In 1930 Marshall published an article that is considered seminal in the formulation of a coherent, modern, national wilderness doctrine. It was called "The Problem of the Wilderness" and appeared in *Scientific Monthly*. He wrote:

> . . . it will only be a few years until the last escape from society will be barricaded. If that day arrives there will be countless souls born to live in strangulation, countless human beings who will be crushed under the artificial edifice raised by man. There is just one hope of repulsing the tyrannical ambition of civilization to conquer every niche on the whole earth. That hope is the organization of spirited people who will fight for the freedom of the wilderness.

In the next few years Marshall continued to develop his thoughts about wilderness, thoughts expressed by Thoreau, Muir, and earlier wilderness writers, but phrased in the modern idiom, drawing on new ideas in psychology. Wilderness must be retained not simply to preserve watersheds, to provide forests for the future, to make havens for plants and animals, to set aside reservations for scientific research, but because man, the intelligent and aesthetic animal, needed it. (How many wilderness areas do we need? he was asked. "How many Brahms symphonies do we need?" he replied.) Like William James, he sought a "moral equivalent of war," and found it in the "harmless excitement of the wilderness," where man's consuming desire for adventure may be appeased. Freudian notions mingled with his love for wild places; civilization has cramped and warped us, he believed, and in frustrating our longing for the freedom of the wilderness we leave ourselves open to the modern ills of tension and anxiety. To plunge into the wilderness and test ourselves against the natural world is to alleviate "the terrific harm caused by suppressed desires."

And he defined wilderness in this way:

> . . . a region which contains no permanent inhabitants, possesses no possibility of conveyance by any mechanical means and is sufficiently spacious that a person in crossing it must have the experience of sleeping out. The dominant attributes of such an area are: first, that it requires anyone who exists in it to depend exclusively on his own effort for survival; and second, that it preserves as nearly as possible the primitive environment. This means that all roads, power, transportation and settlement are barred. But trails and temporary shelters, which were common long before the advent of the white race, are entirely permissible.

Paul Schaefer, an associate of Apperson's in the Adirondack preservation battles for many years, has spoken of his first meeting with Bob Marshall. Appropriately, it was on a peak—Mount Marcy—on July 15, 1932, when Schaefer was photographing (for propaganda purposes) patches of the High Peak area that had burned during a lumbering project. There was another man on the summit when Schaefer and a companion arrived.

"The man was Herb Clark, whom we all knew about as Bob Marshall's guide in the Adirondacks," Schaefer said. "He told us that Marshall had set out that morning at three-thirty to climb fourteen Adirondack peaks by dark. He had just arrived with Marshall's lunch. And sure enough, here came Marshall, right on schedule, heading for us at a dog trot. He was a stocky, powerful, ruddy man, dressed in a well-worn plaid shirt, blue denims, and sneakers."

The men introduced themselves, and while Marshall paused for lunch, Schaefer spoke to him about the endless problems of maintaining a wilderness in the Adirondacks. (Marshall had been spending most of his time in recent years in Alaska, and was out of touch with matters in the eastern wilderness.) Schaefer pointed out the burned-over areas, the high slopes that were still being logged despite the state's attempt to include them in the preserve, and the Closed Cabin Amendment proposal which would be voted on by the people in November.

"Marshall was plainly upset," Schaefer recalled. "He walked back and forth across the summit, and circled it a couple of times, and for a while he was deep in thought. Then he said, in an intense way, 'We simply have to band together—all of us who love the wilderness. We must fight together—wherever and whenever wilderness is attacked. We can't let the American wilderness be destroyed.' Three years later Marshall helped to organize the Wilderness Society in Washington. He first wrote about an organization like that in his 'Problem of Wilderness' article, but I think our meeting on Mount Marcy that afternoon pushed him into making it a reality."

When Aldo Leopold accepted the chair of game management at the University of Wisconsin in 1933, Bob Marshall became the leading spokesman for wilderness in government, and he suggested to Secretary of the Interior Harold L. Ickes that he create a "Wilderness Planning Board" to choose areas that ought to be set aside in perpetuity by Congress. Although this idea was not accepted until 1964, Marshall took an active interest wherever wilderness came under attack.

Such an opportunity arose during the Adirondacks' "truck trails" dispute. Marshall joined with Apperson in opposing the idea, contending that the roads were not needed to fight fires, that it was the observation and preventive steps taken by the Conservation Department and its predecessors since 1908 that were responsible for saving tremendous acreage; moreover, the trails, he believed, would actually increase the danger of fire, inviting many more people into the wilderness (he saw no way of keeping vehicles off the roads despite Commissioner Osborne's promise that they would be barred to the public) and leaving flammable slash along the roadsides. He strenuously objected to the precedent. Writing in *American Forests*, Marshall argued:

> Once a road passable for automobiles is actually built, there will immediately be a strong argument that the Conservation Department is like a dog in a manger in not permitting the general public

> to use it. It will be much easier to open by constitutional amendment a road which already exists than it would be to authorize the cutting of an entirely new road.

He pointed out that dead-end "fire roads" cut through the wilderness in the Great Lakes region "just growed," like Topsy, and eventually became "wilderness highways." Finally, there was the ultimate argument; the roads would destroy the character of the Adirondacks' wild forest lands. With Marshall's intervention, the pure wilderness movement got under way in the Adirondacks; heretofore, even Colvin and Apperson had phrased their arguments chiefly in terms of watershed protection.

Commissioner Osborne responded to the preservationists' attack by halting the truck trails' construction temporarily in 1935. Governor Lehman, equally sensitive to the issue, appointed a committee of five men, representing various interests in the Adirondacks, to study the problem and submit a report to him. Four members filed a favorable report on the truck trails, suggesting a few changes in their routes and recommending that Osborne's restriction on public use be maintained. The fifth member, John Apperson, issued a minority report, commenting acidly that he did not believe foresters were qualified to "supervise forests in their natural state."

Bob Marshall prodded the Association for the Protection of the Adirondacks to take the Conservation Department to court, but the association officially remained neutral, believing the opponents' case was not strong enough. Ninety-five of the proposed trails were built. It would be many years before specially designated wilderness areas in the preserve were finally closed to mechanized traffic; though public use was never permitted, "administrative abuse" of the road system disturbed protectionists until the 1970s.

Bob Marshall had confirmed in a new generation of wilderness lovers their belief that wilderness is not a frivolous ideal of the privileged class, but a necessity in the modern world. Marshall was an ideal of purity, a man dedicated to a cause, despite an illness that threatened his life. To the end he was driven by a boyhood dream. There is something a little disturbing in all this bustling from one mountain peak to another, something of the mania that sustained flagpole sitting or marathon dancing. Pull up a pumpkin and sit down for a while, one wants to say to Marshall. But in a moment he would be up and away again, toiling manfully up another mountain range as a blood-red sun sank behind it. He dropped dead on a train one day in 1939 at the age of thirty-eight.

When the Constitutional Convention of 1938 convened, the preservationists were able to deal with any attacks (some organized by the Empire State Forest Products Association) on the Forever Wild clause. The Constitution itself was revised, Article VII, Section 7, being renumbered Article XIV, Section 1, with three other sections added to include subsequent amendments dealing with highways, reservoirs, the state's responsibility to provide for reforestation on the Forest Preserve, and the right of citizens to bring suit when violations of the article occur. The new article was approved with other parts of the Constitution by the voters of New York in November 1938.

CHAPTER XXII

Dams in the Mountains

It was water—the desire to preserve its sources—that led to the creation of the Forest Preserve in the nineteenth century. It was water—the desire to put it to use—that brought on the bitterest and costliest battle over the preserve in our own century. A student of water resources in New York State has called it "the Black River War."

Two of the great conservation debates of this century concerned water rights. Hetch Hetchy, as we have seen, was primarily a struggle between those who put forth the needs of a great city and those who defended a natural treasure, the survival of which was ostensibly guaranteed by its inclusion in a national park. TVA was primarily a struggle between the advocates of public and private power. A curious twist to the Black River case in the Adirondacks was that, because of the preservationists' manipulations, various arms of the state government were pitted against each other.

The struggle had its roots in 1913 when voters passed the amendment authorizing the use of up to 3 percent of Forest Preserve land for reservoirs (the reservoirs' function being to provide municipal water supplies, maintain the state's canals, and "regulate the flow of streams"). In 1915 the Legislature passed the Machold Storage Law (named for its sponsor, Assemblyman H. Edmund Machold), granting "any person or public corporation" the right to petition the Conservation Commission for permission to form a river regulating district. If the commission approved the petition, the district acquired the right to own real estate, to sue and be sued, to exercise the right of public domain, and to assess taxes among the beneficiaries of its projects. The district became, in law, a state agency, and the members of its board, who were appointed by the governor, became state officials. To raise money for construction, the district was authorized to issue bonds; the bonds, however, became the district's, and not the state's, obligation. The board's function was to prepare a plan to regulate the flow of rivers and streams within the district, and carry out the construction of the necessary dams and reservoirs.

Two districts were formed under this law, one of them the Hudson River Regulating District, which eventually built the Sacandaga Reservoir (its name was changed later to Great Sacandaga Lake) within the Adirondack Park but not on Forest Preserve land. Its existence has been comparatively tranquil. But in 1919 the Black River Regulating District entered upon its stormy career. It began when the city of Watertown joined several villages and private corporations in presenting a petition to the Conservation Commission to form a district. "River regulation," in this case, was a euphemism under which the initiators hoped to harness the Black River to turn the wheels of Watertown's industries. The great age of hydroelectric development was under way. The old system, by which waterwheels or steam drove a central shaft, which in turn transmitted the power to various belts to run the machines, was grossly inefficient. Friction sapped power at almost every step in the process. Hydroelectric power cut most of the losses sustained by mechanical power, and could be transmitted to industries built at some distance from the river. Thus, despite the contention of the Black River Regulating District's incorporators that upriver dams and reservoirs would regulate the river and prevent farmers from being flooded out downstream in spring, the project's true goal was to supply Watertown and its industries with hydroelectric power. To supply such power, the district needed a steady flow, one not subject to seasonal fluctuations.

The Black River, which drains 1,918 square miles in the southwestern Adirondacks, runs from high wooded slopes in Herkimer County southwesterly and then northwesterly to Lake Ontario. Two of its chief tributaries in the Adirondacks are the Moose River and the Beaver River; some of its flow is diverted to the New

York State Barge Canal. Merchants built a mill on the Black River to utilize its power as early as 1808, and industry has used it almost ever since, despite seasonal fluctuations. Aside from a few small dams raised on the river during the nineteenth century, it remained comparatively unregulated at the time of the Machold Storage Law.

The board of the newly created Black River Regulating District adopted a plan for the river in 1920, calling for a total of twelve reservoirs, including the three small ones already in use. Most of the proposed reservoirs were dropped later for one reason or another, but the board went right to work on the first part of its plan, enlarging the old Stillwater Reservoir on the Beaver River. Although the enlargement flooded three thousand additional acres of the Forest Preserve, preservationists evidently felt that this loss could reasonably be included among the 3 percent of the preserve scheduled for flooding under the Burd Amendment of 1913, and there was only a minor court challenge (won by the district) to the plan. The enlargement was completed in 1925. As a former official of the district later explained to Homer C. Martin, a historian of the project: "There were no people around here with wealth, as there were later at Panther Mountain and Higley Mountain. We were lucky to get down before the furor started over state lands."

The other two old reservoirs in the river system, at Old Forge and Sixth Lake on the Moose River, were not suitable for enlargement because resort areas already were growing up around them. The residents would have objected to the unsightly drawdown in summer months that characterizes most reservoirs, and so their usefulness had been marginal. Thus the district formulated plans to build a large reservoir at Panther Mountain and a smaller one at Higley Mountain on the south branch of the Moose River. The two reservoirs would be located partly on the Forest Preserve and partly on that great 100,000-acre rectangle owned by the Adirondack League Club. The club's officers voiced the first objections to the proposal, especially Panther Dam's reservoir, most of which would lie on club land. In his report to the Black River Regulating District, an engineer said that "the chief objection appears to be the fear that a reservoir built partly on state land and partly on their land, will give the public access to their property and thus materially damage it for park purposes." Apparently, however, the club's officers hinted they would raise no strong objection if the reservoir were built wholly on their land.

For a while events moved with almost alluvial imperceptibility. Plans for the two reservoirs were retarded by the onset of the Depression as well as by the reluctance of the reservoirs' "beneficiaries" to agree to pay the necessary taxes. Federal money was not available, partly because, according to some of the reservoirs' proponents, the Roosevelt administration felt that the people of the region didn't "vote right." In 1942, with the Depression over, the board temporarily dropped its plan to build a reservoir at Panther Mountain and decided to approve the smaller one at Higley, but World War II loomed as a new obstacle to the start of construction. The human element seemed the least of the district's problems, for the Adirondack League Club had no objection to Higley, nor did the Conservation Department under Lithgow Osborne. Then, as soon as the war ended and construction became imminent, opposition arose in a gathering storm.

The opposition throughout the ensuing struggle was centered in Schenectady. The aging John Apperson remained a force, but new blood was taking over, none more effectively than an Apperson protégé, Paul Schaefer. Today Schaefer is a tall, white-haired contractor who specializes in the building of Early American period homes; like Apperson, he considers the Forest Preserve his meat and drink.

"I guess you could say I officially became a conservationist at the age of eleven," Schaefer has said. "In 1919 the old Conservation Commission held a series of meetings around the state to interest people in what it was doing. The meetings, I believe, were suggested by Warwick Carpenter. Anyway, I attended one at Schenectady High School that was presided over by Commissioner Pratt and Carpenter. After they showed us some wildlife films they asked if anyone would like to be identified with the conservation movement. I was one of those who said yes, and Pratt gave me a little gold pin—I still have it—that said 'New York State Conservationist' on it, with a picture of a deer and a grouse. I was thrilled."

Like so many of the Adirondacks' most tenacious defenders, Paul Schaefer was introduced to the mountains as a summer resident. His family owned a camp in the park, at first as a retreat where his mother could go to ease her hay fever, but the boy soon took to the mountains with his father and became an enthusiastic hiker and camper.

"I decided that I would collect a library devoted to the Adirondacks," Schaefer said. "I thought at first it might mean buying fifty or sixty books, but then I found that the literature was endless. I began to haunt the bookstores in Albany. Now I have thousands of books and documents."

Schaefer joined several local hiking clubs, among them the Adirondack Mountain Club, which had become a potent force of its own in Adirondack affairs. "I met John Apperson in 1931 when we were fighting the Closed Cabin Amendment," Schaefer said. "I was impressed with him right away—the enormous amount of facts he collected before he would speak out on an issue. He wasn't too enthusiastic about the Adirondack Mountain Club at first. When the club was formed back in the early twenties he and Warwick Carpenter had tried to get the members to make a strong stand on the purchase of the peaks before they were denuded, but the club's founders didn't want to offend George Pratt, who had recently left as Conservation Commissioner and promised to be a valuable supporter, just when they were getting started. Then, for a while my good friend Russell Carson, who became president of the club later on, didn't really see anything wrong with the Closed Cabin Amendment. Appie was upset about that. But pretty soon Russ Carson came around to our way of thinking and the Adirondack Mountain Club became a strong ally in our fight to beat the amendment."

By 1945 the Conservation Department had approved the construction of the dam and reservoir at Higley Mountain. Schaefer and Edmond H. Richard, another Adirondack conservation leader, approached Commissioner Perry B. Duryea, who had succeeded Lithgow Osborne, and asked him what steps they could take to stop the proposed violation of the Forest Preserve.

"You're too late," Duryea told them, pointing out that there was no legal appeal from the Conservation Department's order. "The fight's over."

Schaefer and Richard immediately got in touch with Frederick Kelsey, president of the Association for the Protection of the Adirondacks, who invited them to come to an association meeting in New York City and present their case.

"We went down to 55 Liberty Street one day and gave the board's trustees a half-hour talk with pictures," Schaefer said. "We asked for their help in turning this thing around. But the trustees said it was too late, there was no appeal possible under law. They admitted it was a terrible thing, but they wouldn't help us.

" 'We'd like to help you,' Kelsey said. 'But the association is not used to being involved in lost causes.'

"Ed and I got real mad—we were seething. I started out the door, then I turned around and said, 'Well, we're going to fight this thing. We may get beat, but if we do we'll go down with our flags flying!' "

In October 1945, the leaders of thirty conservation, sportsmen's, and civic groups gathered to organize the opposition to this invasion of the preserve. A representative of the Wilderness Society characterized the Higley reservoir (as well as the one at Panther Mountain, lurking in the background) as a force that "would destroy the largest deer winter-yardage in the Adirondacks, exterminate deer that seek winter food and shelter in the valley, and destroy some of the best natural brook trout waters." Even Conservation Commissioner Duryea was on hand to promise that his department would now work to stop the reservoirs. Early the next year the preservationists formed an organization called the Adirondack Moose River Committee, designed specifically to fight the reservoirs.

There began a spirited battle between the preservationists and the board of the Black River Regulating District. The former published pamphlets, took movies of the land to be flooded, and caused bills to be introduced in the Legislature that would have prevented any further construction of reservoirs within the Forest Preserve. The district, in turn, hired a public relations man, and the preservationists were at first turned back in the Legislature. The Moose River Committee, claiming a membership of one thousand local, state, and national organizations (the Association for the Protection of the Adirondacks at first was not among them), was able to maintain the pressure on the reservoir's proponents.

An object of this pressure was Governor Thomas E. Dewey. In

March 1947, Speaker of the House Oswald D. Heck, a friend and neighbor of Paul Schaefer's, released a statement to the press: "The Governor has advised me that he intends to direct by an appropriate agency a thorough study of all of the ramifications of the flood control and water power program and of its effect upon the forest preserve during the coming months. Pending completion of this study, the State will oppose any attempt to construct a dam in that area."

The study was undertaken by Hickman Powell, a special adviser to the governor. Powell eventually laid a report on Dewey's desk criticizing the Higley proposal, and Dewey at once announced his opposition to it, saying it would provide "little or no flood control" or adequate supply of water for the region. To make certain the project was dead, he filled two vacancies on the Black River Regulating District's board with men who agreed to rescind the Higley proposal.

The preservationists' joy was short-lived. Within a week or two they learned that the political shuffling behind the scenes had not been restricted to the appointment of two new board members. Apparently there had been several trade-offs, for the governor then announced his support for the larger dam and reservoir downstream at Panther Mountain. To the preservationists' further dismay, they discovered that one of their leaders, Ed Richard, had agreed with the district's board not to oppose Panther Dam if the Higley proposal was killed.

"We realized that Panther Dam was a larger project and so a greater threat to the preserve than Higley," Paul Schaefer recalled. "But Ed Richard felt he was bound by his commitment to the district. Finally we got Ira Gabrielson, who was one of the country's most influential conservationists, to come up from Washington and talk to Ed. Ira went to him and said, 'Ed, if you believe now that Panther Dam is bad, you've *got* to come out against it.' "

Richard returned to the fold, and the preservationists presented a united front, supported by most of the state's leading newspapers. *The New York Times*, the New York *Herald Tribune*, the Buffalo *Evening News*, the Albany *Knickerbocker Press*, and, of course, the Schenectady *Gazette* lined up against the dam. Schaefer published a twelve-page magazine, *The Forest Preserve*, crammed with facts and exhortation. In it he called upon Governor Dewey to recognize the desires of the "hundreds of thousands of people" who supported the Forest Preserve:

> A citizen may not have title to his home, but he does have an undivided deed to this Adirondack land of solitude and peace and tranquility. To him belong the sparkling lakes tucked away in the deep woods and the cold, pure rivers which thread like quicksilver through lush mountain valleys. His determination to preserve his personal treasure for posterity has been tempered by memories of campfires, and strengthened by pack-laden tramps along wilderness trails and by mountaintop views of his chosen land. To him the South Branch of the Moose is a River of Opportunity, for he has come to regard it as the front line of defense against the commercial invasion of *his* Forest Preserve.

The battle was renewed late in 1947 with increased bitterness, many of the preservationists believing that the defeat of Higley should have settled the matter, while the district's proponents felt betrayed by the refusal of Richard and other preservationists to live up to a "gentlemen's agreement." The Association for the Protection of the Adirondacks (former Conservation Commissioner Lithgow Osborne was now its president and a staunch opponent of Panther Dam) joined the anti-dam forces, as did the Adirondack League Club. One of the strongest voices was that of Herman Forster, president of the New York State Conservation Council, a coalition of sportsmen's clubs. Other important groups included the Adirondack Mountain Club, the Forest Preserve Association (John Apperson's organization), the Wilderness Society, the National Park Association, the Camp Fire Club of America, and state affiliates of the Garden Clubs of America and the Izaak Walton League. Once again, these and nearly a thousand other clubs and organizations united under the leadership of the Adirondack Moose River Committee, with Ed Richard as its president. The dam's proponents included local municipal governments, the Lewis County Chamber of Commerce, the Lewis County Farm Bureau, and the Carthage Paper Makers.

The preservationists brought the case to the State Supreme

Court, challenging the district's decision to proceed with construction. Among the most important grounds for the suit was that the taking of property for private purposes was in violation of the State Constitution; and the dam's function—to provide hydroelectric power—was a private purpose. In 1949 the preservationists' case was rejected.

"The lawyers were doing the best they could, getting injunctions and so forth," Schaefer said, "but finally they came to us and said, 'We can't do any more. You'll have to get us some more ammunition—maybe something in the Legislature—to give some credence to our injunctions.' 'How about a legislative committee?' I asked them. 'Great,' they said. So I went to my neighbor Oswald Heck, who helped us get Higley killed, and he got a Joint Legislative Committee on River Regulation appointed, with Assemblyman John L. Ostrander of Saratoga as its chairman."

Schaefer acted as an unofficial secretary of the committee, deciding when and where public hearings should be held, and scheduling them around the state. The meetings were attended in force by preservationists ("In New York City, we got a lot of important people from the federal government to add a little weight," Schaefer says), generating an enormous amount of publicity for their cause. "It was not that the proponents were denied the right to be heard," Roscoe Martin wrote, "but simply that the sportsmen's groups through sheer weight of numbers dominated the proceedings. As the hearings continued, the anti-reservoir forces picked up even more support. U.S. Senator Herbert H. Lehman and representatives of the U.S. Fish and Wildlife Service, Federation of New York State Bird Clubs, and New York State Federation of Women's Clubs at one time or another voiced their opposition before the committee."

Events were beginning to move in the preservationists' favor. State Senator Walter W. Stokes (a member of the Adirondack League Club) introduced a bill that said, "No reservoirs for the regulation of the flow of streams or for any other purpose except for municipal water supply shall hereafter be constructed in Hamilton or Herkimer counties on the south branch of the Moose river by any river regulation board." Governor Dewey ("under unusually strong pressure from sportsmen's groups and upstate Republican leaders," according to Martin) signed the Stokes Act into law in the spring of 1950; thereupon the Court of Appeals overturned the Appellate Division's decision supporting the district's right to build Panther Dam, but the district went ahead with plans to contest the Stokes Act. As Martin wrote:

> The situation that had evolved was unusual. A state agency against whose activities a legislative act had been directed was seeking to void the act. The state on its part maintained that the Board of the District had no right as a creature of the Legislature to challenge the constitutionality of a legislative act. An Assistant Attorney-General, E. L. Ryan, argued that the Court of Appeals decision in 1950 had effectively disposed of the Board's case.

The district eventually lost its fight against the Stokes Act, after carrying it all the way to the United States Supreme Court.

To settle the decision the preservationists reverted to the strategy of their spiritual forebears. Assemblyman Ostrander, who had served as chairman of the joint legislative committee, performed another valuable service by introducing an amendment to the Constitution that had the effect of perpetuating (and indeed going beyond) the Stokes Act. It prohibited building any river regulating reservoirs whatsoever on the Forest Preserve. Both houses quickly passed the amendment in 1952. When it was submitted for the second time in 1953, the opposition was stronger; a stand against the amendment was taken by the unfortunate Governor Dewey, who continually shifted from one side of the fence to the other during the Higley and Panther battles, and by the big statewide labor organizations (though their rank and file, many of whom were sportsmen, supported it). The preservationists, however, had the state's press on their side, and the funds to sway the issue. Before the amendment went to the general election that year, Paul Schaefer organized a dinner at the Edison Club in Schenectady for most of the state's political and conservation leaders; Tammany Democrats vied with upstate Republicans in praising the Ostrander Amendment. One of the most outspoken preservationists was Lithgow Osborne, who had been Conservation Commissioner when the department had approved Higley Dam years before but who now was president of the Association for the Protection of the Adirondacks. In November the People of New York voted to amend the Constitution (and undo the Burd Amendment of 1913); the margin in favor of the Ostrander Amendment was 943,200 to 593,696.

There was a last gasp left in the Black River Regulating District. In 1954 its supporters introduced a new amendment in the Legislature, specifically permitting a dam and reservoir to be built at Panther Mountain. Both sides advanced their arguments again. The district's supporters managed to push the amendment through successive sessions of the Legislature, but the people again turned back the dam builders. In November 1955, the vote against the dam was 1,622,196 to 613,927.

"It is almost unbelievable, but in 1945 before we started to fight we were faced with thirty-eight different reservoirs in the Forest Preserve," Paul Schaefer has said. "We didn't get any of them, and events proved we didn't have to destroy the forest to help the people. Watertown now gets St. Lawrence River power. And the floods have not hurt the farmers on the flats below Lyons Falls. The silt deposited by the Moose River there helps them grow the best damn hay in New York State."

CHAPTER XXIII

Judge Froessel's Amendment

"By excessive breeding and abuse of the land mankind has backed itself into an ecological trap," William Vogt wrote in *Road to Survival*, a pioneering study of the population problem, in 1948. "By a lopsided use of applied science it has been living on promissory notes. Now, all over the world, the notes are falling due."

Road to Survival described the problems and even the misery that a part of the world was already facing because of overpopulation. While not yet at bay, the Adirondack Mountains were caught up in the accelerated pace of events that marked the years after World War II, events that were to reach a dramatic climax in 1967.

The Blue Line surrounded 2.8 million acres when it was created in 1892. Through the years the park expanded to envelop more and more territory (the expansion in 1972, absorbing land in Clinton and Franklin counties, and Valcour Island in Lake Champlain, brought the total to just under 6 million acres), and in the intervening time the Adirondack Forest Preserve has grown from 681,000 to 2,425,000 acres. The Blue Line now measures about 120 miles on each side.

On the surface, the park's problems did not seem any more serious than before. The war and its aftermath had introduced pollution to certain areas, notably around the old MacIntyre Iron Mine at Tahawus. Early in World War II there were fears in Washington that the country would be cut off from vital supplies of titanium mined in India and other vulnerable parts of the world. When the mine at Tahawus was found to be rich in titanium its new owner, the National Lead Company, reopened it and with federal help in 1942 extended the railroad thirteen miles from North Creek over Forest Preserve land to the mine just south of the High Peaks.

This war-inspired violation of the preserve has had a unique history. The instrument of violation was the National Emergency Act, under which the federal government took a temporary easement on 220 acres of state land to bring out "strategic materials" from the mine. As if confirming the worst fears of Adirondack preservationists that a foot in the door is forever, or thereabouts, the war came to an end but not the federal intrusion. In 1946, with the National Emergency Act still in effect, the federal government, over the opposition of preservationists, extended the life of its easement until 1967. Before that date came around, in 1962 the government used its power of eminent domain and condemned the land for a one-hundred-year easement on which it pays the state a royalty of $63.50 a year—an obligation which it settled in advance with a check for $6,350.

The mining operation has sometimes polluted the upper Hudson River with its tailings and other effluents and completely destroyed Lake Sanford on the site; its once crystal water, really a widening of the Hudson at that point, was the subject of a well-known painting by Homer Dodge Martin in 1870. The mining company obliterated the lake by draining it and digging a new pit there, diverting the Hudson through a canal. The company went a step further in 1962. Planning to expand the open-pit mine, it simply moved the workers' village of Tahawus, one hundred families in all, with their houses and belongings, to the outskirts of Newcomb, thirteen miles away.

An event that caused a great deal more of an uproar (and led indirectly to the national park proposal and other deliberations during the 1960s) was "the Big Blowdown of 1950." As the prevailing winds in the Adirondacks blow from the west, the root systems grow defensively in such a way that the trees are braced against winds from that direction. But on Saturday, November 25, 1950, the forest was outflanked. Winds of one hundred miles an hour roared through the mountains from the east, toppling thousands of trees. The state estimated later that the blowdown was especially intense on 255,000 acres of the Forest Preserve (with its older trees) and on 168,000 acres of private land.

The Conservation Department asked the attorney general for an opinion on whether it could proceed with plans to remove the fallen timber. On the grounds that the debris was a fire hazard and therefore a threat to the Forest Preserve, the attorney general ruled that the cleanup was legal. The next step was to secure the approval of the Legislature so that bids could be accepted from private companies and the fallen timber sold. The department consulted with the Association for the Protection of the Adirondacks before writing the legislation, and came away with grudging and apprehensive approval. The department advertised for bids and the cleanup proceeded over the next several years. Hunters contended that deer, previously more numerous in the managed forest on private lands, increased on the Forest Preserve where it had been thinned by the storm.

Meanwhile, the Big Blowdown had evolved into what some observers called "the Big Blowup." Pieter W. Fosburgh, the editor of the Conservation Department's official publication, the *New York State Conservationist*, wrote an editorial for the October–November 1951 issue with the approval of Commissioner Perry B. Duryea. Fosburgh asked four questions in his editorial:

1. If our objective is the preservation of our forest, are forests best preserved by prohibiting cutting?
2. What is meant by "forever wild"? Does it suggest an abundance of birds and animals and if so, does our present management policy promote that objective?
3. How does the present management policy, as prescribed by our constitution, contribute to the economic needs of state and nation?
4. Under this policy, are we making the most of the potential recreational values of the Forest Preserve?

In succeeding issues of the publication, the questions were answered by various factions. Employees of the department got first crack at them, and their answers added up to four no's. Outsiders came nowhere near unanimity. Paul Schaefer, however, keynoted the preservationists' replies. He was particularly emphatic in his contention that the department did not have to seek a clarification of its responsibilities in providing trails and campsites for the public, believing that the department had all the legal authority it needed to proceed within reason on the basis of past approval from the various attorneys general. The doubts remained.

Doubts remained about the always sticky subject of roads, for instance. How does one conceive of a roadway network through the wilderness? Mozart is said to have crossed the Alps in a carriage without looking up from his musical scores. The modern motorist from Buffalo or Brooklyn often reveals no greater interest in the wonders of the Adirondacks and merely hopes for a bumpless ribbon of road on which he can pass from one point to another as quickly as possible. Highway departments concur, dutifully setting general road-building standards and improving roads so that cars can go faster through the wilderness. William K. Verner of the Adirondack Mountain Club has explored the consequences:

> As admirable as such standards may be for general purposes the question remains open as to whether the Adirondack Park, by virtue of its very designation, is or should be regarded as set aside for *general* purposes. If this were the case there would be no need to set it aside and provide it special designation. General standards have a way of systematically precluding the search for special standards such as might be properly employed in a park environment.

The question of special standards for roads within the Blue Line would have to await another time, but the solution to another nagging question seemed closer at hand. Historically, roads connecting communities separated by areas of the Forest Preserve could be approved only by a constitutional amendment, voted on by the people of the state. This, of course, was and is in keeping with the spirit of the Constitution. But referenda were also required to approve the taking of a sliver of land or the cutting of trees to rebuild or relocate even a small segment of an existing road. The Forever Wild clause was burdened with a string of qualifying phrases that, as someone has said, made the New York State Constitution read like a highway gazetteer.

Thus, in 1957 the voters approved an amendment setting aside a "road bank" of 400 acres of the Forest Preserve from which small pieces of land can be drawn for use in the rebuilding or relocating (not exceeding a mile in any one case) of existing state highways. If preservationists believed that roadway squabbles would go away for a while, they were in for an unpleasant surprise. A plan was introduced in that year to build a 175-mile superhighway between Albany and the Canadian border. This project, eventually called the Northway and linking Albany with Montreal, was planned to take several hundred acres in the eastern section of the Forest Preserve.

The Northway's proponents seized the initiative and never lost it. They contended that the project was in the public interest, and such an argument proved difficult to contest in the golden age of superhighway building. Its opponents answered logically enough that all sorts of new highways, power lines, ski developments, and what not could be justified in the Forest Preserve on the grounds of "the public interest"; in that case, the preserve would be whittled away in no time at all. The opposing sides eventually arrived at certain compromises on the Northway's route and the voters approved the taking of 300 acres for the project in 1959.

During all these years the State Legislature was busily studying the Adirondack Forest Preserve through its Joint Legislative Committee on Natural Resources. Beginning in 1953, this committee looked into such matters as the Conservation Department's complaint that it did not have the authority to continue building the campgrounds and tent sites needed to accommodate the increasing number of visitors to the park. The Legislature, in effect, was taking notice of "Operation Blowup." The committee was also responsible for introducing the "road bank" amendment and the several acquisitions to the park in the 1950s and 1960s. Perhaps most important, it began to formulate a concept of zoning the Forest Preserve that was to receive a different expression, as we shall see, by the Temporary Study Commission and the State Land Master Plan of the 1970s.

This formulation, too, was an expression of the belief that the precincts of Forever Wild could no longer withstand the population and technological pressures of postwar America. The Joint Legislative Committee drew up a plan to set aside eleven wilderness areas of at least ten thousand acres each in the Forest Preserve, but it was not quite clear what was in store for the rest of the preserve, much to the preservationists' concern. By 1966 the committee's various factions had come up with a number of recommendations, including a proposal for the development of recreational facilities on the preserve, so liberal that they would have permitted the building of restaurants at the end of wilderness trails.

Assemblyman (later Senator) R. Watson Pomeroy, with a clearer head, helped to compose a minority report (the committee was actually split evenly) that defined the chief uses of the Forest Preserve as watershed protection and recreation that was consistent with the Constitution. Pomeroy also believed that the cutting of timber would destroy the wilderness atmosphere in the Forest Preserve.

The dispute in the two decades since the war, reviewed and put in the record by the Joint Legislative Committee, led directly to the major dramas of 1967. All sides had been preparing a long time for the first of these—the Constitutional Convention.

The New York State Constitutional Convention of 1967 put on display the rituals and tactics by which certain philosophical concepts are engraved in the law of our democratic society. The convention began in ritual, convening in the Assembly chambers of the state capitol at Albany on April 4, 1967. Earl Warren, Chief Justice of the United States Supreme Court, addressed the delegates from a rostrum thickly banked with flowers.

The Democratic party controlled the convention, an advantage symbolized by the election of the Assembly majority leader, Anthony J. Travia, as its president. A major issue of the time was to simplify the Constitution, a potentially dangerous movement as it might apply to the complexities of Article XIV. The state conservation organizations, although not well represented among the convention delegates, were well orchestrated for the tactical infighting that was to follow. Such groups as the Association for the Protection of the Adirondacks, the Adirondack Mountain Club, the Sierra Club, and the Izaak Walton League exerted their own individual brands of persuasion upon the delegates and press. Their strength was coordinated through an organization called the Constitutional Council for the Forest Preserve. The council's chairman, David L. Newhouse, was a prominent preservationist from Schenectady.

Preservationists of whatever political stripe were united in their aim, which was to keep hands off the Forever Wild clause. That its present vagueness left the Conservation Department and other agencies unclear about certain of their responsibilities no one could logically deny. But, for the preservationists, this was not a disadvantage. The very vagueness was almost a prohibition in itself. Forever Wild, in an imperfect world, survived best when its edges were blurred; it tended to crumble when subjected to the flinty points of precise legalistic definitions and qualifications. As it stands now, the clause is defined chiefly by the sensibilities of the preservationists. Bureaucrats may maneuver within the confines of those sensibilities, which are flexible and may be reasoned with, but once they get carried away with their own schemes the preservationists can drag them into court. There is safety in that status quo.

"Status quo" was the position adopted by the Democrats at the convention in regard to the Forest Preserve. As in most political bodies, direction was determined by a small group of men and women who knew what they wanted. Tactics dictated that the preservationists control the thinking in the Committee on Natural Resources and Agriculture. Outwardly, the committee seemed to be in nobody's pocket. Its staunchest defender of the Forest Preserve was Watson Pomeroy, the Republican state senator. Most of the Democrats appointed to the committee were from New York City. Aside from Arthur Levitt, Jr. (who, like his State Comptroller father, was a member of the Adirondack Mountain Club), none of them were very much interested in the Forest Preserve and the majority were probably disappointed to find themselves appointed to a committee so remote from their own concerns. Even most members of the committee's staff, who were appointed by their respective parties on the basis of patronage, knew little about conservation issues. An important exception was David Sive, a graduate of Columbia University Law School, who was executive secretary of the Democratic staff. Sive had been active in a number of conservation struggles for the Sierra Club and other environmental groups, and for some time it had been his business to make their views known to the state's Democratic leaders.

The first important break came when Sive was asked to write the press release setting forth convention president Travia's position on the Forest Preserve. Sive composed a strong statement, and Travia, whose home was Brooklyn, recognized it as in the tradition of the downstate protective stance toward the preserve. When the news of Travia's position became public on June 12, most of the other Democratic delegates fell into line. This was particularly important on the Natural Resources Committee, where an early draft of a Forever Wild clause for the new Constitution tended to embrace too many points of view.

Pomeroy was not having as much success bringing his fellow Republicans around to the strict preservation of Forever Wild, not surprising in view of upstate's economic development interests. But he, Sive, and Levitt worked to educate the other committee members, and when public hearings opened at City Hall in May, Paul Schaefer, Herman Forster, and the other preservationists delivered vigorous statements on the virtues of Forever Wild that furthered their education. The old-time exploiters were for the most part absent.

"We knew that the biggest threat at the convention would come not from the exploiters but from the constitutional reformers," Sive said afterward. "They wanted to simplify the Constitution. For instance, Jack B. Weinstein, who was a great constitutional lawyer [and later judge of the U.S. District Court in New York], thought that Article XIV had no real place in the Constitution. In 1966 the Democratic state platform had been written by William Vanden Heuvel, who was close to Bobby Kennedy and who also believed the Constitution should be simplified—those people thought the public should not have to vote on extending a road and such things, that most state constitutions were much too complicated—and so the Democratic platform that year was much weaker on the Forest Preserve than the Republicans'. This kind of approach had us worried at the convention."

But the Democrats lined up behind Travia's strong position and the status quo version of the Forest Preserve article that emerged from the Natural Resources Committee. The preservationists did not expect any serious problems. They held firm in the face of the usual amendments from the floor, intended to open portions of the preserve to cutting or otherwise weaken the article. "When someone wants to destroy the preserve," Sive noted wryly, "he doesn't set out to *repeal* the clause, but just to *amend* it." Sive and several other Democratic staff members wrote strong replies to those proposed amendments for the Democratic committee members—and even for one of the Republican members. Because most of them knew little about the Forest Preserve, these delegates tended to stick to the speeches prepared for them and there were very few extemporaneous remarks.

It was during the final debate that the unexpected occurred. Charles W. Froessel, a retired associate judge of the Court of Appeals and a delegate to the convention, proposed that the public campsites on the Forest Preserve be granted legality under the Constitution.

"It so happens that the Constitution does not authorize that use unless you stretch it to the breaking point," Froessel told the convention. "They have used devious means in order to justify what they have done. All I want to do is to legalize that practice."

The preservationists' forces were afraid that Froessel's amendment would open the way to the "closed cabins" and other recreational frills they had fought for years; explicit phrasing was their enemy. Watson Pomeroy spoke against the amendment. But one of the most dramatic events of the convention took place when Dollie L. Robinson, a delegate from Brooklyn, rose to defend the preserve against amendments of that sort. A graduate of New York Law School who had gone on to work with various labor unions, she had represented the U.S. Department of Labor at the U.S. Trade Fair in Nairobi, Kenya, in 1965. The delegate immediately caught the convention's attention:

> I speak for myself and some who have not yet heard a loon, or seen the morning mist rise from Spruce Lake, or intimately known the forest that has escaped the advance of highways, smog and overpowering noise. Perhaps some of us in many corners of this state and of many different heritages are still overwhelmed by the strug-

gle to leave some rural or urban ghetto, and we have not yet had the time to feel as personally and as deeply as those of you who have picked the blueberries atop Mount Colden, which has so enriched your lives.

For those people who because of accidents of history have not yet achieved the measure of security which they perhaps need before they can know the rarest beauties of the Forest Preserve, for them especially and their children, I urge you to protect it, for I am confident that it will not be long—and other determinations of this convention hopefully may speed the day—when we succeed in applying a small fraction of the genius we apply to flying to the moon to so ordering our economy and body politic that everyone will share some part of our affluence. When that day does come, and those not yet so fortunate are able to pick those blueberries, I beseech you to please, please see that they are not behind a fence, across a thronged road or leased out. I urge you to defeat the amendment of Judge Froessel. Thank you.

Dollie Robinson sat down to tumultuous applause and the banging of President Travia's gavel. She had been the instrument for extending the "future generations" argument for a viable Forest Preserve to previously untouched ethnic groups; though it was not common knowledge even among preservationists that her speech, like that of most of the other Democratic delegates pleading for the Forever Wild clause, had been written by David Sive.

But a more personal sentiment swayed the issue. The preservationists had been caught off guard. Judge Froessel was well liked by many Democratic party members and they were reluctant to vote against him. President Travia almost slipped out of the predicament by declaring Froessel's amendment defeated on a show of hands, but Froessel persisted and asked for a slow roll call. The amendment passed by a vote of 106–60.

Because Froessel had proposed his amendment from the floor and it was loosely worded, the preservationists feared that it would provide the breach in the Constitution that they had fought so successfully against since 1894. Froessel waffled a bit on whether the building of campsites could go on indefinitely. William Vanden Heuvel, who was the chairman of Style and Arrangement, promised that his committee would tidy up the amendment's wording.

On that basis the preservationists decided they could live with it. It was added to the proposed Constitution and stipulated as an exception to the Forever Wild provision: "the use of such lands for public campsites of the kind presently constructed and maintained in areas similar to those in which they are presently located."

As the convention drew to a close, the defenders of Forever Wild believed they had done their job well. The annual report of the Association for the Protection of the Adirondacks was to say: "There was agreement among most conservationists that as a protection for the Forest Preserve there was little to choose between the existing and the proposed conservation article." A constitutional lawyer might not agree. Ralph D. Semerad, professor of law at the Albany Law School, was among those who believed that Vanden Heuvel had not carried out his pledge to sanitize the amendment.

"When the finished product is read, it is obvious that the worst fears of the objecting delegates were realized," Semerad wrote. "It very obviously lends itself to the interpretation that future campsite building is permitted at the option of the Conservation Department. The only safeguards are the restrictions as to the character and location of such sites."

Even more fearsome for the preservationists was the prospect of losing ambiguity, and thus leverage. In any event the voters of the state had the last word. The most controversial sections of the new Constitution submitted to them in November dealt with public education, particularly the sticky issue of state aid to parochial schools, and the voters rejected the entire package by a wide margin. The dramatic statements of Judge Froessel and Dollie Robinson were, so to speak, written in shifting sand.

CHAPTER XXIV

A Modest Proposal

On Sunday, July 30, 1967, a story appeared on the front page of *The New York Times* under the headline: "Huge U.S. Park Urged in Adirondacks." The article described a proposal put forth by Laurance S. Rockefeller, the chairman of the State Council of Parks, and his associates to create an Adirondack Mountains National Park in the heart of New York State's Adirondack Park. The suggested national park, to be made up of 1,120,000 acres of state land and 600,000 acres of adjoining private land, which would be bought by the federal government over the next fifteen years, would become the third largest in the United States. The object of this bold conception was "the preservation and public enjoyment of an outstanding scenic and unique area."

Rockefeller appended a warning: "Without such action these values risk the danger of being seriously impaired or destroyed."

The response to the national park proposal within the state was immediate and emphatic. Men and women who had been at sword's point over the future of the state park came together in this moment to attack the idea of a federal take-over. The proposal, in a sense, never got off the ground, but it exerted a lasting influence on the entire region of upstate New York. It forced all sides to examine the reality of conditions in the Adirondacks in this last third of the twentieth century—the pressures of development, the lack of effective restrictions on potential runaway development on the private land within the park, even the subtle threats to the supposedly invincible status of the park's state lands as Forever Wild. Through all the ensuing uproar the similarity of the region's problems to those of other parts of the country became as plain as the uniqueness of the original park itself.

The proposal had its curious aspects. It had been prepared in some haste and secrecy. Laurance Rockefeller, a brother of then New York governor Nelson Rockefeller, was known to be interested in various conservation projects, including national parks, for a long time. Some years before, he had bought 5,000 acres on St. John Island and donated the land to the federal government for the Virgin Islands National Park. His father, John D. Rockefeller, Jr., had given 35,000 acres in Jackson Hole, Wyoming, to add to Grand Teton National Park. Yet, partial to the idea that parks ought to be open to mass recreation facilities, Laurance himself was never quite comfortable with the dedication of a vast area to the principle of Forever Wild.

Three other men helped Rockefeller prepare his proposal for a national park in the Adirondacks. One was Conrad L. Wirth, who had been the director of the National Park Service from 1951 until 1964 and later a consultant to the New York State Council of Parks. The others were Ben H. Thompson, an official of the council who was formerly with the National Park Service, and Roger C. Thompson, the research director of the New York State Senate Finance Committee, a forester, and, as a historian of the Forest Preserve, a critic of some aspects of the Forever Wild clause. Rockefeller's predecessor at the Council of Parks, which was an agency that made policy on planning, administration, and recreation in the state parks, had been Robert Moses. Having hoped to create "a gigantic playground" in the Adirondacks, Moses chafed under the constitutional provision that kept him out of the park. A few preservationists professed to see a lingering desire within the council for some kind of "management" within the Adirondacks.

The national park idea apparently originated with Laurance Rockefeller. He and Wirth were talking generally about problems in the Adirondacks one day while they were driving around Washington, D.C. When they stopped in a parking lot, Rockefeller suddenly turned to Wirth and asked, "Listen, what would you think about a national park in the Adirondacks?" The former Park Service director was, of course, very much interested.

Rockefeller and his associates went right to work drawing up a plan. With private funds readily available, they surveyed the mountains by helicopter and performed some elementary research. What emerged was a proposal to transfer about 1,120,000 acres of state land to the federal government. The selected land was in the center of the present state park, including the High Peak area, with the large lakes to the west and some smaller lakes and ponds to the south. The more densely populated settlements in this region—Saranac Lake, Lake Placid, Indian Lake, Fourth Lake–Inlet, and Blue Mountain Lake*—would remain as "inholdings" within the national park. The federal government would then buy an additional 600,000 acres of private land over a period of years to put together a national park with a total of 1,720,000 acres. Some private holdings would remain in the area, as they do now within such federal parklands as Grand Teton National Park and Fire Island National Seashore, though none would be permitted to exceed three acres.

It was not clear just how the heart of the Adirondack Park was to be spirited from the protective wall erected around it by the New York State Constitution. Rockefeller's proposal had no official sanction whatsoever. Although the plan bore the state seal, it was not a state document; the decorative seal was dropped in a later printing. (In fact, it carried the Rockefeller Plaza address of Laurance Rockefeller.) Nor had it been drawn up at the request of any government agency such as the National Park Service or the New York Conservation Department.

Probably the most serious previous suggestion for a national park in the Adirondacks had been made as far back as June 1885, when William Hosea Ballou suggested it in an article published in *American Naturalist*. Writing in a period when public opinion was beginning to incline toward a state park in the region, Ballou saw no hope from that direction for the preservation of the mountains and forests.

"Will anyone say that the Government of the United States

* The hamlet area of Long Lake was inadvertently left off Rockefeller's map.

ought not to be charged with the care of the portions of these aged relics which a great State has given over to weeds and bandits?" Ballou asked.

The suggestion was not taken up then, any more than it was in 1967. For a great variety of reasons, nearly everybody who had an interest in the Adirondacks was against the idea of turning the heart of the park over to the federal government. People who detect a sinister motive behind any extension of the federal power might naturally be expected to put their backs up at such a suggestion. A more favorable reception, however, might have been expected on the part of the region's merchants and civic boosters. There was the promise implicit in the proposal of added tourism. As an elderly farmer testified in favor of a national park in another part of the country: "One hundred tourists equal the income from one acre of potatoes, and are a damn sight easier pickin'."

But the prospect of a great federal park in the Adirondacks did not have the allure it might have had elsewhere. The park allegedly was already bringing in nine million tourists a year, while many local people were hoping for diversity of industry. "Our North Country has long felt the adverse economic effect of an already too restrictive policy on the use of our forest lands," a local congressman was quoted in an editorial in the Tupper Lake *Free Press* (this newspaper published the editorial under the heading "Register Your Protest Against the National Park"). Lumbermen objected because the proposal suggested condemning some of the most densely forested private land for inclusion in the park. Sportsmen realized that hunters were usually banned from the other national parks. The owners of the extensive estates or hunting preserves were opposed, too, because of Rockefeller's provision that individual private holdings within the designated area be limited to three acres. One of the landowners opposed to the proposal was Harold K. Hochschild, whose estate, Eagle Nest (Ned Buntline's old stamping ground at Blue Mountain Lake), would have been wiped out in the take-over. The nearby Adirondack Museum, of which Hochschild was the leading founder and supporter, promptly announced that "uncertainties" arising out of the national park proposal were forcing it to postpone the construction of a large building designed to hold its collection of old vehicles. The *Adirondack Daily Enterprise* criticized the museum, calling its statement "a kind of threat." Hochschild replied that the museum was only awaiting "some knowledge of the regulations that may affect us and the conditions under which we could continue to operate."*

Hochschild's uncertainty was reflected throughout the Adirondacks. On one side were those who felt they would rather continue to coexist with the known evil of the state's Forever Wild clause than try their luck with the unknown administration of the National Park Service. Probably the most enthusiastic estimate of the proposal came from Bill Roden, a sportsman and opponent of Forever Wild, who noted that both the Association for the Protection of the Adirondacks and *The New York Times* had come out against a national park. He wrote:

> When I read the positions of these two representatives of the Forever Wild Philosophy, I was even more determined not to make a hasty decision, for if these two dedicated Forever Wild organizations oppose the proposal, there must be something good about the program as far as we in the Adirondacks are concerned.

The preservationists' lack of enthusiasm for Rockefeller's proposal was certainly the chief reason it was not seriously considered in the end. Outwardly, the Association for the Protection of the Adirondacks, the Adirondack Mountain Club (ADK), and other organizations may have taken a stance of open-mindedness on the issue. The ADK's Conservation Committee noted:

> It is the responsibility of all our citizens to determine whether the losses to the State would be offset by gains to the Nation. ADK conservation policy has traditionally supported administration of the preserve under the sole jurisdiction of the New York State Conservation Department. It is difficult to abandon provincial interests and to be objective when we are so close to the Adirondacks, but that is our task at this time.

But the committee's heart really wasn't in it. The Forever Wilders' allegiance, in fact, was not in the deepest sense to the

* It is interesting to note that Hochschild and the probable editorialist, James I. Loeb, later served together on the Temporary Study Commission.

park's administration, federal or state, but to the State Constitution. That document was the source of their power over the administrators. In his *A Wilderness Bill of Rights*, Justice William O. Douglas, a modern patron saint of the boondocks lobby, had written that "the surest security [for wilderness] is by constitutional amendment, as was done in New York respecting the Adirondacks." There was no such guarantee under federal ownership.

To many of the preservationists, the National Park Service seemed a frail fortress. All the great American parks were designed to immerse human beings in the natural landscape. But what is "natural"? Congress has given little direction to the administrators of the national parks, and the Supreme Court even less. The Adirondack Park, however, wrapped in the Forever Wild clause, had become the model for pure wilderness sentiment as made explicit by Aldo Leopold and Bob Marshall. Their disciples hadn't missed the point that some national park administrators changed their policies in response to pressures from various political and economic forces in and out of government. Administrative policy, like foreign policy, was often altered to meet the day-to-day crisis atmosphere familiar to bureaucrats. Policy in the administration of the Adirondack Park was restricted by a more durable concern. What Joseph L. Sax, the environmental lawyer and wilderness enthusiast, has said of the United States Constitution may be aptly applied to that of the state:

"The Constitution, in our legal system, builds a perspective of time into social decision making, which by creating a link with the values that dominated our past acts as a restraining force on the instincts of the moment."

Stephen Mather, in his early attempts to gain support for the national parks, once suggested that people might be lured to them by building tennis courts, golf courses, and swimming pools within their boundaries. Would he have permitted a bobsled run in the Adirondack Park? Certainly the national park administrators have never hesitated to cut trees, lay down roads, and open luxurious hotels when it meant providing easier access for visitors or opening vistas for them when they had arrived. Often the bulk of the tourist facilities and administrative buildings are erected in a national park's most scenic area, attracting large crowds and intruding on the splendor that is the park's *raison d'être*. Allan K. Fitzsimmons, a geographer writing in *Science*, has pointed out the result:

"The Lake-Fishing Bridge area, Grand Canyon Village and the Yosemite Valley complex each have a summer resident employee community with a population in excess of 1,000; and each can provide lodgings for at least 2,500 tourists, not including campers. They each contain hundreds of structures."

Adirondack preservationists, including John Apperson and Paul Schaefer, repeatedly turned back proposed "Closed Cabin" Amendments to the State Constitution that would have permitted tourist cabins and other "enclosed buildings of use to the public for healthful recreation." These skirmishes continued even after World War II.

Yosemite Valley is an obvious, if extreme, example of the complexities of park management. There the management philosophy, shared by Frederick Law Olmsted, was spoken (in a sentence of extraordinary length) by California's state engineer, W. H. Hall, in 1882:

> If in the judgment of men who have studied such things, for their love of the beautiful and the appropriate, who have striven from professional distinction, in the improvement of the great parks of the principal eastern cities, large trees can be cut away with advantage, where it has cost so much of time, money, and skill to raise them, certainly you should be safe from censure if, in opening out the views, caring for the full development of the timber, and clearing up the more unsightly parts of the valley lands of the Yosemite, you apply the axe right freely.

Ever since, Yosemite Valley has been managed both for the convenience of its visitors and for the quality of its views. Kentucky bluegrass was planted to increase the attractiveness of the meadows. Trees have been removed to keep those meadows from being overgrown, a practice begun by the Indians before the white man's arrival. Where roads and ditches have drained the land, robbing the soil of its moisture and driving out some native perennials, weedy annuals have crept in.

"There is, of course, an alternative to management of the vegetation, and that is the acceptance of the landscape which will develop naturally," wrote Robert P. Gibbens and Harold F. Heady, two scientists who studied modern man's influence on the valley's vegetation. "This alternative has been consistently rejected in the past, and, if aesthetic criteria are used, continued rejection is likely in the future."

The pressure to alter the landscapes of our national parks increased enormously after World War II. New highways, faster cars, and the growth of leisure brought more millions to the parks. These visitors threatened to "love the parks to death." Adirondack preservationists were aware that a great stimulus to the added pressure on the national parks was Conrad Wirth. In 1941, there had been 21 million visitors to national parks and monuments, a figure which had swelled to 50 million in 1955. As the director of the National Park Service, Wirth put into operation in 1956 a program called "Mission 66," which was intended to improve park facilities by 1966. Wirth expected the number of visitors to reach 80 million by that year. Instead, there were 137 million.

Because of the ease with which the modern traveler was able to pay a visit to the national parks, a great many of them did not see the landscape "in an absorbed and contemplative way," as Olmsted had hoped. They were a new breed. Bryan Harry, the chief naturalist at Yosemite, commented on some of those visitors. "People used to come for the beauty and serenity," Harry said. "Those who come now don't mind the crowds. In fact, they like them. They are sightseers, and they come for the action."

A distinction ought to be made here between aesthetic preservation, with its emphasis on "scenery" and the public's access to it, and wilderness preservation, with its emphasis on "succession," or the natural processes of an ecosystem, which may or may not conform to the popular notion of beauty. In the latter case, human activity is assigned a priority lower than that of wild plants and animals and the complex web of their relationships. Bob Marshall, in advocating wilderness areas of great size, had both varieties in mind: the first, to enhance one's sense of vastness; the second, to provide for a wide range of stages to take place within the natural community. Those people whose wilderness principles fall short of purity may consider one sort of preservation very much more important than the other.

Although the Adirondack preservationists might not have wanted to see Olmsted's management techniques practiced in the Forest Preserve, they shared his belief that a park should emphasize the works of nature rather than those of man. They also believed (for the most part) with Olmsted that even in a democracy the taste makers can lead the public into accepting a "quality" experience. Quality is a necessity for the minority, and eventually will be accepted just as readily as the tawdry by the majority.

Rockefeller's national park proposal was in essence a reflection of the widening acceptance by Americans that there was relevance in the doctrine of wilderness. Leopold and Marshall had become establishment philosophers. But what Rockefeller and his associates were also saying in this proposal was that wilderness was of necessity severely limited in the modern world. Implicit here was the belief that the Adirondack Park's great size and the complex patterns and nature of the private holdings within the Blue Line gave Forever Wild an uncertain future. Better to carve out the glorious, remote, and still defensible core and preserve it as a wilderness in a national park, and let the beleaguered perimeter fend for itself among the conflicting demands as a state park.

Wilderness as an absolute became a political subject during those years. Its manifestations came in several varieties. Probably the best known non-federal Forever Wild enclave in the United States outside of the Adirondacks was Maine's Baxter State Park. From 1931 to 1962 Governor Percival P. Baxter had given 200,000 acres of wild forest lands and lakes around Mount Katahdin to the people of Maine with the stipulation that it remain "forever wild." Speaking of his gift late in life, Baxter made the prophetic remark:

"While I am living I fear no encroachments on the park, but as time passes and new men appear on the scene, there may be a tendency to overlook these restrictions and thus break the spirit of these gifts."

Indeed, Baxter himself fudged a little before he died, and seemed to acquiesce in granting the state some management leeway in the event of such acts of nature as blowdowns, fire, floods, and insect infestations. The result has been a continuing battle between the state's Baxter Park Authority, attempting to exercise this authority, on the one hand and preservationists on the other, asserting that the Authority often oversteps its mandate. For instance, the preservationists strenuously object to the use of pesticides for insect control, and the salvage and marketing of blown-down timber; they contend that forest management has changed since Baxter's day and that such practices, carried out in a Forever Wild area that is not managed for timber production, are cosmetic and therefore contrary to Baxter's wishes.

Much of the passion of both the preservationists and the developers of natural resources had been focused during the early 1960s on the passage of a National Wilderness Bill. Its object was expressed by perhaps its most tireless adherent in Washington, Howard Zahniser of the Wilderness Society, who owned a camp in the Adirondacks and was certainly influenced by Article XIV of the State Constitution. Zahniser wrote that the bill was intended "to secure the preservation of some areas [in national parks, national forests, and national wildlife refuges] that are so managed as to be left unmanaged—areas that are undeveloped by man's mechanical tools and in every way unmodified by his civilization."

The Wilderness Bill, introduced in Congress in 1956, was fought over bitterly for eight years. Many national conservation organizations enthusiastically supported the bill, under which Congress would designate certain areas on federal lands to be preserved in their natural state. It was opposed not only by ranchers, lumbermen, and miners, but also by many government bureaucrats, especially in the U.S. Forest Service, who believed it violated the "multiple-use" doctrine on national forests. It was also opposed at first by Conrad Wirth, speaking on behalf of the National Park Service. The rallying cry of the bill's opponents was that the preservationists were engaged in "locking up" valuable and indispensable natural resources. They resented the idea of treating land as a luxury rather than as a resource.

The Wilderness Bill was passed by Congress and signed by President Lyndon B. Johnson on September 3, 1964. Millions of acres of government lands in national parks and elsewhere became eligible for complete protection. The act itself contains a definition of wilderness composed by Howard Zahniser in the spirit of John Muir, Aldo Leopold, and Bob Marshall:

"Wilderness . . . , in contrast with those areas where man and his own works dominate the landscape, is hereby recognized as an area where the earth and its community of life are untrammeled by man, where man himself is a visitor who does not remain."

Preservationists in the Adirondacks, as elsewhere, were delighted by the Wilderness Act. Yet the wilderness designation of an area, though removed from administrative whim, was to be made by Congress, and Congress could also take it away. It was the sense of New York's preservationists that they would prefer to have the fate of Forever Wild depend not on either an administrator or a legislator but on the "people" themselves. "This is an odd bit of populism," one of their number, William K. Verner, admits. "Most of us have always been willing to go along with the old public–private land mix in the park."

As the national park proposal slid toward oblivion late in 1967, Laurance Rockefeller flew to Warrensburg to give a talk to the Adirondack Mountain Club. "The weather was bad and the plane was late," recalled Henry L. Diamond, later a New York Conservation Commissioner, who accompanied Rockefeller. "The bar had been open for some time, and when we came in there was an audible growl."

Rockefeller backed off a bit from the proposal during his talk. He implied that its true purpose was to stir some discussion of the park's problems, that it was, in essence, a "trial balloon." Shortly afterward the Conservation Department issued an unfavorable report on the plan and, officially, it was dead.

But in Albany, Governor Nelson Rockefeller recognized both the park's problems and the part his brother's proposal had played in arousing statewide interest in them. He announced that he would appoint a "distinguished group of New Yorkers" to make a study of the Adirondacks.

CHAPTER XXV

Toward a Single Park

The national park proposal's enduring legacy was that it let outsiders in on the secret that the Adirondack Park is largely a private enterprise. Just over 60 percent of the land is owned by individuals or corporations.

Since its creation in 1892, the park had no basis in fact. The Blue Line was really an ecological rather than a political boundary, encircling the forests of a particular mountainous region at the point where they gradually faded into the neighboring flatlands. Where the forests recovered, the Blue Line often expanded through the years to encompass them. The private lands within the park could be lumbered, developed, or left in their natural state, according to their owners' whims.

Rockefeller's proposal suggested that the composite park, private and public, could no longer tolerate a policy of drifting and waiting. Even where the forest remained supposedly inviolable the increasing number of visitors made the term "wilderness" almost a mockery; while 12,000 people had hiked the remote High Peak region in 1953, their number was approaching 70,000 in 1967, subjecting the trails to excessive wear and erosion. Hamilton County in the heart of the Adirondacks remained so far out of the mainstream of American life that it did not have a single traffic light, yet the estimated nine million seasonal visitors to the park were already causing immense changes in many of its more accessible sections.

The Constitution, despite the cracks and strains, gives a large measure of protection to the public land, but until recently there was no such protection for the private land. Motels, cheap eateries, and nightclubs blossomed in that part of the wilderness not covered by the Forever Wild clause. In the town of Lake Placid (built on the shore of Mirror Lake, by the way) the shops and motels intruded between the road and the lake, so that the pedestrian catches only glimpses of the water and boaters see mostly the row of shops and motels.

Gaudy attractions called "theme parks" sprang up beside the roads in parts of the park during the 1950s. (A former cartoonist for Walt Disney named Arto Monaco gave up Hollywood to return to his hometown of Upper Jay and designed what was apparently the first theme park in the United States—Santa's Workshop at North Pole, New York, antedating Disneyland itself.) "When you get right down to it," the operator of one of these theme parks asked rhetorically in defense of his business, "just what is there for the average tourist to *do* in an area which has only scenery?" And yet the flood of tourist dollars was not bringing year-round prosperity to the park's 108,000 residents. Jobs were mostly seasonal, and the unemployment checks began arriving as soon as the tourists left for home.

Like most mountain regions, the Adirondacks have built-in depressive characteristics for the people who live and make their living there. As early as 1961 the federal government had recognized this condition, and declared Essex County (in which two of the region's tourist centers, Lake Placid and parts of Saranac Lake, lie) a depressed area. For all its glories, the central portion of the park also reflects this condition in that there is no true "rural" buffer zone between wilderness and the most blatant and dreariest aspects of civilization. There are few tranquil scenes of mankind's compatible place in the environment—well-kept farms, cows grazing in green pastures, row on row of luxuriant vegetables; one has to go to the fringes of the park, as to the rich soils of the Champlain Valley, for such sights. For the park's core, the physical choices too often seem to be between the pristine and the mucked up.

Population, of course, is scarce. There are 19.1 persons per square mile on the private land, or 11.3 if one takes the park as a whole. When Rockefeller's proposal was made public, out-migration had been a fact for most regions of the park in recent decades, and its population had not risen above the level of the 1880s. Education and income were low compared to the rest of the state. While the nation as a whole was living through boom times, unemployment was high in the Adirondacks, reaching 12.7 percent in Hamilton County in 1968.

Tourism, paper manufacturing, mining, and government agencies supplied a large part of the employment. The opportunities in government service were indeed more a reflection of local inefficiency than the hand of a distant Big Brother at work. In his book *The Sticks*, Burton Bernstein points out that most towns in Essex County have a hierarchy of officials, usually including a supervisor, a town clerk, two town justices of the peace, two councilmen, three assessors, a collector, a superintendent of highways, and a welfare officer.

"In the case of North Hudson, the paid, elected officers number eleven, or five percent of the town's total population of 220," Bernstein wrote. "In such inefficient circumstances, it is not surprising that the government turns out to be the biggest employer in the entire county."

Religion in the Adirondacks is to a greater extent than in most other rural areas Roman Catholic, imported by the French-Canadians who arrived as lumberjacks and the Irish who came to mine the iron and other minerals. In 1977 a priest, relatively new to the area, created a furor of agreement and dissent by writing a column about this "depressed area" for the *Adirondack Daily Enterprise*. Father Carmen Guiliano declared:

> The Adirondacks is a depressed area because the people are depressed and depressing. They don't seem to understand what the beauty of the Adirondacks is all about, except that somehow it can be a source of revenue, money. They talk about growth and even economic prosperity, but the only activities they seem real adept at is manipulating the Social Service Department and-or the Unemployment Insurance Fund. They are plagued with problems such as alcoholism and marital dissension. . . . They don't seem to know how to respond to the God given gift of being responsible for one's own life.

A number of people wrote in reply, some in high dudgeon, to complain that Father Guiliano had tarred the people with a broad brush, that he hadn't been around long enough to notice the many hard-working and ingenious men and women who made a living for themselves in that harsh land and who often came together to produce impressive community projects and buildings out of what sometimes seemed thin air. But Father Guiliano, like the Reverend Lundy a century before, had put on paper what many visitors to a poor area often sense, fairly or not. Hemmed in by more than two million acres of "mustn't touch," many Adirondack natives are burdened with the age-old colonists' feeling of being put upon. A typical instance of this was the complaint of some resort owners who came to the preservationists' belief (through convergent evolution, so to speak) that the state overstepped its responsibilities by building campsites and ski facilities on the Forest Preserve; at cut-rate fees, the competition from the state was formidable.

Adding to the psychological burden is the influx of people "from away." The Adirondack natives are a minority in their own country. In the course of a year the visitors overwhelmingly outnumber the residents. Moreover, outsiders own about 60 percent of the park's private land. Large holdings, individual or corporate, are the rule. More than 50 percent of the private land is held by only 1 percent of the landowners. Seventy-five percent of Hamilton County's 1.1 million acres of private land belongs to thirty-seven individual owners.

Ironically, many of the famous old camps are gone. Taxes, the scarcity and cost of servants, the insufficiency of sun, and the abundance of blackflies have combined to drive away many of the wealthy families who once made a tradition of summering in the Adirondacks. (It is even suggested that their puny scions have lost their enthusiasm for hunting and fishing on the surrounding Forest Preserve, which bars their planes and motor vehicles.) Stephen Birmingham, the social chronicler, puts forth another reason for the falling away of a part of the upper crust:

> Mountains are no longer chic. Eastern summer vacationers have been turning more and more to the Hamptons of Long Island, to the New Jersey shore, to Fire Island, to Cape Cod, to the islands of

> Martha's Vineyard and Nantucket. The beach is winning out over the woods. Part of this may be laid to the "new equality" of women. The forms of recreation the mountains offer—hunting, fishing, canoeing, hiking, camping—have always been those that appeal more to males than females.

The old places have, many of them, gone on the block. Sometimes they have been taken over by institutions or nonprofit groups such as the Boy Scouts and foundations. Sagamore, perhaps the finest example of the Adirondack camp, was given by the Vanderbilt heirs to Syracuse University, and is now owned by a foundation, while the surrounding 1,500 acres are part of the Forest Preserve. The taking over of these properties by tax-exempt groups gnaws at the local rate base, but the state has made up for that in part, paying taxes on its Forest Preserve holdings to local governments, often at assessments higher than that for private owners.

If a part of the old guard has defected, the masses have rushed in to fill the vacuum. The women in Birmingham's circle may shun the rugged arts of canoeing and camping, but a hardier breed has evolved from below and crowds the lakes and woods. Vacationers of all tastes travel to the Adirondacks, stretching the present services and encouraging the development of additional ones that threaten to blot out the natural landscape they presumably have come to enjoy.

Many of the visitors want to become at least part-time residents of the wilderness. In the late 1960s newspaper advertisements laid out the enticements, extolling vacation homes by lakes and streams. The lures included badminton areas, shuffleboard courts, tetherball, cocktail lounges, and enough other frills to dash wilderness enthusiasts into unrelieved gloom. "Urban conveniences," one ad proclaimed, "include year-round water supply and full-width well-built roads." People were being lured to the wilderness by turning it into suburbia, and sometimes into Atlantic City. Where would it all end?

"The great parks cannot be protected for the pleasures that people take in their natural values if we administrators respond to every demand made by the public," Stanley A. Cain of the U.S. Department of the Interior had said in a speech delivered in 1966 on the fiftieth anniversary of the National Park Service. "It is all too easy to measure 'success' by counting visitors and to respond to demands by adding some new development here and some more there, until what was sought to be preserved has been irretrievably lost. There is a saturation point beyond which the wilderness experience cannot be had. Parks need to apply the familiar rangeland concept of carrying capacity."

This sentiment, which the Rockefeller proposal had not dealt with, took hold as the 1960s drew to a close. Park administration began to de-emphasize "body counts" and look for ways to ease the impact of all those bodies on the parklands in their care. But in New York, the Conservation Department had almost no authority to regulate the potential for runaway growth on the 3.75 million acres of private land that made up more than 60 percent of the Adirondack Park. A law of 1924 had given the department the authority to prohibit signs on some private land within the park, but this authority did not extend into incorporated villages or onto active business property.

"Some people might say, in fact, that if it weren't for the 'sign law' there wouldn't be any Adirondack Park at all," William K. Verner said of this period, "for the sign law represents about the only positive manifestation of control over the specialized character of a region a 'park' presumably is intended to designate."

Even that regulatory power was seldom exercised. One summer in the late 1960s cardboard signs advertising a circus in Tupper Lake appeared on telephone poles along the road between Tupper Lake and Long Lake. A resident protested to the Conservation Department. A department official gave the American Legion, which was sponsoring the circus, thirty days to take down the signs. The circus (which never opened because of a local zoning law in Tupper Lake) would have completed its performance and been on its way long before the thirty days had elapsed.

"If there is no God, everything is permitted," Ivan Karamazov said in an earlier time. Almost everything was permitted on most of the land in one of the nation's great parks because of the lack of a higher authority. Obviously the 107 towns and villages which lie wholly or partly within the park are not the same as the other towns in New York State because the Legislature drew the Blue Line around them and thus said they are different (but did nothing else about it). Most of the Adirondack towns are small. In 1968, thirty-nine of them had less than a thousand people, and four had less than a hundred. Saranac Lake was the largest town lying wholly in the park, with a population of 6,000. Despite Tupper Lake's zoning law that kept out the circus, the towns had very little protection through zoning. They were mostly poor and self-absorbed, intent on improving the local economy and incapable of integrating their development with the best interests of the state-owned wilderness land around them. Patchwork local zoning was no longer sufficient to preserve the qualities for which the park was created.

Ideas of regional zoning, like ideas about easing the impact on parklands, were in the air by the late 1960s. Early in 1968, Governor Nelson Rockefeller released a report by the State Commission for the Preservation of Agricultural Land, noting that much rich farmland was being lost to developers. The report described the difficulty that rural towns had in fending off corporate developers and recommended more state and regional planning. At nearly the same time, the governor was grappling with some of the issues his brother's national park proposal had raised about the Adirondacks. On September 19, 1968, he made the classic response to a problem by appointing a committee, the Temporary Study Commission on the Future of the Adirondacks, directing its members to review in depth the problems of the area and to develop alternatives for the future of the Adirondacks to best serve the people of the state.

The fate of such commissions is generally dismal. If a politician wants to sweep a nagging problem under the rug, he appoints a commission. The commission produces a report, the report is filed away, and that is the end of the matter. But in this case, the governor assembled a group of men who were for the most part talented, imaginative, and, perhaps most important, seriously concerned about their subject. There were no "grass roots" Adirondack natives among them, but, since few people believed that this commission was different from any other, no one set up more than a perfunctory outcry back in the mountains.

"Most of the members of the Temporary Study Commission

were conscientious and very hard-working," Harold K. Hochschild, who eventually became its chairman, said afterward. "There were a few exceptions. Lowell Thomas showed up for the first meeting, but we never saw him again. Then there was another member—a very nice fellow, by the way—who didn't do much work. I heard later that he accepted the appointment because he liked to ski and he thought this was a good chance to get to the mountains. But we held most of our meetings in New York City."

The commission's staff, under its executive secretary, Harold A. Jerry, Jr. (a native upstater, a former state senator, and a skillful state planner), compiled an enormous amount of material in its various studies and field investigations, providing the commission with its direction. But despite the number of able members serving on the commission, its leadership was weak at first and the work was concentrated on problems of the Forest Preserve, about which there was a consensus that the final report ought to stress the inviolability of the Forever Wild clause. Harold Hochschild remained in the background through the early meetings, deferring to the nominal leadership. Finally the others convinced him to take the lead in their deliberations, and when the chairmanship became vacant in 1970 Hochschild assumed that position and drew the commission together so that it functioned efficiently for the rest of its existence.

The Temporary Study Commission thus was prepared to face down the single serious threat to its integrity. In 1970, responding to the environmental problems that plagued the state, and the growing public awareness of them, the Legislature created a superagency called the Department of Environmental Conservation that absorbed the old Conservation Department and several other state agencies. As a part of the reorganization, Governor Rockefeller seemed to be supporting (perhaps on the advice of his brother Laurance, who favored mass recreation opportunities in the Adirondacks) the transfer of the many facilities in the Adirondack Park, such as ski areas and campsites, to the office of Parks and Recreation. There was also some pressure from the governor's office for the commission to wind up its business early and submit its report, because its views were stronger on the side of strict preservation than many bureaucrats preferred. Hochschild believed that these developments violated the governor's earlier pledge to the commission that the state would make no policy decisions about the Adirondacks until the members had had the time to prepare a comprehensive report. He and several other commission members visited the governor's office, carrying in their pockets the resignations they planned to offer if Rockefeller indicated he would not honor his pledge. Rockefeller reaffirmed his support for the commission, and its members went on with their work.

Harold Hochschild was by wealth and experience perfectly equipped to deal with Nelson Rockefeller on equal terms. Then a stocky, energetic man in his middle seventies, he had been chairman of the board of the giant, worldwide mining firm which is now known as Amax. He had strong ties to the Adirondacks, too. He began coming to the family's estate at Eagle Nest for summer vacations in 1904, and was one of the boys who made the first penetration of the central Adirondacks by automobile in 1906. Tales of Ned Buntline were still in the air at Eagle Lake. As a young man, Hochschild became a friend and admirer of William West Durant, the once flamboyant Adirondack entrepreneur who had fallen on lean times.

Later, his mining ventures took him all over the world, but he always returned to the Adirondacks. His love for the mountains and his talks with Durant aroused a more than ordinary interest in the region's history. This interest evolved into one of the classic Adirondack books, *Township 34*, which he had privately printed in 1952. In the usual course of events, a museum gives birth to books. Hochschild, being an unusual man, turned his book into a museum. He collected a great many documents, paintings, and artifacts of historical worth bearing on his interest. Some well-to-do men and women who were interested in the region had formed the Adirondack Historical Association, and Hochschild became its president in the late 1940s; out of it grew the Adirondack Museum in Blue Mountain Lake. The museum, which is one of the finest of its size in the country, is mainly supported by contributions from the Hochschild family and other individuals and has as its theme "the relationship of man to the Adirondacks."

On the Temporary Study Commission there was the belief that unplanned development on private land had become, as its report later phrased it, "a grave and growing threat to the entire park." There was a vivid example of that kind of development in the southeastern corner of the park at Lake George, once a tranquil resort that had been described in an early-nineteenth-century travel book as "rendered peculiarly interesting from the unrivalled exhibition of the beautiful and romantic scenery presented by the lake and its environs." Now the beauty and the tranquillity, and even "Millionaires' Row," were submerged in the most garish sort of strip development. About that time, to show what might be in store for the Adirondacks, Hochschild had a collection of photographs, taken of the modern Lake George, exhibited at the Adirondack Museum. Some staff members at the museum worried that they might be in for adverse criticism because of the unrelieved ugliness captured by the photographs. Instead, Hochschild received a lesson in the depth of environmental concern then prevalent in the region. Most of the people who came from Lake George to see the exhibition were pleased by the attention lavished on their hometown, while those from other towns in the park expressed the hope that similar manifestations of progress would soon be visited on them.

Of even greater concern to the commission members was the imminent arrival in the park of the second-home developers. Neighboring Vermont, just across Lake Champlain, was already suffering from a glut of those instant communities, with their attendant strain on local services and pollution of adjacent lakes and streams. Schuyler Jackson, a state planner in Vermont, has described the reality of much second-home development:

> What is being built now is investment housing, not second homes. It has all the dynamics of the New Jersey boom which started in the 1950's and, by the time the buildings got to the third generation owner, they were falling apart. I think that these condominium projects are absolute and utter disasters and they are going to be a millstone around communities' necks when the ownership loses interest in them, when they change and begin to deteriorate and the public service facilities, which are privately owned, begin to fall apart. When such things as the sewer systems fall apart, the communities are going to be asked to fix them. When the investment sours the investor leaves and doesn't care who picks it up.

A member of the Temporary Study Commission who was especially concerned about the development taking place on private land was Richard W. Lawrence, Jr., a lawyer and businessman who made his home in Elizabethtown in the eastern Adirondacks. (Many of the most ardent spokesmen for well-planned development in the park are residents of the Champlain Valley region who are familiar with what has happened in Vermont.) Lawrence believed that the state should create an independent park commission to deal with the area's private lands.

"I discussed my idea with the staff members first, but they seemed to be against it," Lawrence said afterward. "They thought that the new Department of Environmental Conservation ought to administer the entire park. Harold Jerry, the staff director, called a meeting of his assistants and asked me to lay out my idea in detail to them. I did, and I said I thought that planning for private lands was going to be difficult in the Adirondacks and that the direction should be set by a group of commissioners appointed by the governor, and not by bureaucrats in Albany. The staff bought my idea, and slowly prepared the commission members for it."

Harold Hochschild was determined to write a strong report and see that its major recommendations were translated into state policy. Through the late summer and into the autumn of 1970 the commission and its staff worked to sort out their ideas and data and put together a document that would stand up under public scrutiny.

On December 15, 1970, Hochschild submitted the Temporary Study Commission's Report to Governor Rockefeller. With the report went 181 specific recommendations and a series of detailed technical reports on various issues dealing with the Adirondacks. The commission recommended among other things that Article XIV, Section 1, of the Constitution be retained without change, that a wild, scenic, and recreational rivers system be established for the park, and that "no further large-scale impoundments should be built within the park for municipal water supply except as a last resort after all other alternatives have been shown to be infeasible." Almost in passing, the commission said that "there should be no participation by the federal government in the management of state or private land in the Adirondack Park."

By far the commission's most notable point was its first recommendation:

"An independent, bipartisan Adirondack Park Agency should be created by statute with general power over the use of private and public land in the Park."

In effect, the commission was advising the state to assume the chief responsibility for regulating the uses of private land within the park. It gave two reasons for taking this step. The commission believed, first of all, that local governments, with large areas and small populations, did not have the resources to formulate comprehensive planning for the entire area. Of more importance to the park itself, "vast open space acreages" were of such relevance to the wilderness concept that planning for them could not very well be left wholly to ill-equipped local governments if the best interests of the state were to be served. However, the commission did not recommend a tyranny over the park's towns, but rather a partnership, a recognition of the strong home-rule provision in the New York State Constitution and a reflection of the dominance of Republicans on the commission. With advice from the new agency, local governments ought to be able to devise a plan for small-scale land use, especially in their comparatively populous sections. The agency would retain the authority to regulate large-scale development on those "vast open space acreages."

The commisssion saw the Adirondack Park Agency "as a planning and land use control agency only." It recommended that the Adirondack Park Agency prepare a comprehensive plan for the park and that it have planning power over all the private land, eventually sharing some of this power with local governments. As for the state land, the agency should have planning power consistent with the Forever Wild clause and subject to consultation with the Department of Environmental Conservation. The department would continue to administer the state land.

The commission also included with its report the draft of an "Adirondack Park Agency Act," relieving the governor's office of that little chore. The old battle lines were drawn up once more as the bill went to the Legislature.

"If the Adirondacks are to be saved," Harold Hochschild told Rockefeller, "time is of the essence."

CHAPTER XXVI

The Legislative Battle

For the first time since 1894 the preservationists were on the offensive. Instead of defending the status quo, they had formed a positive, well-reasoned plan of action, as revolutionary in its way as was Forever Wild, yet by its very nature it was eventually to stir far deeper antipathies than wilderness preservation. The Adirondack Park Agency Act went beyond telling people what they could not do on state land. It was telling them what they could not do on their own land.

On May 10, 1971, Governor Rockefeller sent a bill to the Legislature that would create the agency. He strongly urged the Legislature to act on it, and, echoing Harold Hochschild, said that "time is critical." To many political pundits the governor's written support seemed no guarantee that the legislation would even reach a vote before adjournment for the year. It was already late, and the Legislature had many other bills still to consider. The economy was beginning to slow down, along with the Vietnam War, and Rockefeller was putting in an "austerity state budget" for 1971–72; the climate was not favorable for the creation of a new state agency. Rockefeller's presidential ambitions were temporarily dormant at this period when Richard Nixon was in firm control of the Republican party and certain to run for a second term in 1972; Rockefeller, then, was more intent on mending fences within the state and keeping upstate Republicans in line.

There was much grumbling from upstate politicians about the

proposed Adirondack legislation. The familiar complaint that it would "lock up resources" was heard. One of the bill's most outspoken opponents was James DeZalia, chairman of the Essex County Board of Supervisors. In urging the Legislature to defeat the bill, he resorted to the sort of exaggeration that was to become a routine practice in attacking the new agency. He argued that "these proposals call for the removal of fire spotting towers, exposing the property and homes of the people in the Adirondacks to destruction by fire." (This was not so, as the plan was merely to remove some towers in wilderness areas where aerial spotting had proved to be more efficient.) DeZalia also contended that "people acquiring property by purchase, gift or inheritance, must apply to the agency for a permit to continue its former use." (This was not so either.)

But the upstate opposition was by no means monolithic. The *Adirondack Daily Enterprise*, which is the only daily newspaper in the park and which was later to become under its new management a vitriolic foe of the agency, commended the Temporary Study Commission's report. In an editorial in 1971 the newspaper ridiculed "the constant cries and groans" about locking up the area's resources and the presence on the commission of people who were not born "Adirondackers" but had moved there later on. The editorial concluded:

"The Adirondack Park must be considered as a whole and some action must be taken if it is to survive as a special place in this country. Some planning effort must be made and this cannot be restricted to areas already owned by the state."

The conservation organizations were once more well organized. David L. Newhouse of Schenectady, the president of the Constitutional Council for the Forest Preserve (which had been coordinating the Forever Wilders' strategy during the 1967 Constitutional Convention), called up his forces. The council had only two hundred members, but they in turn belonged to and reflected the views of nearly a hundred conservation organizations. Among those which endorsed Newhouse's call for swift action on Adirondack legislation were the National Audubon Society, the Wilderness Society, the Sierra Club, and the Association for the Protection of the Adirondacks. Arthur M. Crocker, the president of the last-named organization, accompanied Newhouse and other conservation leaders to

Albany, where they asked Rockefeller's aides to push the legislation.

In 1967 the conservation bloc had worked chiefly through the Democratic party at the Constitutional Convention. In the present struggle, they had to adjust their strategy. The traditional overwhelming support from downstate was not readily apparent. While the conservationists expected some opposition there from conservative Republicans who were against regional planning on principle, they also found scattered opposition among contractors, municipal groups, and even labor unions, which disliked a close rein on development. However, the AFL-CIO took a favorable view of the bill, perhaps in part a reflection of the influence exerted by lawyer David Sive and Frederick O'Neal, a member of the Temporary Study Commission who was then also the president of Actors' Equity.

Clearly, the Republicans were the key to success this time. Rockefeller's wealth and business connections made him an enormously powerful governor. His party enjoyed a majority in both houses of the Legislature that session, and some members usually thought twice before voting against his wishes. But in a session of austerity budgets there had been many rows and disappointments, forcing Rockefeller to admit that he could not push the legislators too roughly. Although he supported the Adirondack Park Agency bill, he was reluctant to twist arms.

"I'm no environmentalist. I'm a power broker," Rockefeller told Harold Hochschild in the spring of 1971. "But I'll support the bill if you can show me there's real statewide support for it."

Hochschild passed the word to the conservation organizations to lobby hard for the bill. Peter S. Paine, Jr., a New York City lawyer who had served with Hochschild on the Temporary Study Commission, toured the Adirondacks (where his family had owned a home for many years) and other parts of the state, urging its passage. Other conservationists kept in constant touch with their legislators, trying to avoid the pitfalls they knew lay ahead.

The most dangerous pitfalls were dug by a few legislators whose constituencies were in, or close to, the park. Assemblyman Glenn Harris, a Republican from Canada Lake in the park, had a meeting with Rockefeller and asked him to delay a vote on the bill until the next session.

"I told him that the people in my area just can't see setting up an agency to override local home rule and zoning laws," Harris said afterward. "He told me 'we have to have something, Glenn, or the land developers are going to run away with the Adirondacks.' I told him that just wasn't true."

Still fighting a rear-guard action, Harris (a powerful and able legislator who would become the Assembly's minority whip in the near future) approached Speaker Perry B. Duryea, Jr., about modifying some parts of the bill. The Legislature was due to adjourn in early June and the bill's proponents were running out of time. Conservationists from all over the state gathered in Albany on Saturday, June 5, 1971, for last-minute lobbying.

The key to passage was the Assembly, where the most outspoken opposition had concentrated. The sessions that weekend ran on until the early hours of the morning. Conservationists rushed from the gallery to the corridors and back again, trying for a word with their legislators. Rockefeller had refused to ask the Democratic leaders to support the bill and conservationists grew apprehensive that the Legislature might divide on the issue roughly along party lines.

Assemblyman Peter A. A. Berle of Manhattan, an ardent and articulate conservationist, began to take over the floor fight for the bill. He was given aid and comfort by William K. Verner, the Adirondack Museum curator, who had put together a "little black book" crammed with facts and figures from which Berle would be able to answer almost any conceivable question on the subject. In caucus, Berle reminded his fellow downstate Democrats that their constituents were all taxpayers in the Adirondack Park, contributing their share to the taxes the state paid to local governments there for Forest Preserve lands; until now, he told them, those people had little to say about how the park was run—they had been subject to "taxation without representation."

For a time Harold Hochschild had watched the proceedings impassively, perhaps even nodding off now and then. But as reports came to him that the bill his commission had so carefully put together was about to be gutted by compromise in the party caucuses, he took over the negotiations. With Peter Paine he went to Speaker Duryea's office. Duryea, a son of the former Conservation Commissioner, had ambitions at that time to succeed Rockefeller as governor and he was trying to placate Harris and the other Adirondack Republicans. Harris wanted to write a grandfather clause into the bill that would give local governments in the park several months after the bill's passage to prepare zoning ordinances that would not be subject to review by the new Adirondack Park Agency. Duryea and his counsel asked Hochschild if he would agree to the compromise.

Hochschild sat back in his chair, stared for a moment at the Republican leaders, and then shook his head. "No," he said simply.

The older man had made his final concession. He had made it plain that he would prefer no bill at all if the gutting was to continue.

"It was now June, so Duryea's plan had been to give the towns until September to get up an ordinance," Hochschild said later. "Well, you know that those towns had been squabbling for years over zoning without being able to produce a plan—less than ten percent of them had passed even token zoning—but I knew that now they would rush something through and get in under the wire. I had to give Duryea some deadline, so I said we'll let them have until July 1. Duryea's counsel said that the towns couldn't get anything through that fast. He was right, of course. A few towns managed to push something through in a hurry, but those plans were full of flaws and eventually they would have to be upgraded."

Hochschild had his way and the bill finally went to the floor on Sunday evening, June 6. The legislative leaders had ordered the clocks stopped in the chambers just before three o'clock, which they had established as the time of adjournment in their earlier resolutions, thus avoiding a vote on a new resolution. Some downstate Democrats who had opposed the bill or were indecisive received word from their leaders to cast a favorable vote when the Republicans agreed to support two housing bills sought by New York City. On Monday, the Assembly voted 123–24 in favor of the Adirondack Park Agency bill, and the next day the Senate approved it, 22–14, just before adjournment.

The time scramble continued. There were frantic moments for some Adirondack towns, which hoped to squeeze in some marginal second-home developments before the Adirondack Park Agency (APA) settled on a master plan. The new agency in turn had to draw up two master plans for the park. One, covering the state land, needed only the governor's approval. The other, for the private land, had to be prepared for the Legislature's approval by 1973.

The advantage was all on the agency's side. One or two enterprising consulting firms talked several town officials into letting them prepare local zoning ordinances, but the resulting ordinances were very much alike and all were more suitable for suburban villages than for a rural, mountainous area. The agency, however, already had in hand the groundwork for its public land master plan, inheriting the great mass of detailed material compiled by the Temporary Study Commission, as well as several experienced members of the commission's staff. Although one of the commission's recommendations had been that none of its members be eligible for a position on the new agency, Rockefeller chose to ignore it and appointed Richard W. Lawrence to be the APA's chairman and Peter Paine one of its members. Because he and his wife were preparing to sail on a Cunard liner from Montreal to Europe within a few days, Lawrence considered declining the appointment.

"I talked it over with my wife," Lawrence said later, "and she listened to me for a while and finally she asked, 'Well, would you rather see someone else handle it?' Ah, vanity! It rose up in me at that. Of course no one else could handle it as well as I could, I admitted to myself. So there I was, with a new job."

In designing a master plan for the Forest Preserve, the agency basically resorted to the classification system discussed by the Joint Legislative Committee on Natural Resources a decade earlier. It divided the preserve into seven categories: wilderness, primitive, canoe, wild forest, intensive use, travel corridors, and, finally, wild, scenic, and recreational rivers. The basis for classification was each area's "characteristics and capacity to withstand use." For instance, fifteen areas (one of them a so-called canoe area) containing nearly a million acres were classified as Wilderness. Each had to contain at least 10,000 acres of land and water. "All non-conforming uses," such as roads, power lines, tent platforms, and snowmobile trails, were ordered to be removed by the end of 1975. No motorized vehicles of any kind, including snowmobiles and aircraft, were to be allowed in the area.

Wilderness Areas, then, were to be managed for their own sake —in other words, to be left severely alone. Restrictions were gradually less inflexible in other areas. Snowmobiling was permitted on designated trails in Wild Forest Areas, which made up a total of more than a million acres, while the large campgrounds, the boat-launching sites, and the ski facilities at Whiteface and Gore mountains were confined to Intensive Use Areas.

The Adirondack Park Agency held nine public meetings on the plan. They were attended by a thousand people and were the basis for some modifications in the plan's text and map. The final version of the State Land Master Plan was prepared in cooperation with the Department of Environmental Conservation and submitted to the governor on June 1, 1972. Seven weeks later Rockefeller announced that the plan had become state policy.

The master plan for private land was another matter. Several important developers had already announced their intentions to build major second-home projects in the park. Courtney Jones, a prominent conservationist who lives in the Adirondacks, described one of those projects at the time in *The Living Wilderness:*

> One subdivider, Horizon Corporation of Tucson, Arizona, thinks it has already found paradise in the Adirondacks. Early in 1972, Horizon purchased 24,000 acres in St. Lawrence County and announced its desire to become "the premier developer" in northern New York. Most of Horizon's experience has been in land speculation and lot sales rather than in the construction and servicing of seasonal homes, but officers of the company have stated that they can envision as many as 10,000 houses on the property. The project would include access roads, golf courses, skiing facilities and several dams on the scenic Grass River. Since there are no existing controls in the town where the project is located, the Adirondack Park Agency is all that stands in the way of what a *New York Times* editorial called "an undisguised assault on a primeval area of forest and wetland."

Local conservationists spread the alarm and underlined for their colleagues around the country the importance of having a strong regional land use plan to control a development of this size.

Fortunately for the incipient agency, which did not have its private land use plan approved by the Legislature, Horizon was slow to act, and the land use plan's final approval by the Legislature effectively discouraged the developer. Furthermore, the arrival of a proper-sized ogre on the scene at that time gave weight to Harold Hochschild's message that time was of the essence. As an agency staff member later said, "If there had been no Horizon, we would have had to invent one."

At another point in the park there was an even more imminent crisis. Louis Paparazzo, a successful developer in Connecticut, chose the town of Altamont for a development of 18,500 acres on forested land. He planned to build 4,000 units and eventually house 20,000 people. In this case, Altamont had passed a zoning ordinance of sorts some years before and thus the Adirondack Park Agency was unable to act under its interim powers. The town approved Paparazzo's project (which basked in the seductive name Ton-Da-Lay) and the issue seemed to be closed.

But the state was not yet beaten. The Environmental Conservation Law, under which the Department of Environmental Conservation had been created in 1970, gave the new department a mandate to "conserve, improve and protect [the] natural resources and environment, and control water, land, and air pollution, in order to enhance the health, safety, and welfare of the people of the state and their overall economic and social well-being." Under this law, the department assumed the Water Resources Commission's old power to regulate the sources and distribution of public water supplies. It also took over the Department of Health's power to regulate sewage disposal. Conservation Commissioner Henry L. Diamond, a protégé of Laurance Rockefeller, promptly used this mandate to call a public hearing on the Ton-Da-Lay proposal and strike it from the landscape.

Diamond ruled that among other things the developer had not provided adequately for the protection of watersheds, the safety of its waterworks, and the adequacy of its septic tank system. Moreover, he declared that the development would adversely affect the health, safety, and welfare of the people of New York and their natural resources, and that, in fact, the development was not justified by public necessity.

"We have taken a view now in any permit proceeding before

the DEC that we will look at the full environmental impact of the permit," Diamond had said in 1970 when discussing the new mandate.

Paparazzo took the matter to court. (In 1974 the Appellate Division of the Supreme Court of the State of New York criticized the department's environmental impact assessment in the case but upheld its right to deny Ton-Da-Lay a water supply permit.) It was but the first of a series of major legal challenges to the state's newly asserted right to regulate the pace and extent of development on the park's private lands.

The agency sent the Adirondack Park Land Use and Development Plan to the governor and members of the Legislature in March 1973. It was composed of a map and accompanying text, sorting the park's private lands into six categories for both the kinds and the intensity of development. The plan, based on inventories of the land's physical characteristics, such as soil, vegetation, waterways, topography, and existing uses, had been compiled after detailed field studies by the staffs of the Temporary Study Commission and the agency itself, as well as other state agencies. Its coverage was exhaustive and sometimes, for the reader, exhausting.

The original draft, circulated several months earlier by the agency, had stirred the anticipated admiration and wrath, and was somewhat modified in response to the latter. Peter Paine, Courtney Jones, and other conservationists went on the road, explaining and defending the plan's purpose, which was essentially to preserve the park's "open space character." There was opposition from many local government officials, state legislators, and businessmen in the Adirondacks, who did not like being told what to do with their land by "outsiders" and believed the zoning restrictions would be destructive to the area's economy. They described the plan as a blow against home rule. (Frank C. Moore, a former lieutenant governor of New York, once described home rule as "the right to be misgoverned by your friends.")

In the Legislature the attack on the plan was led by Assembly minority whip Glenn Harris and Senator Ronald Stafford. They sponsored a bill to delay a vote on the plan for at least another year, contending that the people ought to have more time to read and consider such a complex document. Governor Rockefeller argued against the "delay bill." In 1971 he had let the conservationists carry much of the responsibility for pushing the original agency act through the Legislature. Now, two years later, he was beginning to turn his thoughts again toward national office and believed that a successful land use program in the Adirondacks would gain him the support of conservationists throughout the country if he should run for the presidency in 1976. When a reporter reminded him at a press conference that some Adirondack residents said they hadn't had time to read the plan, Rockefeller replied, "If the matter is urgent they'll find time to read it. I'm busy too, but I found the time."

The conservationists got a nasty shock, however, when both houses of the Legislature passed the "delay bill" by decisive margins. Harold Hochschild later explained what had happened:

"Legislators usually try to go along with colleagues on an issue that those colleagues consider to be a local matter. They want to be treated the same way when issues come up that are important to them locally. So in 1973 many of them went along with Harris and Stafford. They had nothing to lose in that case. They knew that Rocky would veto the delay bill, and then of course the second time around they couldn't vote against his veto."

Rockefeller vetoed the bill after the Easter recess, sending it back to the Legislature with the message that "no matter how well intended such a delay may be, its inevitable impact would be to create a dangerous time gap during which irreversible damage can be done to the Adirondacks."

The horse trading then began in earnest. The conservationists, as a group, were not nearly as effective this time as they had been in 1971.

"Land use planning was foreign to the wilderness types," one of them has said. "Peter Paine and a few others who were well versed in the issues did most of the work. The rest of us didn't understand the bill much better than the developers did."

Rockefeller and Duryea ran the legislative battle this time, and they made a number of concessions to Harris and Stafford. The only one that was resented by the conservationists was a relaxation of certain restrictions on building along shorelines. The governor also agreed to authorize a twelve-member Local Government Review

Board to advise and monitor the agency, offered more funds to help towns with their own planning, and promised that the state would not phase out the traditional payments of taxes to towns on the state land within their boundaries. The last point was especially important to Adirondack communities at that time; legislation to reduce assessments on state-owned lands had been on the books for some years, but local legislators had managed to stave off its implementation. Senator Stafford now was able to obtain a permanent freeze on the reductions as a trade-off with the governor.

Rockefeller also agreed to enlarge the agency to eleven members. The final bill provided for eight members (none of whom can be state officials or employees) to be appointed by the governor, in addition to the commissioners of commerce and environmental conservation and the secretary of state. At least five of the appointed members must be legal residents of the park.

The heart of the plan remained intact. It was not designed to halt development in the Adirondacks, but to guide that development so that the region retains the quality that caused it to be designated a park in the first place. The Adirondack Park Agency, an independent commission of the New York State Executive Department, is given the authority to approve all the new land uses of potential regional impact in each area as described in the plan; later, a part of this regional authority is to be handed on to the individual local governments after each has drawn up a plan of its own that the APA certifies as fitting into the overall purpose of park preservation.

The six categories into which the plan divides the park's 3.8 million acres of private land determine whether the APA approves or rejects an application for development. One of these land use categories is Hamlet, which generally describes the existing concentrations of settlement; the plan prescribes no guidelines for the intensity of building in those areas and suggests that future development be concentrated there. Another category is Industrial Use, which recognizes areas devoted actually or potentially to mining or manufacturing. Other categories are called Moderate Intensity Use, Low Intensity Use, and Rural Use. Each of these areas is designated chiefly for residential or second-home development, the intensity depending on the nature of its soils, topography, and other physical characteristics, as well as its accessibility to Hamlet areas.

The areas in which development is most severely limited are called Resource Management. Building is usually restricted there because of shallow soils, steep slopes, elevations over 2,500 feet, or the proximity to wetlands, wild and scenic rivers, or "critical wildlife habitat." On those areas, development is limited to fifteen "principal buildings" per square mile, or an average lot size of 42.6 acres.

The plan also divides all the proposed projects on private lands into two classes. Class "A" is made up of large projects having a potential impact on a wide area of the park. They must be approved by the APA itself. Class "B" projects are those of primarily local significance, and they are to be regulated by the individual local government once its plan has been approved by the APA.

Governor Rockefeller sent the plan to the Legislature, which approved it overwhelmingly as an amendment to the Adirondack Park Agency Act of 1971. On May 22, 1973, the governor signed the legislation before two hundred conservationists who were gathered in the Red Room of the state capitol at Albany.

"The Adirondacks are preserved forever," Rockefeller said with satisfaction.

"Forever" carries a lot of weight in a Constitution. Its weight is less easily gauged when it issues from the mouth of a governor who has one eye cocked on national office.

CHAPTER XXVII

The Spirit of '76

On a damp evening in the fall of 1975 the southern Adirondack town of Northville suddenly came alive. People from miles around converged on the Northville Central School auditorium, their emotional fires burning as if for an old-fashioned revival meeting. A high school band, the Starlighters, arrived by bus from Malone, several hours away beyond the northern fringes of the park, and the blare of their bugles and the beat of their big drums kept the air in a flutter. With the floor of the auditorium overflowing, latecomers were directed to the balcony until more than 700 people were present, their eyes focused on the stage, which was set out with panelists' tables and pots of chrysanthemums. A leggy young woman clad in an abbreviated spangled costume pranced onto the stage and manipulated a baton with great flair and energy.

"This is a victory dance for the Adirondack people," proclaimed the master of ceremonies, as the crowd sent up a thunderous cheer.

The meeting that evening was one of a series of protests sponsored throughout the park by the League for Adirondack Citizens' Rights, an organization whose avowed aim was to destroy the Adirondack Park Agency. Each member of the audience, upon paying a dollar for admission, was handed an "Adirondackers' Survival Kit," a folder of stiff paper decorated with the league's emblem—two long-fingered hands reaching out to touch each other across a rugged summit, below the motto "Hands Across the Mountains." Inside the folder was a variety of literature, all of it uncomplimentary to the APA, and some of it requesting new members and donations. The message, bristling with phrases such as "Civil Rebellion," "Fascist-type Bureaucracy," and "Regulation Without Representation," was written in the pugnacious spirit of 1776.

After the breathless baton twirler had left the premises the rest of the evening's events reflected the tone of the Survival Kit. The only levity was occasioned by several references to a recent assault on an APA official. As its featured speaker the league imported a man from Maryland who had written a book highly critical of the Rockefellers, the sinister force behind the APA. The speaker, however, proved something of an embarrassment to his conservative hosts by devoting much of his talk to an attack on the Vietnam War and what he called the gullible souls who had voted Richard Nixon into office.

But from then on the procession of people stepping forth to "testify" against the APA lent to the evening (for those who had attended the league's earlier speak-outs) a feeling akin to that of watching television reruns. It seems that the league was trotting out the same cast each time, a repertory company of developers, businessmen, homeowners, and housewives, all of whom harbored grievances against the APA. The group's leader was Mrs. Ruth Newberry of AuSable Forks, the widow of a variety chain proprietor named C. T. Newberry and one of the first residents to become seriously disenchanted with the new state of things in the park.

According to APA officials, the trouble began when Mrs. Newberry learned that the agency's restrictions might interfere with the eventual sale of holdings like her own to subdivision developers. Mrs. Newberry saw the matter as one of intolerable infringements on a citizen's rights. She might have gone on seething in isolation if a combination of circumstances—the awkward attempts of a new agency to live up to its mandate and the inbred resistance of a rural population to government directives—had not presented her with an opportunity to press her complaint in the populist tradition.

In a world burdened by red tape, many of the park's residents saw the APA as another layer of bureaucracy further impeding their attempts to get on with their lives. The landowner who wanted to start building, or sometimes even renovating, was faced with an intimidating array of local and state agencies from whom he had to extract permits. Among several cases crying out for some form of redress to come before Mrs. Newberry's notice was that of Joey Hickey at Star Lake. Although Hickey had obtained a local permit when he set about putting up a combination store and home on his land, he was unaware that he also needed one from the APA. The agency ruled that Hickey was violating several regulations, mostly on the grounds of its own ill-considered interpretations of the law that his "mom and pop" business, combined with his living quarters in the same structure, constituted two principal buildings on a lot zoned for but one. The agency ordered Hickey to stop construction shortly before he had planned to open the store; the alternative it offered him was criminal prosecution, then the only remedy at the APA's disposal. Rain seeped into the unfinished structure, and Hickey's neighbors lamented with him on the injustice of the new regulations. It was many months after Hickey opened the store that the APA finally came to its senses and permitted him to move his family into the apartment on the second floor.

Meanwhile, serious damage had been done to the new agency's image. Mrs. Newberry rounded up some developers and small landowners like Hickey, all with grievances of one kind or another, and organized the League for Adirondack Citizens' Rights, with herself as president. She skillfully blended a dozen or so of the more exploitable case histories to arouse rabid antagonism against the APA throughout the park. In a series of protest gatherings and the pages of a splashy newspaper called the *Adirondack Defender*, these residents told of their unfortunate encounters with the APA. Mrs. Newberry found a valuable ally in William M. Doolittle, who had become the publisher of the *Adirondack Daily Enterprise* in 1971 and a little later the president of the Saranac Lake Chamber of Commerce. Earlier he had been a newspaperman in New Jersey, where he grew "distressed" by what he considered exclusionary zoning in the suburbs. He took sides quickly in the Adirondacks, seeing the issue as a "civil rights battle." Doolittle believed that what amounted to zoning 53 percent of the park's private land for 42.6-acre lots was a violation of the "due process" clause of the Fourteenth Amendment—and that the best solution to the region's environmental problems would have been an Adirondack Mountains National Park!

Doolittle was sometimes accused by APA sympathizers of

fighting battles for the large developers, but he denied it. "I shed no tears for the developers," he once said. "They take their chances, and I personally think that they get away with too much. But I believe the APA's zoning restrictions are often confiscatory. The people of the state did not have the will to buy up all the private land in the park, so the APA simply took it."

Apparently he and some of the APA's staff took an immediate dislike to each other, and this pushed him into a hard-line position. He became associated behind the scenes with Ruth Newberry. He gave her the idea for her "Hands Across the Mountains" emblem as well as the theme that the current situation in the Adirondacks bears striking similarities to the American Revolution. This was the theme that was hammered into audiences at the league's speak-outs, as it was that evening in Northville, where Mrs. Newberry, her light gray hair pulled back severely, her trim figure resplendent in an emerald pants suit, talked of radical tactics in patrician accents. Joey Hickey, who had become an instant celebrity in the park by telling his story before enthusiastic crowds, furnished the emotion.

"I don't know how New York State can try to run my property because they can't even run their own," Hickey roared, winding up his talk. "Let's get our freedom back! Let's get our land back! And let's *kill* the APA!"

Rhetoric of this sort had increased in the Adirondacks ever since the APA began its full-scale operations in 1973, leading to name-calling, violence, and even some reasoned efforts at solutions. Attempts were being made in the Legislature to destroy the APA. From many angles, the original park legislation and its offspring, the agency (called by its supporters a national model for land use planning), were under intense fire. What was the source of the widespread antipathy? Was the APA, and by extension regional planning, "un-American"? Despite the spreading stain of tacky residential and commercial development, and the obliteration of untold acres of greenery and productive land by concrete, the country was slow to embrace the obvious solutions suggested by planning on a wide scale. As we shall see, the obstacles were sometimes thought to be legal as well as psychological.

One of the great contradictions of our society is the nearly paranoid rejection of effective planning by a large proportion of the people. Men and women who carefully arrange their personal lives or their businesses are horrified when government proposes a comprehensive and long-term plan for the land or its natural resources. The pioneer attempt at well-organized resource planning on a nationwide scale in the United States took place under Franklin D. Roosevelt at the beginning of his first administration. As Samuel Eliot Morison wrote, "Roosevelt's National Resources Planning Board aroused more frenzied opposition from senators such as Taft, Tydings, and Byrd, than anything else in the New Deal." It was a way of seeing the country as an organic whole, and it was thought to be "un-American." The board itself tried to analyze the opposition to its work in 1934:

> Those with special privileges to protect and preserve naturally object to any public planning that may dislodge them from a preferred position where they are able to exact tribute from their fellow men. . . . When men express sincere opposition to all governmental planning, it can only mean a grave misunderstanding of what planning really is, or an opposition to some special detail of planning that seems undesirable, rather than to the general principle.

But resource planning disintegrated in the convulsions of World War II and the great burst of laissez-faire that followed it. Public parks as well as cities and suburbia suffered. Then Hawaii created a pioneering but poorly administered land use commission in 1961, and slowly the notion spread that perhaps development could be structured to shield a community from its most unappetizing aspects. By the late 1960s, here and there, environmentalists and civic leaders were taking some bold steps toward effective regional planning. The Vermont Legislature, shocked into action by the aesthetic nightmare of explosive, badly planned vacation-home and strip development in the southern part of the state, passed a sweeping set of land use regulations. In California the Legislature approved a San Francisco Bay Conservation and Development Commission to review the filling and development of local wetlands, and later, in the 1970s, an ambitious Coastal Zone Act, creating a state commission and several regional conservation commissions to experiment with zoning and regulation along the entire California coast. California also joined Nevada in a Tahoe Regional Planning Agency to control the unsound development that was creeping over a number of small communities around Lake Tahoe.

It was planning of this sort that struck many residents of the Adirondacks as a personal insult. Although the state is the largest single landowner in the park, paying taxes to the towns, and much of the private land is owned by people from other parts of the state, a tendency spread among residents to look on the APA as a hostile army that had invaded "their" Adirondacks. When a severe national recession set in soon after the agency imposed its regulations, these residents ignored the fact that development had slowed down all over the United States. They found a convenient scapegoat in the APA for their own economic troubles.

It was a difficult situation at best. The Legislature had charged the agency with carrying out the most detailed yet comprehensive land use plan put into law in America. On a large scale the APA moved effectively, restraining (if sometimes only by its presence) the large, carelessly planned vacation-home developments that might have had a severe impact on the park. It also prepared, quickly but thoroughly, a set of regulations to save the park's waterways in the Wild, Scenic, and Recreational Rivers System. Because the waterways had been the chief highways for travel and transportation in many parts of the Adirondacks during the nineteenth century, their well-being had not been as carefully nurtured by conservationists as had that of the forested lands. Now, by putting restrictions on development along their shores, many segments of lovely streams and rivers were certified as Forever Wild. In a series of public hearings, the APA listened to people who owned land along the rivers, and in many cases modified the regulations to suit individual needs.

But the new agency stumbled on some smaller project applications that were anything but insignificant to landowners. While most of those matters could have been cleared up by patience on either side, tempers or intransigence often prevailed. The agency might have been wise to move slowly at first, taking pains to work with local governments and build goodwill. Instead it tended to act in the bureaucratic tradition, imposing its complex regulations on a confused public, and sometimes, according to critics, changing the ground rules after the fact.

"We were afraid of being nickeled and dimed to death," a staff member said later. "We were afraid that after stopping the big fellows we would be overrun by a lot of piddling eyesores that would all add up to a mess. We also wanted to let it be known that we were in earnest."

It is, of course, a common failing among idealistic young men and women, full of good intentions and an eagerness to serve, to antagonize what they might unconsciously consider the ignorant wretches they have come to set straight. Whether they are empire builders in Africa or social workers among the slums of London's East End, they are not likely to make the best impression on their clients. Sometimes they are simply ignored. A character in Rose Macaulay's *The Towers of Trebizond* sums it up:

> "It must be rather like the country parts of Turkey, which have taken so little notice of poor Atatürk, it's wonderful how people go on in their old ways of thought long after they have been revolutionized and reformed; it's so discouraging for reformers, the way reformation often don't seem to do more than scratch the surface, so that the mass of the people stay just as they were."

In the Adirondacks, the residents were more likely to grow truculent about what they thought of as outside interference. Many of them took a dislike to the APA's chairman, Dick Lawrence, a dedicated and intelligent man, but one who often seemed to lack the common touch. He had no fear of being disliked. Unfortunately, this willingness "to take the heat" wasn't always an asset to the struggling young agency.

"Dick did a tremendous job in getting the agency off the ground," a conservationist who worked with Lawrence has said. "But he found it difficult to unbend with some of the people he had to work with. He wasn't at ease with reporters. The editor of one important newspaper had given us a lot of help in getting the APA law passed in the first place. But Dick wouldn't give him the time of day, and turned down his request to let him attend an agency meeting. This editor soured on the agency and began to attack it in print."

There were public relations blunders that ought to serve as warnings for regional planning groups in the future. To its capable staff of planners, lawyers, and ecologists, the agency might have added a community relations expert—and even a psychologist—who could have bridged the gap by interpreting the goals and techniques of the planning effort for local government officials, the press, the business community, and the public at large. Too often, the planners and the residents were not hearing what each other was saying.

The agency seemed to take forever to process the simplest applications for home building. The siting of a public television transmitter that promised great benefit to the area was infuriatingly delayed. The first person to whom the APA issued a criminal summons for a zoning violation turned out to be a state forest ranger. The second man to receive one arranged to be served just as he was setting out on an expedition at the head of his Boy Scout troop.

In that climate it was easy for those who had personal grievances to whip up popular hostility against the agency. Absurd rumors spread, including one that if a woman lived in a certain land use zone, the APA would restrict the number of children she could bear.

The town of Clare voted to secede from the park. Aggrieved parties hurled eggs at and dumped manure on APA property. An agency lawyer, returning to its headquarters in Ray Brook late one evening to pick up some documents, found a man inside trying to set the place on fire; after a struggle, he subdued the intruder and sat on him until the police arrived. In the town of Fine an elderly woman slapped an agency official who had come to inspect a relative's property and broke his glasses. Joey Hickey and other rural orators rekindled passions whenever they tended to flag.

"Just to illustrate how stupid the Adirondack Park Agency is," Bill Doolittle of the *Daily Enterprise* commented acidly, "can you imagine getting into a full-scale war with *Joey Hickey?*"

Further polarizing the issue was the Local Government Review Board, which had been created by the APA Act to advise and monitor the agency. The various county boards of supervisors almost invariably appointed men and women to the Review Board who were among the most antagonistic critics of the agency in their own areas, thus effectively cutting off meaningful discourse between the two bodies. The Review Board's ultimate concern came to be the search for ways to get rid of the agency and replace it with a regulatory body remarkably similar to itself.

Under fire, the APA struggled to make its procedures more palatable to the public.

"Together these regulations constitute the most comprehensive and enlightened system of land use controls anywhere in the United States," said Robert F. Flacke, a businessman and the town supervisor of Lake George, who became the APA's chairman late in 1975. "But we have also got the makings of a regulatory nightmare."

The agency streamlined application procedures, rescinded some of the more petty restrictions on small landowners, and carefully investigated grievances; a number of them turned out to be based on misunderstandings, errors, or distortions. At the agency's urging, the Legislature amended the APA Act in 1976 to eliminate the criminal penalties and provide for a wide range of civil remedies.

Here and there cracks appeared in the monolithic local opposition to the APA. A real estate dealer spoke in favor of regional zoning at a symposium sponsored by the APA for businessmen, remarking that "our hearts and our pocketbooks are both served by the sensible regulation of land." And he went on with the tentative offer of an olive branch:

"I believe we will eventually turn the APA administrators into Adirondackers, the same as we did some years ago with the game wardens—the *then-hated* game wardens of the Conservation Department who are now our friends and neighbors."

While the real estate man's words were spoken optimistically, some conservationists and planners found a disturbing note if the thought was to be carried on another step. The agency's future remains cloudy. Even if the terms of the APA Act survive the constant attacks mounted on it by Adirondack legislators in Albany, much depends on the day-to-day decisions of the agency members, who are appointed by the governor, and the staff members who live in the park and are often subject to uncomfortable social pressures. Like the real estate man, William Doolittle takes the longer view and finds an optimistic note of his own.

"You can't conquer China," he once said. "Conquerors come in and take over, but then they become residents themselves or the residents begin to infiltrate their ranks. Pretty soon the Adirondacks will swallow the APA."

If either the agency's members or the staff undergoes a rapid turnover and becomes susceptible to political and social pressures, the framework of the land use plan will be nibbled away. Decisions will inevitably be based on expediency rather than on the long-range needs of the land. In the future, a governor of a certain political persuasion could, by exercising the executive rights of appointment, change the public-spirited nature of the Adirondack Park Agency to the park's detriment.

But besides the Legislature and the Executive, the third arm of government was taking a more active role in events, prompting Commissioner Peter Paine of the APA to some gloomy musings in 1976. Recalling Rockefeller's national park proposal, he said, "I'm not sure that Laurance wasn't right. If we lose a big lawsuit it could be a disaster."

CHAPTER XXVIII

Challenge in the Courts

Conservationists have almost always been well prepared to put up a fight against anyone who challenged the laws protecting the forests and waterways of the Adirondack Park. ("The power of the conservation organizations in Albany is *unbelievable*," an opponent of the APA recently said with disapproval and perhaps hyperbole.) Having lived by the New York State Constitution, now in the 1970s they had to come to grips with the United States Constitution. Not Ruth Newberry, but "the taking issue," seemed for a while the greater menace.

As the earth fills up with people, certain restrictions on human activity are inevitable. The restrictions will be imposed at first either by human beings themselves working through government or, ultimately, by nature working through dwindling space and resources. The matter is seen to be urgent only in those areas where crowding decreases society's ability to function properly. City dwellers are more accustomed to adapting to these restrictions than country people are; they pass building codes, lower the speed limits, or keep people from shooting off guns in the neighborhood.

Wherever the state imposes restrictions on the use of land, a conflict is touched off between the state's policing powers and the individual's rights of private property. "It's my land, and I can do with it what I want," became a common refrain in the Adirondacks, as it does anywhere else, when the state clamps on land use controls. If a person living in a remote area is not aware of the blight brought on by runaway development in more congested areas, he or she is likely to come up against those restrictions with a sense of even more anger and misunderstanding than is usual among city dwellers. At the heart of the opposition to the APA was the firm conviction of most landowners that what the agency was trying to do was somehow alien. The state, by passing the APA Act, had taken their property. And that is a violation of the Constitution. That is un-American.

It was the specter that threatened to upset the plans to put some order into America's haphazard development in the last years of the twentieth century. Conservationists, government planners, and even lawyers proceeded slowly with the job that had to be done, constantly casting apprehensive glances at what is known as "the taking clause" in the Fifth Amendment of the United States Constitution:

". . . nor shall private property be taken for public use, without just compensation."

These words mean exactly what they say. Yet, by reading into them something else, the whole process of sound land use planning had been slowed, causing developers to grow more aggressive and planners more timid. It is worth looking carefully at "the taking issue" to understand the nature of much of the opposition to the APA.

> Many people seriously believe that the Constitution gives every man the right to do whatever he wants with his land. Foreign concepts like "environmental protection" and "zoning" were probably sneaked through by the Warren Court! Many more people recognize the validity of land use regulation in general, but believe that it may never be used to reduce the value of a man's land to the point where he can't make a profit on it. After all, what good is land if you can't make a profit on it. The courts have never adopted either of these philosophies.

The above quotation comes from *The Taking Issue*, a book that was prepared by the U.S. Council on Environmental Quality (CEQ) in 1973 to examine the curious history of this clause and how the "philosophies" it spawned came to have "an independent existence above and beyond the law." Contrary to popular belief, there have always been many restrictions on the use of land, ever since the first settlers arrived in North America. Colonial history is full of such examples. New Amsterdam, for instance, appointed street surveyors to prevent the building of unsightly houses and fences, while in Boston a local ordinance prohibited slaughtering in certain areas of the city. The Puritan colonies imposed all sorts of restrictions on the behavior and property of their people.

The CEQ's book painstakingly examines the drafting of the Bill of Rights by James Madison, and concludes that neither he nor any of his colleagues were troubled about regulating the use of land:

> Such regulations had been standard practice in England and throughout colonial times and seemed to have provoked no serious controversy. There is no evidence that the founding fathers ever conceived that the taking clause would establish any sort of restrictions on the power to regulate the use of lands.

Throughout the nineteenth century the courts strictly interpreted the clause, insisting on compensation for the owners only when the state actually took land for some public purpose. This was true even if the owner lost his investment or his livelihood when the state prohibited certain uses of the land. The police power was interpreted as being entirely distinct from the power of eminent domain.

The case of *Mugler* v. *Kansas* made the point very well. Mugler was a brewer whose business was ruined when the state outlawed the manufacture and sale of intoxicating liquors. He sued, on the grounds that the state had in effect taken his business away from him and ought to compensate him for it. In 1887 the U.S. Supreme Court ruled against him, deciding that his property was not taken from him or destroyed for the purpose of public use, but a prohibition was simply put upon his use of the property for a business that the state considered to be contrary to the public welfare.

"Such legislation does not disturb the owner in the control or use of his property for lawful purposes, nor restrict his right to dispose of it," Justice John Marshall Harlan wrote in his opinion, "but is only a declaration by the state that its use by anyone, for certain forbidden purposes, is prejudicial to the public interests."

This interpretation was not seriously disputed until 1922, when Justice Oliver Wendell Holmes took a position whose results were incalculable. The coal-mining regions of Pennsylvania were plagued by the phenomenon of land subsidence, in which portions of the land's surface, and the buildings upon it, often tumbled into the void left by mine shafts beneath. The state passed the Kohler Act in 1921, which prohibited mining within municipalities where it might cause buildings or roads to collapse.

When the Pennsylvania Coal Company announced its intention to dig a mine under the home of a couple named Mahon in Pittston, the Mahons asked the state to intervene. The state invoked the Kohler Act against the coal company. The company went to court, claiming it had bought the mineral rights to the property from its previous owners many years before, and the Kohler Act was thus taking the company's property without compensation.

Eventually the Supreme Court ruled in favor of the coal company, with Justice Holmes formulating the decision. In his opinion, the difference between the police power to regulate land and the power to seize land by eminent domain differed only in degree. He set forth a balancing test: did the property's decrease in value outweigh the benefit to the public of the regulation in question? In this case, he thought it did:

"The general rule at least is while property may be regulated to a certain extent, if regulation goes too far it will be recognized as a taking."

Since that time, the U.S. Supreme Court has usually averted its eyes from cases in which the state's power to regulate land use was challenged. The balancing test remains the rule. States and municipalities have been wary of going beyond minimal regulation, for fear of tipping the balance, but the emergence of a breed of bright and aggressive environmental lawyers in the 1970s is slowly changing the picture. Joseph L. Sax of the University of Michigan Law School has found fault with judicial thinking on this issue because it tended too often to underestimate the full benefit to the public of land use controls. The courts in many cases have measured only the regulations' cost to the developer and not the cost of the development to the broader community around it.

"Frequently," Sax writes, "the use of any given parcel of property is at the same time effectively a use of, or a demand upon, property beyond the border of the user."

According to the authors of *The Taking Issue*, today's courts are more likely to uphold regulations "having multi-purpose goals." Regional and statewide land use plans fit this criterion. The history of "the taking clause" and a fair application of the balancing test brand the notion that a man can use his land in any way he wishes as simply another native myth.

The basis of going to court over "the taking issue" is, of course, economic. The usual plaintiffs in these cases are developers—individuals or companies that have bought property for the purpose of subdividing it into lots or building some sort of resort facilities. The issue, however, has struck a sympathetic note among a wide range of people who believe that restrictions on the big developers cut into jobs and sales on all levels in the park. The economy of the Adirondacks, always frail at best, and sometimes almost moribund, is a sensitive point.

One of the most difficult arguments to combat is that conservationists are "elitists," condemning minorities or the poor to further misery so that they can enjoy their leafy preserves, bird watching, and wilderness hikes. This is a familiar theme wherever environmental health has become a source of controversy. In the Adirondacks it was carried to its extreme by William Doolittle in his editorials.

"Groups like the Sierra Club and the Association for the Protection of the Adirondacks, deep down, despise people," Doolittle wrote in the *Daily Enterprise* at the end of 1976. "After all they are the crest of a wave of self hatred, misnamed environmental protection, which has swept the land. It is fed by fear of the future and a desperate need to run backward into a sentimental reconstruction of the past."

Beneath the diatribe runs the argument that is expressed in some other rural areas in the phrase "payrolls or pickerel," that one must choose between a sound economy on the one hand and clear air, unpolluted streams, and good fishing on the other. Into this argument William Doolittle, Ruth Newberry, and their followers injected the indictment that certain selfish, well-to-do people are fighting to preserve a healthy environment for their own frivolous ends.

But there is a more serious side of the contention. Has the Adirondack Park Agency been guilty of both "taking" the property of large developers and depressing the region's economy? Recent court decisions seem to be swinging back to an insistence on Aldo Leopold's concept of *property responsibility* as well as *property rights;* they are upholding the state's authority to recognize the interconnectedness of a region's land uses and thus regulate them. Doubt has been cast, as we have seen, on the idea that regulation legally destroys the value of property. A close look at what has happened in the Adirondacks also tends to destroy the theory that the APA undermined the region's economy.

The APA began to regulate certain properties in 1973. At about that time, real estate sales fell off in the Adirondacks, causing its critics to blame the APA as the source of the trouble. (These critics like to refer to the State Land Use Master Plan as SLUMP.) But 1973 was the year a serious recession settled over most parts of the country. Condominium sales began to diminish in Florida. The second-home industry was badly hurt in northern New England. Real estate transfers throughout New York State decreased by about 13 percent between 1973 and 1975. The rate of decline reached about 23 percent in the Adirondack Park, but the drop was just as high in the state's other rural areas, such as those parts of the Catskill Mountains and Adirondack counties lying outside the park where the APA did not function.

Residents of the park complained of low income and the departure of its young people because of a scarcity of opportunities. Yet neither condition was new to the Adirondacks. Incomes were low and jobs scarce in the park long before the APA went into business. This has been almost universally true of isolated rural areas in our time, regardless of land use laws. In fact, New York experienced an unprecedented decline of 140,000 permanent residents throughout the state between 1970 and 1975.

The weather, the soil, and the topography have combined to keep the Adirondacks from developing a thriving economy. Twentieth-century technology has done little to make over the area and conditions change slowly. (A local real estate dealer recalls that as late as the 1930s many residents paid their automobile premiums for only eight months of the year; during the other four months they put away their cars because of the ice and snow.) Civic leaders for a long time have tried to lure light, non-polluting industries to the Adirondacks, but without much success. Part of the problem lies in transportation difficulties posed by the mountains' distance from both the sources of certain raw materials and mass markets in the cities.

The sophisticated modern industry that settles in the Adirondacks faces another problem. Like many underdeveloped areas, the Adirondacks have a shortage of skilled labor. A classic story of a beleaguered region's attempts to improve the economy by imposing a large industry on itself is that of Naples. When Alfa Romeo opened a large auto assembly plant there, local boosters believed it would give new life to southern Italy's sagging economy. Instead, unemployment remained high and many small businesses failed. Economists discovered that the plant had swallowed almost the entire pool of skilled technicians in the city, leaving small manufacturers without the labor to carry on. Similarly, certain new industries in the Adirondacks would fill their manpower needs by draining off skilled workers from resident companies or importing them from outside the park. In Appalachia, Maine, Florida, California, or the Adirondacks, the unemployables generally remain just that—unemployable.

In the 1970s the park's residents still relied heavily on the old standbys for work: government, tourism, mining, and forestry. As noted before, small towns, each with a government structure, tend to employ an unusually high percentage of the population to keep that structure functioning, in many cases with money provided by the state from taxes on Forest Preserve lands within their borders. Yet with the present reluctance to increase local taxes, there is little likelihood that there will be an expanding job market in that direction. The mining of iron, titanium, and other minerals remains a good source of jobs but it is hard work and not for everybody; mining's future in the region, moreover, is uncertain. Jobs in the tourist industry are often seasonal and at the mercy of bad weather, recessions, and gasoline shortages.

Surrounded by Forever Wild, forestry continues to thrive on the park's private lands. A number of wood products companies, including the International Paper Company, the St. Regis Paper Company, and Finch, Pruyn and Company, employ park residents either inside or outside the Blue Line. In addition to the land owned by large companies, millions of acres of forest lands in the park are managed for wood products by the owners of some of the great estates and even smaller holdings. Litchfield Park, composed of 28,000 acres near Tupper Lake, still practices silviculture on the principles laid down by Gifford Pinchot. The estate built a million-dollar processing plant that includes a chipper-canter rig designed to exploit the whole tree, including smaller parts that used to be discarded. In recent years Litchfield Park employed fifty workers in the woods and at its Tupper Lake plant, and another fifty at its conventional plant in Potsdam.

Yet the owners of many woodlands are in trouble. Taxes have sometimes risen beyond the value of their cutting operations. It is likely that the members of the Temporary Study Commission had this very much in mind. Despite the commission's inspiriting references to "open space," some local residents believe that the designation of large areas as Resource Management would not be possible without implying that, in the long run, taxes on such land would not keep rising.

If a community reduces the taxes on woodlands (which may make up a large part of its taxable property), the other local landowners will have to provide the difference. An eventual solution in this case may be for the state to subsidize in part towns within the Blue Line, thus obligating all of New York's taxpayers to share to a greater extent in the park's upkeep. As one Adirondacker has said: "It would be a chance for the state to show an interest in the people as well as the trees of the park."

These problems are endemic to the region and the park. The APA did not bring them on, but it may be able to help find a way to solve, or at least ease, some of them. To date, there is no sound evidence that the APA has had an impact for good or ill on the park's economy. Its regulations may yet benefit the landowners' economy as well as their environment. In 1975 an anonymous author in the *Yale Law Journal* seized on this as more than a probability:

> If a developer or other landowner complains of a "loss" suffered because his property is worth less regulated than unregulated, he must be asked how much it would be worth were all properties around it unregulated also. A program which like the Adirondack program preserves the attractiveness of the region for vacation home dwellers ought in the long run to cause an overall gain in vacation home property values.

One of the bitter ironies of recent environmental battles is that in some cases conservationists have been pitted against other pressure groups that ordinarily they would like to think of as having much in common with themselves—among them, labor unions and civil rights organizations. Most conservationists like to believe they are not trying to preserve portions of the environment simply for selfish reasons, but that their victories benefit the entire community as well as future generations. Yet they still hear charges that their concerns are frivolous and their outlook elitist. These charges can be shrugged off during a public hearing or in a newspaper's editorial columns, but they must be defended when they form the grounds of a challenge in court.

Lawsuits amounting to nearly fifty million dollars were filed against the Adirondack Park Agency in the first two years of its existence. Some were based on the "taking clause" of the Fifth Amendment. Others challenged the agency on various points of state law. One of the agency's most satisfying victories came on a challenge to its authority to regulate development on aesthetic grounds.

In that case, two developers named Clifford W. McCormick and James E. LaPan were given a permit by the APA for a subdivision on Oseetah Lake, which is a part of the Saranac River. A principal condition attached to the permit was that no boathouses could be built along the shore. The developers went to court, charging that the agency's prohibition was "arbitrary, capricious, discriminatory, unreasonable, unlawful and unconstitutional." The implication was that aesthetic considerations, where no other environmental harm was being done, were frivolous.

Justice Edmund L. Shea of the New York State Supreme Court

ruled otherwise. In an important decision that demonstrated how far the courts have come in their view of environmental planning, Justice Shea stated that "aesthetic considerations alone generate a sufficient impact on the public welfare to warrant an exercise of the police power where such considerations relate to unique features of a locality." He went on to point out that the Legislature had recognized the Adirondack Park as a "unique and natural area," and that the APA's stipulation served to carry out its duty "to preserve the aesthetic and scenic value of the park," and was therefore neither arbitrary nor unreasonable.

An equally important ruling affecting the APA's authority was made three thousand miles away. In 1972 the city of Petaluma, California, forty miles north of San Francisco, became alarmed by its own rapid growth and the attendant social and environmental problems. Its citizens approved a plan to slow down local growth, restricting new housing to 500 units a year and halting annexation for five years. A builders' association joined with civil libertarians to contest the plan.

Civil rights groups have been concerned about exclusionary zoning, in which certain suburban towns apparently tried to close their gates to minorities and the poor from nearby cities. Although Petaluma seemed to be planning for a different purpose, the civil libertarians believed that the city was setting a dangerous precedent and decided to support the builders in court. The basis of their case was that such zoning infringes on people's rights to travel and settle where they choose. Conservationists and planners supported Petaluma.

In reversing a lower court's decision the U.S. Court of Appeals in California found in favor of Petaluma, ruling in 1975 that the concept of public welfare was far broader than the right to travel.

"We conclude," Judge Herbert W. C. Choy wrote for the court, "that the concept of public welfare is sufficiently broad to uphold Petaluma's desire to preserve its small town character, its open spaces and low density of population to grow at an orderly and deliberate pace. . . . The federal court is not a super zoning board."

The courts have not given government planning agencies a blank check. Great care must be taken to design land use plans that are fair, comprehensive, and for the greater public welfare. Lawyers must defend these plans skillfully in court, for they are certain to be challenged by powerful and often well-intentioned corporations or organizations. The APA's early experience in defending itself in court was gratifying to the conservationists and planners who had fought for its creation, but, like the exercise of foreign policy, land use regulation at present remains less the supervision of a well-ordered, long-range plan than the coming to grips each day with a new crisis.

The tumult continues among the Adirondacks' grandeur and green wealth. As William K. Verner has said: "We are living through the *creation* of the Adirondack Park, and sometimes it is agonizing."

Conclusion

"Adirondack" Murray, surveying in some awe the Forest Preserve his *Adventures in the Wilderness* had helped to create, maintained that New York State doesn't own the land, but holds it in trust for the people. This is a conception agreeable to our own time; stewardship is an antidote for arrogance, an alternative to a hasty decision when, in fact, we are not sure of our competence to make a decision.

Foresters since Gifford Pinchot have grumbled that the Forever Wild clause keeps them from getting on with their work in the state's largest forest; but that was exactly what the framers of the clause had in mind in 1894, preventing both private individuals and state agencies from having their way in the preserve. Property owners in the park today complain that the Adirondack Park Agency's regulations discriminate against them in relation to all the other citizens of the state; but that was exactly what the framers of the APA Act had in mind in 1971 as they pursued their dream of a unified park. The history of the Adirondack Park is the account of how the people of New York State exercised their stewardship on those six million acres. It may not be very far out of line to say that this history describes a vision of Arcady, often blurred and flawed but persistently alluring.

"Whose vision prevails?" it may be asked. Is the maintenance of the Forest Preserve and the regulation of the private lands simply an elitist pastime? On one level, yes. Although no group is without its purely selfish individuals, the conservationists and planners (almost indistinguishable from each other today in the Adirondacks) work in a long tradition of idealism, going back to Muir and Pinchot and beyond. Like Olmsted or John Ruskin, they are of the nineteenth century in that they believe in the role of the taste maker. By pointing out and shining their discriminating light on the object of their passion—a various and renewable natural world—they once induced the masses (those of the masses, at any rate, with a tendency toward self-improvement) to elevate their own tastes and aspirations.

But twentieth-century democracy looks on the taste maker with a fishy eye. Its suspicions are not groundless, for taste is an appendage of power. In the past it was a function of those who held the keys to power—the elite—to set the standards for art and fashion. The medieval church institutionalized its icons, a later aristocracy its cherubs, minuets, and gardens, the beneficiaries of the Industrial Revolution their novels, bibelots, and public parks. Today, however, an elite is hardly distinguishable, and people defend their tastes in aesthetics or recreation as jealously as they do their property rights.

If wilderness and land use policies have been set in the Adirondacks by the few, no tyranny is implied. Public notions evolve or fluctuate, and ours is not an era for eternal verities. Policies stand only until they are seen as impeding common aspirations, and then they are swept away. The New York State Constitution bestows on "forever" about as much longevity as we are likely to see in a democracy, but a new generation may interpret its stewardship in other terms.

Forever Wild and the APA survive in the Adirondacks now because they are in tune with sentiments that are in the ascendancy. There is so little in our present environment (in the broadest meaning of the word) to stimulate the senses. Our cities, which evolved from mud and thuggery into diverse centers of commerce and culture, are in many places sinking into unpicturesque decay. (Compare them with the views that linger on—overshadowing even the ground tone of human misery—of the Paris of the 1920s, old Vienna, Prague, Dresden, the English cathedral cities of Henry James's travels, Venice before the poisoned air crept over it like a stain, even Greenwich Village.) Many of our suburbs are sprawling and tacky. There is a paucity in daily life of old inns, fine china, satisfying textures. Sensuousness has retreated from our environment to the museums or the homes of the well-to-do, and it often seems that to appease our hunger for authenticity we have nowhere to turn but to nature. So there is increasing support for wild situations, with or without portable TV's. Not to preserve such areas, which form only a tiny proportion of the country's land mass, removes one of the cultural options open to society. Similarly, crowding and blight are hastening an acceptance of land use planning far beyond what its proponents might have hoped for even a few years ago.

All this may change. Such a conjecture does not imply that the public's present commitment to wilderness or land use planning is insincere, but that change may come about through dire necessity. It is by no means certain that the doomsday prophets are wrong and that mankind's biological and chemical excesses will not exact a fearful price. In *An Inquiry into the Human Prospect*, Robert L. Heilbroner concludes that "whether we are unable to sustain growth or unable to tolerate it, there can be no doubt that a radically different future beckons."

In the face of such prospects it is fruitless to predict with any confidence the shape of things to come in the Adirondacks. Some future energy crisis may force the federal government to take an "easement" in the Forest Preserve and harvest wood for fuel or materials, just as it did on a restricted scale to extract titanium during World War II. New pressures from an increasing population or changing values may undo the most carefully planned regulations to preserve open space on private lands. In the years ahead we may find ourselves squirreling away tracts of wilderness as early monks hid illuminated manuscripts, gold chalices, and other treasures from the menace of their own Dark Ages.

But for now we must go on behaving as if our values have substance. In New York there is a long tradition of land stewardship, and the decisions made by the Adirondacks' broad constituency during the last century have carried this treasure reasonably intact into our own day. There will be new challenges and decisions just ahead for all Americans as they try to accommodate wild and viable green spaces in their changing society.

Primarily because of the Forever Wild clause in their Constitution and a strong land use planning law, both of them refined by experience, the people of New York State retain their options.

And that, in the modern world, is no small privilege.

Notes

The following titles appear often in the notes. For convenience, I will cite them only by the author's last name or, in one case, by a shortened version of the sponsoring commission's name.

Alfred L. Donaldson, *A History of the Adirondacks*, 2 vols. (New York, 1921).

Harold K. Hochschild, *Township 34: A History, with Digressions, of an Adirondack Township in Hamilton County in the State of New York* (privately printed, 1952).

Marvin W. Kranz, *Pioneering in Conservation: A History of the Conservation Movement in New York State, 1865–1903* (Ph.D. Thesis, Graduate School of Syracuse University, 1961).

Temporary Study Commission on the Future of the Adirondacks, *The Future of the Adirondacks*, 2 vols. (Blue Mountain Lake, N.Y., 1971). Referred to hereafter as the Temporary Study Commission.

Roger C. Thompson, *The Doctrine of Wilderness: A Study of the Adirondack Preserve-Park* (Ph.D. Thesis, State University College of Forestry, Syracuse, 1962).

Norman J. Van Valkenburgh, *The Adirondack Forest Preserve: A Chronology* (mimeographed, State of New York Conservation Department, 1968).

William Chapman White, *Adirondack Country* (New York, 1975; updated and reprinted from the original edition, New York and Boston, 1954).

The titles of all other works are given in full, with dates, when they first appear in the references. Two other volumes were of enormous importance in locating sources and should be in the library of anyone seriously interested in the Adirondacks and their history. They are:

Adirondack Mountain Club, *Adirondack Bibliography* (Gabriels, N.Y., 1958).

Adirondack Museum, *Adirondack Bibliography Supplement, 1956–1965* (Blue Mountain Lake, N.Y., 1973).

Preface

p. xi
else furnish William H. H. Murray, *Adventures in the Wilderness; or Camp-life in the Adirondacks* (Boston, 1869; reprinted by Syracuse University Press, 1970), pp. 9–10.

CHAPTER I

p. 3
United States Hotel For a description of this period, see George Waller, *Saratoga: Saga of an Imperial Era* (Englewood Cliffs, N.J., 1966), and White, pp. 87–88.

p. 4
fishing parties White, p. 86.
angler Thomas F. Gordon, *Gazetteer of the State of New York* (Philadelphia, 1836), pp. 475–76.
her trip Harriet Martineau, *Retrospect of Western Travel* (London, 1838), pp. 263–71. See also White, pp. 100–01.
Great Rocks White, p. 52.
visited by them H. D. Thoreau, *The Maine Woods* (Riverside Edition; Boston and New York, 1892), p. 86.

p. 5
virtual isolation Donaldson, Vol. I, p. 102.
formidable For a discussion of the geology of the Adirondacks, see Walter C. O'Kane, "The Building of the Adirondacks," *The Living Wilderness*, Vol. XI, No. 16 (March 1946), pp. 10–12, and Peggy Byrne, "Mr. Anorthosite," *The Conservationist*, Vol. XXX, No. 3 (December 1975), pp. 10–13.
before the Hudson's White, p. 5.
Totten and Crossfield For an account of early land dealings in the Adirondacks, see Donaldson, Vol. I., and Hochschild.

p. 7
chiefly beavers Robert Boyle, *The Hudson River: A Natural and Unnatural History* (New York, 1969), p. 86.
mercantilist policy Kranz, pp. 4 ff.

p. 8

Alanson and Norman Fox Boyle, *op. cit.*, p. 78, and White, p. 90.
public highways Thompson, p. 57.
Erie Canal Carl Carmer, *The Hudson* (New York, 1939), p. 219, and Boyle, *op. cit.*, pp. 58, 64.

CHAPTER II

p. 10

down every year Quoted in Ulysses P. Hedrick, *A History of Agriculture in the State of New York* (Albany, 1933), p. 153.

p. 11

if not impossible Kranz, pp. 16–17.
fertilize it *Ibid.*, p. 47.
staff of assistants William H. Goetzmann, *Exploration and Empire* (New York, 1966), p. 355.

p. 12

Williams College Donaldson, Vol. I, pp. 36–37, 152–53.
many falls Boyle, *The Hudson River*, p. 71.

p. 13

hunting grounds Russell M. C. Carson, "The First Ascent of Mount Marcy," *High Spots*, Vol. XIV, No. 3 (July 1937), pp. 9–12.
Abominable Pass William K. Verner, "Painting Indian Pass," *The Conservationist*, Vol. XXII, No. 6 (July 1968), p. 28.

p. 14

to a man John Burroughs, *Indoor Studies* (Boston, 1904), p. 269.
Thoreau's psyche James McIntosh, *Thoreau as Romantic Naturalist* (Ithaca, N.Y., 1974), p. 18.
in the country H. D. Thoreau, *Journal* (Boston, 1906), Vol. XII, p. 387.
Switzerland Joel Tyler Headley, *The Adirondack; or, Life in the Woods* (New York, 1849).

p. 15

man and nature Kenneth Clark, *Landscape into Art* (Edinburgh, 1956), pp. 77–78.
for taxes Thompson, p. 60.
quantities of bark Hedrick, *op. cit.*, pp. 139, 143.
producing lumber Thompson, p. 58.

p. 16

inevitable book Amelia M. Murray, *Letters from the United States, Cuba and Canada*, 2 vols. (London and New York, 1856).

p. 17

best here S. H. Hammond, *Wild Northern Scenes* (New York, 1857), pp. 83–84.

CHAPTER III

p. 18

intellect inert William J. Stillman, *Autobiography of a Journalist* (Boston, 1901), pp. 199–200.

p. 19

and went home *Ibid.*, pp. 208–09.

p. 20

will be shot *Ibid.*, pp. 233–47.

CHAPTER IV

p. 23

Ned Buntline For an informative and entertaining account of Buntline, his character, and his stay at Eagle Nest, see Hochschild.

p. 24

days on end Quoted in Maitland C. DeSormo, *The Heydays of the Adirondacks* (Saranac Lake, N.Y., 1974), pp. 91–92.
in 1705 Kranz, p. 27.

p. 25

in 1869 For an illuminating account of the Murray phenomenon, see Warder H. Cadbury, "Introduction and Notes," in the edition of Murray's *Adventures in the Wilderness* published by Syracuse University Press, 1970.

p. 26

a chapel bell! William K. Verner, "The Adirondack Painters," *The Conservationist*, Vol. XXII, No. 5 (April–May 1968), p. 11, and Cadbury, *op. cit.*, pp. 34, 70.

p. 28

to keep up Murray, "Reminiscences of My Literary and Outdoor Life," *The Independent*, Vol. LVII (1904), pp. 194–95.

p. 29

out of the woods Thomas Bangs Thorpe, "The Abuses of the Backwoods," *Appleton's Journal*, December 18, 1869, pp. 564–65.

p. 30

a large public Cadbury, *op. cit.*, p. 72.
lavish abundance Murray, "The Adirondacks," New York *Tribune*, October 23, 1869.

CHAPTER V

p. 31
railroads For an account of railroads in the Adirondacks, see Hochschild; also see DeSormo, *The Heydays of the Adirondacks*, pp. 99–119.

p. 32
uncles and cousins Theodore Roosevelt, *Diaries of My Boyhood and Youth* (New York, 1928), pp. 241–55.

p. 33
they treat Quoted in Paul Russell Cutright, *Theodore Roosevelt the Naturalist* (New York, 1956), p. 18.

p. 34
near the bottom Donaldson, Vol. I, pp. 320–22.
out of season White, p. 134.
with royalty Donaldson, Vol. I, pp. 320–22.

p. 35
quicker than I could DeSormo, *op. cit.*, pp. 240–41.
hotels For an account of Adirondack hotels and the Durants, see Hochschild.
nighttime dash White, p. 127.

p. 36
build its nest Quoted by DeSormo in Warrensburg–Lake George *News*, September 30, 1965.
seen at night L. Francis Herreshoff, "Naphtha Launches," *The Rudder*, November 1965.

CHAPTER VI

p. 37
electricity Mildred P. (Stokes) Hooker, *Camp Chronicles* (privately printed, 1952; reprinted by the Adirondack Museum, Blue Mountain Lake, N.Y., 1964), p. 44.

p. 38
one hamper *Ibid.*, pp. 4–5.
camp Donaldson, Vol. I, p. 6.

p. 39
unpeeled logs White, p. 147.
Durant For details on Durant and his achievements, see Hochschild and Donaldson.

p. 40
different from it Donaldson, Vol. II, p. 92.
Putnam Camp For a description of Putnam Camp, its routine, and its dis-

tinguished residents, see Elizabeth Putnam McIver, "Early Days at Putnam Camp, 1941," a paper reprinted by the Adirondack Museum.

p. 42

felicity For James's letters about his experiences in the Adirondacks, see his letters to Pauline Goldmark in Josephine Goldmark, "An Adirondack Friendship: Letters of William James," *The Atlantic Monthly*, Vol. CLIV (September–October 1934), pp. 265–72, 440–47.

unaltered *Ibid.*, letter to Fanny Morse.

p. 43

in winter This letter is reproduced in *James Jackson Putnam and Psychoanalysis*, edited and with an introductory essay by Nathan G. Hale, Jr. (Cambridge, Mass.: Harvard University Press, 1971), pp. 23–24.

Litchfield For accounts of Litchfield and his homes, see Joseph K. Lane, "Prospect Park," *Civic News* (Park Slope Civic Council, Brooklyn, N.Y.), April 1966, pp. 12–15; Stephen Birmingham, "The Beautiful, Bedeviled Adirondacks," *Holiday*, Vol. XXXVI, No. 2 (August 1964), p. 42; M. Foster, "American Game Preserves," *Munsey*, Vol. XXV (June 1901), pp. 385–86; and James S. Whipple, "First Wild Boar Hunt in the United States," *State Service*, Vol. III, No. 5 (May 1919), pp. 61–64.

CHAPTER VII

p. 46

withdrawn "Wachusett," according to Cadbury (in Murray, *Adventures in the Wilderness*, 1970, p. 40), was probably the pen name of George B. Wood, whom he does not otherwise identify.

health For his thoughts on health and the wilderness, see Murray, 1970, Introduction, pp. 66–68, and Appendix, pp. 92–93.

Trudeau Much of the material on Trudeau comes from Edward Livingston Trudeau, *An Autobiography* (Philadelphia, 1916). See also Donaldson, Vol. I, pp. 244 ff., and White, pp. 165–78.

p. 47

Trudeau's tern Edward S. Gruson, *Words for Birds* (New York, 1972), pp. 126–27; see also John Bull, *Birds of the New York Area* (New York, 1964), p. 479.

p. 48

church Lundy is quoted in Donaldson, Vol. I, pp. 230–31.

p. 50

fair Hooker, *Camp Chronicles*, p. 33.

spool Donaldson, Vol. I, pp. 243–44.

p. 51

fine wine *Ibid.*, p. 241.

Stevenson Stevenson's life in the Adirondacks is described in Margaret (Balfour) Stevenson, *From Saranac to the Marquesas and Beyond* (New York, 1903); some of Stevenson's letters from the Adirondacks are quoted in Paul F. Jamieson, *The Adirondack Reader* (New York, 1964).

p. 52
research projects White, pp. 318–19.

CHAPTER VIII

p. 54
done now Quoted in Henry Hope Reed and Sophia Duckworth, *Central Park: A History and a Guide* (New York, 1972), p. 3. Much of what follows is based on that history.
our reach *Ibid.*
trees and plants *Ibid.*, pp. 14–15.

p. 56
scenery-making Quoted in F. L. Olmsted, Jr., and Theodora Kimball, *Forty Years of Landscape Architecture: Central Park (Frederick Law Olmsted, Sr.)* (Cambridge, Mass., 1973), p. 212.

p. 57
nature's beauty George Catlin, *Letters and Notes on the Manners, Customs, and Condition of the North American Indians*, 2 vols. (London, 1841), pp. 261–62.
true re-creation? H. D. Thoreau, "Chesuncook," *The Atlantic Monthly*, Vol. II (August 1852), p. 134.

p. 58
Yosemite Valley For an account of the establishment of the original park, see H. Duane Hampton, *How the U.S. Cavalry Saved Our National Parks* (Bloomington, Ind., 1971); see also Goetzmann, *Exploration and Empire*.

p. 59
National Park Service For this and the following quotations from Olmsted, see Holway R. Jones, *John Muir and the Sierra Club: The Battle for Yosemite* (San Francisco, 1965).

p. 61
another treasure For an account of the opening of Yellowstone, see Hampton, *op. cit.*

p. 62
shadows and turmoil Gustavus C. Doane, "The Report upon the So-called Yellowstone Expedition of 1870 to the Secretary of War," *Senate Executive Document* 51, 41st Cong., 3rd Sess. (SN 1440) (Washington, D.C., 1871).

p. 63
appropriate them *Congressional Globe*, 42nd Cong., 2nd Sess., Part I, p. 697.
Yosemite Valley? Quoted in Jones, *op. cit.*, p. 27.

CHAPTER IX

p. 65

hog down William K. Verner, "Wilderness and the Adirondacks: An Historical View," *The Living Wilderness*, Vol. XXXIII, No. 108 (Winter 1969), p. 38.

p. 66

stage lines Murray, in *The New York Times*, February 13, 1872.
North Woods J. B. Harrison, in *Garden and Forest*, July 17, 1889, pp. 345–46.

p. 67

the common object J. B. Harrison, in *Garden and Forest*, July 24, 1889, pp. 358–59.
George Perkins Marsh For a biography, see David Lowenthal, *George Perkins Marsh: Versatile Vermonter* (New York, 1958).

p. 70

pluck and ability New York *Tribune*, March 5, 1883.
future generations For background material on Colvin, see Donaldson and White.

p. 71

the Pacific states Verplanck Colvin, "Ascent of Mount Seward and Its Barometrical Measurement," *New York State Senate Documents*, 1871, No. 68 (republished in the 24th Annual Report of the New York State Museum, pp. 178–80).

p. 72

their inability White, p. 203.
of the Hudson Quoted in Donaldson, Vol. I, p. 162.
largest panther White, pp. 204–05.

p. 73

surrounded him Verplanck Colvin, *Report on a Topographical Survey of the Adirondack Wilderness of New York* (Albany, 1873), p. 6.

p. 74

valley of the Hudson Albany *Argus*, April 10, 1872.
Franklin B. Hough For background on Franklin B. Hough, his work, and the condition of the forests, see Kranz and Van Valkenburgh.

p. 75

becomes law? *The New York Times*, June 10, 1871.

p. 76

scientific forest management "Report of the Commissioners of State Parks," *New York Senate Documents*, 1873, No. 102.

p. 77
with his views Van Valkenburgh, pp. 26–29.

CHAPTER X

p. 79
on the north Manufacturers' Aid Association of Watertown, N.Y., *Attractions and Commercial Advantages of Watertown, N.Y.* (Watertown, 1876), p. 21 (cited in Thompson, p. 67).
I do Frederick Mather in *Forest and Stream*, Vol. I (October 30, 1873), p. 179.

p. 80
It don't pay! For an account of New York State's fisheries and game protection, see Kranz.
any other heathen Quoted in Peter Matthiessen, *Wildlife in America* (New York, 1959).

p. 81
Wolves . . . in the Adirondacks Temporary Study Commission, Vol. II, Tech. Rpt. 2, p. 27.

p. 82
put on them *Ibid.*, pp. 21, 31–32; see also Kranz.
white-tailed deer For discussions of deer in the Adirondacks, see Temporary Study Commission, Vol. II, Tech. Rpt. 2, and Kranz.

p. 83
no personal interests William J. Stillman, "The Adirondacks Today," *The Nation*, Vol. XXXIX (August 14, 1884), p. 131.

p. 85
so that they die *Forest and Stream*, Vol. XII (March 20, 1879), p. 130.
people's hunting ground *The New York Times*, November 13, 1873.
in those counties Van Valkenburgh, pp. 30–31.
for charcoal *The New York Times*, August 31, 1883.

p. 86
unappreciative hand *The New York Times*, July 12, 1881.
high places William K. Verner, "Wilderness and the Adirondacks: An Historical View," *The Living Wilderness*, Vol. XXXIII, No. 108 (Winter 1969), p. 38.
luxury? Kranz, p. 195.

CHAPTER XI

p. 88
Zuyder Zee F. L. Oswald, in *North American Review*, January 1879, p. 135.

p. 89

effect of forests on climate For a good description of one aspect of this subject, see Howard W. Lull and Kenneth G. Reinhart, *Forests and Floods in the Eastern United States* (Northeastern Forest Experiment Station, U.S. Forest Service, Upper Darby, Pa., 1972).

p. 90

ecosystems intact H. W. Vogelmann, "Rain-making Forest," *Natural History*, Vol. LXXXV, No. 3 (March 1976), pp. 22–25; see also Vogelmann's "Precipitation from Fog Moisture in the Green Mountains of Vermont," *Ecology*, Vol. XLIX (1968), pp. 1205–07.

the farm Antonin Rousset, *The Forest Waters the Farm* (New York, 1886).

bed of stones Forest Commission, *First Annual Report for the Year 1885* (Albany, 1886).

p. 91

treatment of the land Howard L. Cook, "Flood Abatement by Headwater Measures," *Civil Engineering*, Vol. XV (1945), pp. 127–30.

p. 92

still be present Kenneth G. Reinhart, "Effect of a Commercial Clearcutting in West Virginia on Overland Flow and Storm Runoff," *Journal of Forestry*, Vol. LXII (1964), pp. 167–71.

higher each year David C. Smith, *A History of Lumbering in Maine* (Orono, Me., 1972), p. 233.

destroys the forest Stillman, "The Adirondacks Today," *The Nation*, Vol. XXXIX (August 14, 1884), p. 131.

p. 93

any other source Forest Commission, *op. cit.*, pp. 18–25.

rights-of-way J. P. Kinney, *The Development of Forest Law in America* (New York, 1917).

p. 94

railroad franchises in the Adirondacks For details on the spread of railroads in the area, see Hochschild, Donaldson, and Cadbury in Murray, *Adventures in the Wilderness* (1970).

utilizing counsel Stillman, *op. cit.*

to be nonsense Utica *Morning Herald*, November 23, 1883.

CHAPTER XII

p. 96

year-round contracts Thompson, pp. 70–71.

suggested an aqueduct Donaldson, Vol. II, p. 165.

p. 97

Board of Forestry as well Kinney, *The Development of Forest Law in America*, p. 210.

will be called to answer New York *Tribune*, November 27, 1883.
Morris K. Jesup For Jesup's background, see Donaldson, Vol. II, pp. 172–73; see also Geoffrey T. Hellman, *Bankers, Bones and Beetles: The First Century of the American Museum of Natural History* (Garden City, N.Y., 1969).

p. 98
cutting any trees Gifford Pinchot, *Breaking New Ground* (New York, 1957), p. 33.
not entirely new There are good accounts of the interest taken by New York City's business community in the Adirondacks in Donaldson, Kranz, and Thompson.

p. 99
better water supply Chamber of Commerce, "Save the Adirondacks and the Waterways of New York State (New York, 1883), p. 45.

p. 100
commerce destroyed New York *Tribune*, December 14, 1883.

p. 101
acquired by the state New York *Tribune*, January 12, 1884.
original blaze Dan Brenan, *Verplanck Colvin: Father of the Adirondack Forest Preserve* (unpublished ms., Adirondack Museum Library).
pack-baskets Donaldson, Vol. II, p. 166.

p. 102
belittled his work Brenan, *op. cit.*
of the commonwealth Donaldson, Vol. II, pp. 173–74.

p. 103
holding an audience New York Board of Trade and Transportation, "Annual Banquet" (New York, 1885), pp. 6–8.
water when set free Brooklyn Constitution Club, "The Forests of the Adirondacks" (New York, 1885), p. 3.

p. 104
diphtheria *Ibid.*, p. 4.
early in 1885 Sargent Commission Report, *New York Assembly Documents*, 1885, No. 36, pp. 1–57.

p. 105
supply of man *Ibid.*, p. 66.

CHAPTER XIII

p. 107
must be stopped Forest Commission, *First Annual Report for the Year 1885*, p. 86.
no taxes on it *Ibid.*, p. 80.
assessed and taxed *Laws of New York, 1886*, Chapter 280.

p. 108
the new Forest Preserve Both Kranz and Van Valkenburgh provide basic information on problems in the new Forest Preserve.

p. 109
to secure evidence S. A. D. Puter, *Looters of the Public Domain* (Portland, Ore., 1908).

p. 110
put them through *The New York Times*, September 17, 1889.
everybody is satisfied *The New York Times*, October 26, 1889.

p. 111
great scenery Quoted in *The New York Times*, August 4, 1887.
that is spiritual Charles Baudelaire, *Intimate Journals*, trans. by Christopher Isherwood (Hollywood, Calif., 1947), p. 56.
Liver Pills Gillian Tyndall, *George Gissing: The Born Exile* (New York, 1974), p. 258.
its successors Quoted in *Garden and Forest*, July 10, 1889, p. 333.

p. 112
spit on the carpet Quoted in Alfred Connable and Edward Silverfarb, *Tigers of Tammany* (New York, 1967), pp. 136–37.
Western Hemisphere Quoted in Olmsted and Kimball, *Forty Years of Landscape Architecture: Central Park*, p. 66.

p. 113
enchanted scene *Ibid.*
sedentary occupations *Ibid.*, p. 130.

p. 114
discordant incursions For a good summary of Central Park's troubles, see Reed and Duckworth, *Central Park: A History and a Guide*, esp. pp. 42–43.
John Muir For details on John Muir and the struggles that swirled around Yosemite, see Jones, *John Muir and the Sierra Club: The Battle for Yosemite*, and Linnie Marsh Wolfe, *Son of the Wilderness: The Life of John Muir* (New York, 1945).

CHAPTER XIV

p. 119
Bernhard Eduard Fernow For a thorough account of Fernow and his work, see Andrew Denny Rodgers, *Bernhard Eduard Fernow: A Story of North American Forestry* (Princeton, 1951).
forestry officials Quoted in Jenks Cameron, *The Development of Governmental Forest Control in the United States* (Baltimore, 1928).

p. 121
Trudeau's garden Adelaide Crapsey, quoted in Jamieson, *The Adirondack Reader*, p. 141.
aromized atmospheres Quoted in Forest Commission Report, 1891, *New York Assembly Documents*, 1892, No. 34, p. 137.
within the Forest Preserve counties Kranz, Thompson, and Van Valkenburgh are all valuable references for this period.

p. 122
in the southwestern Adirondacks White, p. 150.

p. 123
to market *The New York Times*, January 22, 1890.
astonishing Warrensburg *News*, February 27, 1890.
Forest Commissioner New York *Tribune*, January 23, 1891.
Theodore B. Basselin New York *Herald*, January 13, 1891.

p. 124
the Adirondack Park *Laws of New York, 1892*, Chapter 707.

p. 125
State government Quoted in Charles Z. Lincoln, ed., *Messages from the Governors*, Vol. IX (Albany, 1909), pp. 298–300.

CHAPTER XV

p. 127
its preservers *Garden and Forest*, April 18, 1894, p. 151.
to the judiciary The primary source for this landmark in Adirondack history is *Revised Record of the Constitutional Convention of 1894* (Albany, 1900), 5 vols. Good secondary sources are Kranz and Thompson.
David McClure See Borden H. Mills, Sr., "David McClure and the Forest Preserve," *Ad-i-ron-dac*, Vol. XIII, No. 6 (November–December 1949), pp. 118–19.

p. 128
sit as legislators Thompson, p. 81.

p. 129
We carefully considered that For an enlightening discussion of these exchanges by a constitutional lawyer, see Temporary Study Commission, Vol. II, Tech. Rpt. IB, pp. 7–8.

p. 130
certain regions of the Adirondacks *Revised Record of the Constitutional Convention of 1894*, Vol. IV, pp. 141–45.

p. 131
recreational interest group Thompson, p. 431.

p. 132
Delaware and Hudson's plans evaporated For the railroad companies' post-convention hanky-panky, see Hochschild and Van Valkenburgh.

CHAPTER XVI

p. 133
Gifford Pinchot Pinchot tells his own story in Gifford Pinchot, *Breaking New Ground* (New York, 1947).

p. 134
William Seward Webb For background on Webb and his career, see Hochschild and Thompson.

p. 135
ready for it Charles H. Burnett, *Conquering the Wilderness: The Building of the Adirondack & St. Lawrence Railroad by William Seward Webb, 1891–92* (Norwood, Mass., 1932).

p. 136
Adirondack acres Pinchot, *op. cit.*, p. 74.

p. 137
more lasting trouble For further details on this period of Adirondack history, see Thompson and Van Valkenburgh; see also Fisheries, Game and Forest Commission, *Second Annual Report* (Albany, 1897), pp. 376–460.

p. 138
fraud and devastation James P. Gilligan, *The Development of Policy and Administration of Forest Service Primitive and Wilderness Areas in the Western United States* (Ph.D. thesis, University of Michigan, 1953), p. 57.

p. 139
to the older man For the relationship between these two conservation leaders, see Pinchot, *op. cit.*, and Wolfe, *Son of the Wilderness: The Life of John Muir.*

p. 141
sturdy pins Pinchot, *op. cit.*, p. 145. For a description of this relationship between Pinchot and Roosevelt, and its effects on the conservation movement, see Frank Graham, Jr., *Man's Dominion: The Story of Conservation in America* (New York, 1971).

p. 142
President of the United States Donaldson, Vol. I, pp. 155–57.
completely false Mary Jane Nardacci, in *Adirondack Life*, Vol. VII, No. 3 (Summer 1976), p. 62.

CHAPTER XVII

p. 143

camp-site grabbers *Forest and Stream*, Vol. XLVII (November 21, 1896), p. 401.

to the people Charles Reznikoff, ed., *Louis Marshall: Champion of Liberty* (Philadelphia, 1957), Vol. II, p. 1024.

p. 145

car was going forward Hochschild, pp. 409–10.

of the future Percy Lubbock, ed., *The Letters of Henry James*, Vol. II (New York, 1920), p. 35.

p. 146

Melvil Dewey For a description of Dewey and his attitudes, see White, pp. 135–39; see also Stephen Birmingham, *The Right People* (Boston, 1968), pp. 265–68.

personal qualifications Quoted in Birmingham, *op. cit.*, p. 266.

p. 147

no brains Quoted in Kranz, p. 498.

Association for the Protection of the Adirondacks For the formation of this organization, see Donaldson, Vol. II, pp. 210–13, and Thompson, p. 96.

its big game For a discussion of game laws in the Adirondacks, see Kranz, esp. pp. 217 ff.

p. 148

dangerous job John B. Burnham, "The History of the Adirondack Deer," *High Spots*, Vol. XII, No. 1, January 1935, p. 10.

Harry V. Radford White, pp. 226–27, and Donaldson, Vol. I, p. 206; see also Royal Northwest Mounted Police, "Report of the Bathurst Inlet Patrol, 1917–18" (Ottawa, 1919; copy in the Adirondack Museum Library).

CHAPTER XVIII

p. 150

the water users The annual reports of the Fisheries, Game and Forest Commission (and in its later guise, the Forest, Fish and Game Commission), as well as those of the Forest Preserve Board, are invaluable sources for much of what follows. Excellent secondary sources are Kranz, Thompson, and Van Valkenburgh.

p. 151

bought as well as the forest Forest Preserve Board, *Fourth Annual Report* (Albany, 1901), p. 6.

William K. Fox See Van Valkenburgh, pp. 77–78, 80.

retain the woods From Fred B. Cook, *The Forest Preserve* (unpublished), quoted in Van Valkenburgh, p. 71.

p. 153
revenue obtainable Bernhard E. Fernow, in *Fourth Annual Report of the New York College of Forestry for 1901* (Albany, 1902), p. 11.

p. 156
as a deer slayer See Van Valkenburgh, pp. 69–71, for a description of Woodruff's nest feathering.

p. 157
severe criticism Thompson, p. 109.

p. 158
prison for a year *Forest and Stream*, Vol. LXX (February 8, 1908), p. 219, and Vol. LXX (April 4, 1908), p. 538.
for the public benefit Fred B. Cook, *op. cit.*, quoted in Van Valkenburgh, p. 99.

CHAPTER XIX

p. 159
Hetch Hetchy For a scholarly and readable account of this major conservation episode, see Jones, *John Muir and the Sierra Club: The Battle for Yosemite.* See also Wolfe, *Son of the Wilderness: The Life of John Muir*; Samuel P. Hays, *Conservation and the Gospel of Efficiency: The Progressive Conservation Movement, 1890–1920* (Cambridge, Mass., 1959); and, of course, John Muir's own writings about Yosemite.
beneficial uses John Ise, *Our National Parks Policy: A Critical History* (Baltimore, 1961), p. 86.

p. 161
never have succeeded Robert Underwood Johnson, *Remembered Yesterdays* (Boston, 1923).

p. 162
a frenzy Quoted by Roderick Nash in *The Call of the Wild (1900–16)* (New York, 1970), p. 15.

p. 163
San Francisco's water *Congressional Record*, 63rd Cong., 1st Sess.

p. 164
a subsequent court case White, p. 134.
proponents have dreamed Thompson, p. 180.
Water Supply Commission Walter McCulloh, "Water Resources of the State of New York," *Journal* (Association of Engineering Societies), October 1911; see also "New York's Conservation of Water Resources," *The American Review of Reviews*, January 1910.

p. 165
Forest Products Association Thompson, p. 396.
Louis Marshall For an idea of Marshall's breadth and depth of interests, see Reznikoff, ed., *Louis Marshall: Champion of Liberty.*

p. 167
in this climate *Ibid.*, Vol. II, pp. 1028–29.
any other way *Ibid.*, p. 1019.

p. 168
the lumbermen Quoted in Thompson, p. 209.
described boundaries *Laws of New York, 1912*, Chapter 280.

p. 169
a wild forest land Van Valkenburgh, pp. 99–100, 107–8.

p. 170
Burd Amendment Kranz, pp. 534–36.
and *private power companies* John G. Agar, "State Policy of Forest and Water Power Conservation," in *The Revision of the State Constitution* (New York State Constitutional Convention Commission, Albany, 1915), Vol. II.
for fire control Egburt E. Woodbury, "Opinion of the Attorney-General," June 29, 1915.

p. 171
sick to behold them Louis Marshall, in Reznikoff, *op. cit.*, Vol. II, pp. 1022–23.
hot-air balloons Van Valkenburgh, pp. 18–19.

CHAPTER XX

p. 172
George D. Pratt Thompson, p. 164.

p. 173
John S. Apperson Much of the material that follows on Apperson and the Schenectady conservationists is based on the author's interviews with Paul Schaefer, November 5, 1975, and August 20, 1976, and on letters and documents in Mr. Schaefer's extensive library at Schenectady.

p. 174
Warwick S. Carpenter This section is based primarily on a letter from Carpenter to Apperson, dated July 7, 1962, now in the Adirondack Museum Library.

p. 176
assured to the public *Ibid.*

p. 177

his name to the 'gift' See Reed and Duckworth, *Central Park: A History and Guide*, esp. pp. 42–43, 46.

Stephen Tyng Mather See Robert Shankland, *Steve Mather of the National Parks* (New York, 1951).

p. 178

God Almighty *Congressional Record*, 63rd Cong., 1st Sess., 50, pp. 2972–74.

p. 179

Yosemite National Park Stewart L. Udall, *The National Parks of America* (New York, 1966), p. 10.

Aldo Leopold For extensive discussions of the wilderness movement, and of Aldo Leopold's part in it, I am indebted to Gilligan, *The Development of Policy . . .*, and to Roderick Nash, *Wilderness and the American Mind* (New Haven, Conn., 1967).

on the map? Aldo Leopold, in his foreword to *A Sand County Almanac* (New York, 1949). This book is a distillation of Leopold's thought on the wilderness and is an American classic.

p. 180

unlovely human mind *Ibid.*, p. 176.

Leopold argued Aldo Leopold, "The Wilderness and Its Place in Forest Recreation Policy," *Journal of Forestry*, Vol. XIX, No. 7 (November 1921), pp. 718–21.

p. 181

Mather's hands! Gilligan, *op. cit.*, p. 108.

p. 182

into our wilderness Aldo Leopold, in *American Forests and Forest Life*, Vol. XXXII (1926), p. 411.

keeping them alive? Aldo Leopold, "Wilderness as a Form of Land Use," *Journal of Land and Public Utility Economics*, Vol. I (1925), p. 401.

CHAPTER XXI

p. 184

tucked away in the Adirondack mountains *Adirondack Daily Enterprise*, August 2, 1976.

Bobsledding For good discussions of the bobsled controversy, see Thompson and Van Valkenburgh.

p. 186

so treated Louis Marshall, in Reznikoff, ed., *Louis Marshall: Champion of Liberty*, Vol. II, p. 1063.

is located *Ibid.*, p. 1067.

p. 187
cannot be done *Association for the Protection of the Adirondacks* v. *Alexander MacDonald*, 278 Appellate Div. 73, pp. 81–82.
Thomas, a skiing enthusiast From the author's interview with William K. Verner, March 15, 1975.
Robert Moses From the author's interview with Harold K. Hochschild, October 10, 1975.

p. 188
in thrall Thompson, p. 416.

p. 189
when they were governor From the author's interview with Paul Schaefer, November 5, 1975.
hazardous to the campers From the author's interview with John Collins, Sr., November 1, 1975.

p. 190
were often scarce Rodney C. Loehr, ed., in *Forests for the Future: The Diaries of David T. Mason* (St. Paul, 1952).
or county highway system Lithgow Osborne, "Truck Trails in the Adirondacks?" *American Forests*, Vol. XLII, No. 1 (January 1936), pp. 3–6.
attorney general's approval "Opinion of the Attorney-General," April 15, 1935, and December 3, 1935.

p. 191
Robert Marshall See White, pp. 208–11, and Thompson, p. 166.
genuine excitement Robert Marshall, "Impressions from the Wilderness," *Nature Magazine*, Vol. XLIV (1951), p. 481.

p. 192
Clepper Henry Clepper, *Leaders of American Conservation* (New York, 1971).
freedom of the wilderness Robert Marshall, "The Problem of Wilderness," *Scientific Monthly*, Vol. XXX, No. 2 (February 1930), p. 148.
Brahms Quoted in Nash, *Wilderness and the American Mind*, p. 203.

p. 193
entirely permissible Marshall, "The Problem of Wilderness."

p. 194
making it a reality Schaefer interview, November 5, 1975.

p. 195
entirely new road Robert Marshall, "Comments on Commission's Truck Trails Policy," *American Forests*, Vol. XLII, No. 1 (January 1936), pp. 6–7.
their natural state Van Valkenburgh, pp. 171–72.
remained neutral Verner interview, March 15, 1975.

p. 196

Constitutional Convention of 1938 See Van Valkenburgh, pp. 174 ff.
Forest Products Association Schaefer interview, November 5, 1975.

CHAPTER XXII

p. 197

Black River War Roscoe C. Martin, *Water for New York* (Syracuse, 1960), p. 146. Much of this chapter is based on Martin, Thompson, the author's interview with Paul Schaefer, November 5, 1975, and on documents, letters, and pamphlets in Mr. Schaefer's library.

p. 200

for park purposes Quoted in Thompson, p. 248.
vote right Martin, *op. cit.*, p. 153.

p. 203

in that area Quoted in *The Forest Preserve*, No. 2 (November 1947), p. 6.

p. 204

his *Forest Preserve* *The Forest Preserve*, No. 3 (July 1948), pp. 3–4.

p. 205

before the committee Martin, *op. cit.*, p. 163.
strong pressure *Ibid.*

CHAPTER XXIII

p. 208

falling due William Vogt, *Road to Survival* (New York, 1948).

p. 209

unique history The historical background for this paragraph is based on the author's telephone interview with Robert Bathrick, New York State Conservation Department, March 2, 1977.
Lake Sanford on the site Paul Schaefer, "The Adirondacks: Pattern of a Battle for Woods and Water," *The Living Wilderness*, Vol. XI, No. 16 (March 1946), p. 18; see also White, pp. 317–18.
Big Blowdown of 1950 Van Valkenburgh, pp. 195–97; see also "Editorial," *New York State Conservationist*, October–November 1951, p. 1, and succeeding issues of that magazine.

p. 210

Forest Preserve? *New York State Conservationist*, *op. cit.*

p. 211

preservationists' replies Paul Schaefer, in *New York State Conservationist*, February–March 1952, pp. 3–4.

park environment William K. Verner, "Draft Report on Erosion of 'Forever Wild' for Subcommittee of Adirondack Mountain Club Conservation Committee," February 3, 1970 (unpublished typescript).

p. 212

existing state highways Van Valkenburgh, p. 214.

eastern section of the Forest Preserve Van Valkenburgh, p. 217, and White, p. 217; see also New York *Herald Tribune*, March 2, 1959.

Committee on Natural Resources Thompson, White, and Valkenburgh, and the annual reports of the Joint Legislative Committee all provide background on the committee's work.

p. 213

of our democratic society This account of the 1967 convention is based primarily on two sources: *Proceedings of the New York State Constitutional Convention of 1967*, Vols. I, II, and III, Albany, 1968; and the author's interview with David Sive, March 24, 1977.

CHAPTER XXIV

p. 219

Laurance S. Rockefeller Conrad L. Wirth, Ben H. Thompson, and Roger Thompson, "A Report on a Proposed Adirondack Mountains National Park" (issued by Laurance S. Rockefeller, 1967).

p. 220

Conrad L. Wirth Part of the account of the proposal's background is based on the author's telephone interview with Conrad L. Wirth, March 16, 1977.

p. 222

weeds and bandits? William Hosea Ballou, "An Adirondack National Park," *American Naturalist*, Vol. XIX (June 1885), pp. 578–82.

Against the National Park Tupper Lake *Free Press*, October 12, 1967.

Harold K. Hochschild Hochschild interview, October 26, 1975.

of old vehicles *Adirondack Daily Enterprise*, September 12, 1967.

p. 223

kind of threat *Ibid.*, September 22, 1967.

to operate *Ibid.*, October 6, 1967.

are concerned Bill Roden, in *ibid.*, August 9, 1967.

at this time "The Adirondack Mountains—A National Park?" (mimeographed, Adirondack Mountain Club, September 12, 1967).

p. 224

respecting the Adirondacks William O. Douglas, *A Wilderness Bill of Rights* (Boston, 1965), p. 99.

of the moment Joseph L. Sax, "America's National Parks," *Natural History* (Supplement), October 1976, p. 79.
within their boundaries *Ibid.*, p. 83.

p. 225
hundreds of structures Allan K. Fitzsimmons, "National Parks: The Dilemma of Development," *Science*, Vol. CXCI (February 6, 1976), pp. 441–42.
right freely W. H. Hall, quoted in Robert P. Gibbens and Harold F. Heady, *The Influence of Modern Man on the Vegetation of Yosemite Valley* (University of California, Division of Agricultural Science, Berkeley, 1964), p. 33.

p. 226
likely in the future *Ibid.*, p. 34.
137 million Udall, *The National Parks of America*, p. 11.
contemplative way Quoted in Sax, *op. cit.*, p. 79.
come for the action *Ibid.*, p. 83.

p. 227
these gifts Percival Baxter, in a letter to Governor John Reed of Maine, May 20, 1960.

p. 228
National Wilderness Bill For an account of the legislative battle for a Wilderness Bill, see Graham, *Man's Dominion: The Story of Conservation in America*, pp. 289–309; see also Michael McCloskey, "The Wilderness Act of 1964: Its Background and Meaning," *Oregon Law Review*, Vol. XLV (1966), pp. 288–321.

p. 229
who does not remain Public Law 88-577, in *U.S. Statutes at Large*, Vol. 78, pp. 890–96.
audible growl Henry L. Diamond, personal communication.

CHAPTER XXV

p. 231
Disneyland itself Burton Bernstein, *The Sticks: A Profile of Essex County, New York* (New York, 1972), pp. 111–12.
only scenery? Thompson, p. 348.
depressed area Bernstein, *op. cit.*, p. 81.

p. 232
in 1968 Temporary Study Commission, Vol. II, Tech. Rpt. 4, p. 20.
entire county Bernstein, *op. cit.*, p. 146.
one's own life Father Carmen Guiliano, in *Adirondack Daily Enterprise*, January 25, 1977.

p. 233
thirty-seven individual owners Temporary Study Commission, Vol. II, Tech. Rpt. 1A, pp. 54–55.

p. 234
males than females Stephen Birmingham, "The Beautiful, Bedeviled Adirondacks," *Holiday*, Vol. XXXVI, No. 2 (August 1964), p. 92.
on the block White, pp. 232–33, 310–11.

p. 235
carrying capacity Stanley A. Cain, "Fiftieth Anniversary of the National Park Service, 1916–1966," reprinted in *The Living Wilderness*, Vol. 30, No. 94 (August 1966), pp. 16–19.
law of 1924 *Laws of New York, 1924*, Chapter 512.
to designate William K. Verner, unpublished draft of Adirondack Mountain Club Conservation Committee Report, 1973.
had elapsed *Ibid.*

p. 236
Preservation of Agricultural Land See highlights of this commission's report in "Can We Preserve Good Farm Land?" *The Conservationist*, Vol. XXII, No. 4 (February–March 1968), pp. 27–33.

p. 237
meetings in New York City Hochschild interview, October 26, 1975.
its existence Much of this account of the Temporary Study Commission and its workings is based on the author's interviews with Hochschild, October 26, 1975; Richard W. Lawrence, Jr., March 2, 1977; and Peter S. Paine, New York City, September 16, 1974.

p. 239
its environs Gideon M. Davison, *The Fashionable Tour* (Saratoga Springs, N.Y., 1822).
picks it up Schuyler Jackson, in St. Lawrence University, *Fourth Conference on the Adirondack Park, 1974* (Canton, N.Y., 1976), p. 91.

p. 240
members for it Lawrence interview, March 2, 1977.
to Governor Rockefeller See Temporary Study Commission, Vol. I.
infeasible *Ibid.*, p. 16.
in the Adirondack Park *Ibid.*, p. 24.

p. 241
Adirondack Park Agency *Ibid.*, p. 9.
control agency only *Ibid.*
of the essence Letter of Harold K. Hochschild to Governor Nelson A. Rockefeller, December 15, 1970.

CHAPTER XXVI

p. 243
its former use Warrensburg–Lake George *News*, April 22, 1971.
owned by the state *Adirondack Daily Enterprise*, February 4, 1971.

well organized Much of this account of the legislative struggle to enact the Adirondack Park Agency bill is based on the author's interviews with Harold K. Hochschild, October 26, 1975; Richard W. Lawrence, Jr., March 2, 1977; and William K. Verner on various dates during 1975 and 1976.

p. 244
support for it Hochschild interview.

p. 245
just wasn't true Amsterdam *Recorder*, May 21, 1971.

p. 246
upgraded Hochschild interview.
before adjournment *Laws of New York, 1971*, Chapter 706.

p. 247
a new job Lawrence interview.
designing a master plan Adirondack Park Agency, *Adirondack Park State Land Master Plan* (1972).

p. 248
forest and wetland Courtney Jones, "Challenge in the Adirondacks," *The Living Wilderness*, Vol. XXXVI, No. 120 (Winter 1972–73), p. 28.

p. 249
from the landscape Natural Resources Defense Council, *Land Use Controls in New York State* (New York, 1975), pp. 73 ff., 88–94.

p. 250
by your friends Quoted in Lake Placid *News*, October 16, 1975.

p. 251
against his veto Hochschild interview.
done to the Adirondacks For an account of this political struggle and Governor Rockefeller's messages, see Association for the Protection of the Adirondacks, "Seventy-second Annual Report" (June 1973).
developers did From the author's interview with Courtney Jones, October 29, 1975.

p. 252
six categories See Adirondack Park Agency, *Adirondack Park Land Use and Development Plan and Recommendations for Implementation* (1973).

p. 253
preserved forever *The New York Times*, May 23, 1973.

CHAPTER XXVII

p. 254
came alive Much of this chapter is based on the author's attendance at various meetings in the Adirondacks, interviews with state officials and local citizens,

and the reading of local newspapers (especially the *Adirondack Daily Enterprise*) during the years 1975–77.

p. 257

simply took it From the author's interview with William M. Doolittle, October 28, 1976.

p. 258

the New Deal Samuel Eliot Morison, *The Oxford History of the American People* (New York, 1965), p. 986.

principle *Report of the National Resources Planning Board* (Washington, D.C., 1934).

p. 259

around Lake Tahoe For details and helpful discussions of these pioneering planning cases, see U.S. Council on Environmental Quality, *The Quiet Revolution in Land Use Control* (Washington, D.C., 1971); Elizabeth N. Haskell, *Managing the Environment: Nine States Look for New Answers* (Washington, D.C., 1971); and U.S. Council on Environmental Quality, *The Taking Issue* (Washington, D.C., 1973).

p. 260

in earnest From the author's interview with Gordon Davis (former APA counsel), March 2, 1977.

just as they were Rose Macaulay, *The Towers of Trebizond* (London, 1965), p. 267.

p. 261

a state forest ranger *Adirondack Daily Enterprise*, October 3, 1975.

Boy Scout troop From the author's interview with Mary Prime (APA commissioner), Lake Placid, October 28, 1975.

Joey Hickey? Doolittle interview.

p. 262

regulatory nightmare Robert F. Flacke, in a statement at the annual convention of the Environmental Planning Lobby, Albany, N.Y., October 3, 1976.

friends and neighbors John M. Wilkins, in a statement at an APA seminar for businessmen, Lake Placid, N.Y., December 6, 1975.

p. 263

swallow the APA Doolittle interview.

a disaster Paine interview, September 16, 1974.

CHAPTER XXVIII

p. 265

these philosophies U.S. Council on Environmental Quality, *The Taking Issue*, pp. 1–2. Much of the following account is based on this book.

p. 266

the use of lands *Ibid.*, p. 104.

public interests Quoted in *ibid.*, p. 119.

p. 267

as a taking Quoted in *ibid.*, p. 136.

p. 268

of the user Joseph L. Sax, "Taking, Private Property and Public Rights," *Yale Law Journal*, Vol. LXXXI (1971), p. 149.

of the past *Adirondack Daily Enterprise*, November 22, 1976.

p. 269

in Florida *The New York Times*, December 1, 1975.

did not function For discussions of economic problems in the Adirondacks, see Adirondack Park Agency, "Comprehensive Report," Vol. I (February 1976), and Adirondack Park Agency, "Adirondack Economic Profile" (February 1976).

p. 270

labor to carry on William Murray, "Letter from Naples," *The New Yorker*, August 26, 1974, pp. 61–62.

p. 271

trees of the park John Stock, in a statement to the New York State Assembly Environmental Committee, Saranac Lake, N.Y., May 1, 1976.

p. 272

property values Anonymous, "Preserving Scenic Areas: The Adirondack Land Use Program," *Yale Law Journal*, Vol. LXXXIV (1975), p. 1719.

p. 273

nor unreasonable Justice Edmund L. Shea, copy in the files of the Adirondack Park Agency, Ray Brook, N.Y.

Petaluma, California See *The New York Times*, August 17, 1975, and March 13, 1976; see also *Audubon*, Vol. LXXVII, No. 6 (November 1975), p. 126.

p. 274

agonizing William K. Verner, in a statement at an Adirondack Park Agency public hearing, Ray Brook, N.Y., March 21, 1975.

Conclusion

p. 275

trust for the people Murray, *Adventures in the Wilderness*, p. 74.

p. 277

future beckons Robert L. Heilbroner, *An Inquiry into the Human Prospect* (New York, 1974), p. 94.

Index

About the Author

Frank Graham, Jr., was born in New York City in 1925. Graduated from Columbia College in 1950, he was publicity director for the Brooklyn Dodgers for four years, and then became assistant managing editor of *Sport.* Since 1958, Mr. Graham has been a free-lance writer specializing in nature and conservation, and has written several books, among them *Since Silent Spring* (1970), *Where the Place Called Morning Lies* (1973), and *Potomac: The Nation's River* (1976). He and his wife, Ada, have also collaborated on a number of books for young readers in the fields of natural history and the environment. Since 1968 he has been a field editor for *Audubon* magazine. In 1976 Mr. Graham received an honorary Doctorate in Humane Letters from Colby College. The Grahams live in Milbridge, Maine.

A Note on the Type

This book was set in Caledonia, a Linotype face designed by W. A. Dwiggins. It belongs to the family of printing types called "modern face" by printers—a term used to mark the change in style of type letters that occurred about 1800. Caledonia borders on the general design of Scotch Modern, but is more freely drawn than that letter.

Composed by Maryland Linotype Composition Company, Inc., Baltimore, Maryland. Printed and bound by The Haddon Craftsmen, Inc., Scranton, Pennsylvania.
Typography and binding design by Virginia Tan

Map by Rafael Palacios